CONSCIOUSNESS

CONSCIOUSNESS

SEPARATION AND INTEGRATION

Neil Rossman

STATE UNIVERSITY OF NEW YORK PRESS

Published by
State University of New York Press, Albany

© 1991 State University of New York

For information, address State University of New York Press,
State University Plaza, Albany, N. Y.   12246

Production by Marilyn P. Semerad
Marketing by Bernadette LaManna

Library of Congress Cataloging-in-Publication Data

Rossman, Neil, 1937–
     Consciousness: separation and integration / Neil Rossman.
        p.   cm.
     Includes bibliographical references.
     ISBN 0-7914-0407-2. — ISBN 0-7914-0408-0 (pbk.)
     1. Consciousness.   I. Title
     BF311.R6545 1991
     126—dc20   89-48909
                                                                            CIP

     10   9   8   7   6   5   4   3   2   1

BF
311
$.R6545$
1991

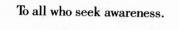

To all who seek awareness.

CONTENTS

PREFACE

Like all philosophical work, this book is incomplete. In this case, however, due to the subject matter, the incompleteness is radical. The subject matter is consciousness and the attempt is to understand it from the "inside"—the only way the experiential phenomenon of consciousness can be properly understood. But this cannot be done in a complete or final fashion, for every attempt to understand consciousness is itself an expression of consciousness and this latter expression cannot itself be understood without generating an infinite regress. But there is an additional dimension of difficulty, for consciousness is, I think, developmental and historical; it is unfolding. As such, it is not clear whither it proceeds. So any examination of consciousness is limited to an exploration of consciousness as it now displays itself, the causes and conditions which have been at work in producing the present situation, and the apparent direction of development.

Within this context, I have attempted to provide a rather general overview of the "structure" of consciousness and various of the "elements" which comprise consciousness. I am aware how much further detail is needed for almost everything I discuss; but I thought it worthwhile to present the larger perspective in some detail since much of what I discuss is often ignored in contemporary analytically oriented philosophy of mind. Contemporary philosophy of mind is brilliant in the questions it poses and the analyses it provides; but it tends to omit, for reasons I touch on in the text, the lived dimension of consciousness. I have tried to provide that focus.

As I indicate in the text, consciousness has developed in such a manner that separation, which is a condition of the emergence of humanity, has, for the most part, become deep seated and pervasive alienation. The deepest dimensions of this development—those relating to the experience of self as an ongoing, separate entity—are often not remarked upon, but are simply taken for granted. As a result, whatever problems flow from or are undergirded by this movement of consciousness are not properly understood and so not adequately confronted. Perhaps some of what is found in this book will stimulate increased awareness and exploration of these matters.

Many people over many years have played a significant role in the development of the ideas and approaches explored in this work. Two of my earliest teachers, Kai Nielsen and the late Sidney Hook, helped me understand not only the nature and importance of commitment in one's philosophical work, but also the beauty of creative passion. Nonna Holy, slowly and patiently, helped me to see how concepts need to be grounded in concrete, lived experience and how easy and tempting it is to get lost in a world constructed of concepts. George Groman, first as a teacher, then as a chairperson, and finally as a colleague and friend, has always been kind, encouraging and supportive. For many years, Marguerita Grecco has been an attentive, patient and supportive friend and colleague. My wife Maxine has been and continues to be helpful and loving. Finally, the many students at LaGuardia Community College who attended various of my courses inspired me with their energy and their insistence that what we discussed and explored had to be real and relevant in the best sense of these too easily distorted words.

Sydney Shoemaker and Charles Landesman, respectively, read earlier versions of Chapters 2 and 5. I thank them for their helpful responses. Gerald Myers read the entire manuscript and provided many useful suggestions. An initial version of Chapter 2 was written at Cornell University, while I was attending a National Endowment for the Humanities Summer Seminar, during the Summer of 1985. I want to thank the Endowment and Sydney Shoemaker, the leader of the Seminar, for their support. First drafts of Chapters 1 and 3 – 7 were written while I was on sabbatical leave from F. H. LaGuardia Community College during the academic year 1985–86. I wish to thank the College and City University of New York for this leave.

Janet Palazzolo and Jeanne Young cheerfully provided the typing from my near illegible handwritting.

Philosophy of Mind and the Problem
of Personal Integration

Chapter One

I

It is not an exaggeration to say that since the writings of Descartes, mentality or consciousness has become the central area of philosophical attention and investigation. But it is not just mentality as mentality which has taken center stage; it is rather mentality as grasped and experienced self-reflectively. Indeed it is largely through the writings of Descartes that this has occurred, for it is he who explicitly and systemically directed the gaze of awareness inwardly and in so doing helped create a world, the world of self-reflective consciousness or self, within the larger non-self-reflective world.

Recently, say over the last thirty years or so, activity within this and related areas has expanded at an even greater rate than usual. The expansion has been so great that even the names given to the enterprise have undergone change. What was once called "philosophy of mind" and "philosophical psychology" is now called "philosophy of psychology" or "cognitive science," and, most recently, "neurophilosophy." These developments suggest that besides the great deal of work that is being done within the discipline, there is also a great deal of self-conscious work being done on the nature of this work. Not only has attention been directed at the content of the discipline; it has also been directed at the goals, presuppositions, tools, and methodology of the discipline.

This, of course, is a healthy and positive situation and the work that has been produced is both important and impressive. But while there is much good here, there have also been some unfortunate developments. As work has proceeded, the discipline has become more and more narrowly focused.[1] The focus has been on a cluster of questions which relate to the ontology or nature of the mental; and the primary concern has been to understand and explain the similarities and differences between the mental and physical or, better yet, to show there is an identity of the mental and physical, with the former reduced to the latter. Understandably, a good deal of this theorizing is directed at avoiding as much as possible the absurdities and embarrassments of dualism, especially substance dualism. But what is unfortunate is that as a result of such emphases what can be called "lived consciousness" or "lived sense of self" has been largely, perhaps entirely, ignored.

For example, when consciousness in its phenomenological presence is investigated, it is almost never in its own terms or in its character as a dimension of a life being lived; rather it is investigated as a phenomenon which is at least potentially embarrassing for some form or other of materialism. Similarly with self, for when it is treated, it is not from the standpoint of *being* a self or living a life—well or ill—as a self, but from the standpoint of personal identity, conceived in a general, abstract and impersonal fashion. As we have become more and more knowledgeable concerning the workings of the brain and both in imagination and actuality are able to separate out parts of the brain from each other and the brain from the rest of the body, questions about personal identity have become more complex and intriguing. But from this standpoint, the question of personal identity becomes, to a significant degree, a matter of physiological, or even sometimes logical, structure and is no longer entirely, or even primarily, a question of psychological structure or of psychological experience.

There is, of course, no doubt that questions concerning the nature of the mental and its relationship to the physical are both relevant and crucial. Indeed, it seems reasonably clear that, at the very least, the mental is physically based. The idea of freely flowing, unattached mentality is, I think, defective in a profound fashion. Even though many people talk about such a phenomenon and on the surface there does not appear to be anything incoherent about such talk, I think such talk is a symptom of deep seated distortions within consciousness. With consciousness properly experienced and understood, claims of this sort would be seen as unintelligible.[2] We would then not talk about a disembodied mentality or disembodied mental states or properties.

These remarks, however, do not commit me to a form of materialism within which it is not possible to discuss consciousness. Whatever ontology my views ultimately entail — some form or other of materialism or a dual aspect theory or something else — I wish to discuss consciousness and sense of self, not as embarrassments we have to explain or explain away, but as fundamental constitutents of the kind of life we lead—indeed, as the very phenomena which make human life what it is.

However important the ontological question, it leaves quite untouched a more fundamental and, apparently, inescapable question. For whatever ontology I endorse, *I still must determine how to live*. This is unavoidable; and adopting any version of materialism or dualism does not, at least at this point in the development of consciousness, solve the problem of how to live. To be sure, if certain theories are adopted and, more so, turn out to be true, we may need to see how our everyday concepts can be understood and modified in light of what these theories teach us. And, I suppose, as an extreme outcome of the *deep acceptance* of certain theories, our experience of life may, over an extended period of time, come to be radically altered. Certainly, if consciousness is developmental and historical, as I think it is, it can change; and perhaps it can even change to the extent that the felt reality that one must determine how to live is no longer felt at all.

These last remarks, of course, are prompted by the recent wave of attacks on what has come to be called, with an unfortunate use of emotive language, "folk psychology" (FP). The suggestion that FP be eliminated and replaced by the insights and language of a mature neuroscience is radical to an extent that is almost impossible to state. Whether proponents of elimination are aware of it or not, it is not just a call to change how we think and talk about experience, but is a call to alter how we see and experience the world at its most fundamental levels — levels, it might be added, at which most, perhaps all, of us are not even aware.

To make such a proposal, one must have a conviction that what is called folk psychology is distorting, deceiving, and systematically wrong. And wrong not just in its presentational or representational content, but also, more radically, wrong in the modes by which it presents or represents. From this point of view, the basic categories of the mental, *i.e.*, belief, desire, and the like, are seen to be defective, virtual fantasies creating a totally mistaken sense of experience. To be convinced of this is to be convinced that all of us, as we walk about, are in systematic and complete error about the way the world is, and the way we and others are. And, again, this is not just error about this or that, but is systematic, structural error or illusion. Obviously, this is no small claim.

It is, however, quite interesting how both those who attack and those who defend FP do not see the depth of the suggestion for elimination. For example, Horgan and Woodward, defenders of FP, claim that "the wholesale rejection of FP would . . . entail a drastic revision of our conceptual scheme."[3] This, however, is the least of the matter, for how could such a revision take place? There is here not only the suggestion that our "conceptual scheme" could undergo a "drastic revision," but an implication that there is something outside the conceptual scheme in terms of which the revision would be accomplished. But what could this possibly be? What, other than elaborations, modifications and alterations of the conceptual scheme could alter the conceptual scheme? It appears Horgan and Woodward's remarks are undergirded by an assumption that there is some neutral, non-conceptualized, perhaps abiding and unchanging, realm of mentality which, with the proper conceptual scheme, will be adequately conceptualized. Implicit in this kind of talk about drastic revision of our conceptual scheme is a split between content and form, or conceptual system and life, such that the one can be separated from the other without significant or fundamental alteration of either.

This, however, is a very problematic model. For there appears to be a mutual interconnection between mentality in its various manifestations and FP. There are not two separately existing realms which are somehow accidentally and contingently pasted together. Rather, FP is constitutive of mentality as mentality is constitutive of FP. The seeds of mentality not only have developed as they have, but have developed at all, because they have produced and, in turn, been permeated by FP. If, per impossible, FP is rejected in total, there would be nothing left over which could be called mentality. To attempt to eliminate FP is not just to remove an extraneous, replaceable feature of how we see and experience life in its various aspects; it is to remove our very seeing and experiencing of life.

These remarks, however, should not be taken to imply that FP cannot and ought not be modified, developed and altered. Not only is such change possible; in many instances it is needed. These, however, would be changes within FP; they would be developments and refinements of FP, not replacements of FP with something else. As I have suggested, such a wholesale replacement is impossible and unintelligible.

Yet, it is probably possible, *over an extended period of time*, to alter FP so radically that the way we now see and experience life would be only dimly recognizable. Such change, however, cannot occur by way of the discovery or creation of a new language for dealing with mentality. If FP is constitutive of how we see and experience life, in depth change will occur only as we come to identify and "work through," concretely and personally, the elements which constitute our sense of the world and our lives. Any suggestion concerning what is ultimately real and how we ought to talk which derives from elements extraneous to how we see and experience life will simply roll down the back of the complex depths of how our folk psychological concepts constitute our experience of life.

II

While it is somewhat surprising that defenders of FP fail to see the full character of the call for the elimination of FP, it is not surprising that opponents of FP do not fully appreciate the matter. Paul Churchland, certainly one of the staunchest critics of FP, chides functionalists for their alleged conservatism concerning FP.[4] The implication, of course, is that Churchland and other eliminative materialists are not conservative, but are genuine radicals. But I doubt Churchland appreciates the full force of his radicalism. In *Matter and Consciousness*, he writes that the bottom up approach — *i.e.*, the focus on the material bases of behavior rather than on the mentalistic phenomena stressed by FP — will produce " . . . a new and more adequate set of concepts with which to understand our inner life."[5] This suggests there is some inner life separate from the concepts of FP, that removal of the concepts leaves an unconceptualized inner life which can then be more adequately understood with the new concepts developed by neuroscience.

However, it is again not clear what this inner life would be — unless, that is, it is something entirely different from the inner life which is experienced as consciousness. And, of course, that's what Churchland has in mind. The inner life which can survive the elimination of FP is not the inner life which enables us to relate to the world in the manner we do. The outcome of Churchland's proposal would be the elimination of what is universally experienced as our inner life and the provision of another inner life which cannot function — at least without considerable explanatory detail of how it could — as the inner life of a reflective creature must if the creature is to survive. That is, the inner life which enables us to act in the world as we do is FP; it is not the brain states which can be described separate from FP. We can, of course, recognize that brain states provide the physical basis of the inner life expressed by FP; but this is far indeed from replacing the inner life expressed by FP with a set of descriptions of brain states.

That Churchland accepts a distinction between an inner life that exists separate from FP and can be radically severed from FP can be seen still more clearly if we look at one of his arguments against FP. In the context of a rejection of various folk theories concerning the physical world, Churchland writes about FP: " . . . it would be a *miracle* if we had got *that* one right the very first time. . . . "[6] This is a very interesting and revealing remark, for it suggests that at that time, there existed something to be got right or wrong; that at the dawn of reflective consciousness there was already in existence a mental life which could have been adequately understood by a set of concepts and theories. But how could there have been such a mental life or set of concepts and theories by means of which that mental life could be adequately grasped? These are all elements of consciousness, and, as such, need to develop, and come to be over extended periods of time. They are not and cannot be present, "fully formed," at the dawn of reflective consciousness. There was thus nothing to have gotten right or wrong; there was only the beginning in pre-reflective awareness of what has come to be our reflective mental life.[7]

Although just how one would prove this is uncertain, consciousness, and especially reflective consciousness, is developmental and historical. In part, the awareness which is consciousness develops in terms of a secondary awareness of the original, primordial awareness. This secondary awareness or understanding is, in part, creative and so also expansive and enlarging. And this enlargement of consciousness, of which FP is one inherent and central dimension, includes the sense we develop of ourselves and our lives. Thus, if we are to alter and improve our understanding of ourselves and our lives, we must work through FP. One can miss this, I think, only if one's attention is not on consciousness, but on something else, such as brain states. If consciousness is held to *be* brain states, then it is understandable how one might say that we could have got things right the first time, for presumably—though this too is questionable—the brain states that were mental states five or ten thousand years ago would be the non-numerically same brain states that would be mental states today.

If consciousness is developmental and historical, the sorts of entities which are conscious are developmental in a way in which entities which are not conscious, say rocks and trees, are not. Rocks and trees do, of course, undergo change; but such change is simply mechanical and physical, involving no elements of awareness at all. Even beings somewhere between rocks and trees, on the one hand, and human beings, on the other—dogs and cats for example — do not undergo change in the unique manner in which reflective creatures do. Dogs and cats—that is, pre-reflective creatures—do not undergo changes which involve representational or symbolic systems which can be directed onto the environment, the creature doing the representing or the mode of representation itself. Though dogs, cats, and the like, do direct themselves onto the world in definite ways, *i.e.*, act or at least behave, they are severely limited by their inability to develop the awareness which issues in reflective self-awareness and the development of modifiable and expandable symbol systems. The emergence of such reflective awareness and its peculiar mode of operation thus constitutes a new stage in the development of consciousness, a stage which I call "reflective consciousness." Since this development is expressed by and manifested in FP — indeed, comes about in part through the development of FP — the latter is constitutive of reflective consciousness, and is in fact an essential part of what enables us to experience life in the peculiar self-reflective fashion we do.

The language and concepts of FP seem to play an essential, constitutive role in our having the sort of inner life that we have. But if this is so, it tells dramatically against the eliminativist's goal of having the language of FP replaced by a language of neuroscience. To talk about spiking frequencies and the like rather than about pain or belief or desire would, I think, accomplish either of two things. If, over some extended period of time, reflective creatures came to the point of talking exclusively in terms of spiking frequencies and the like, it is not clear how they would be able to act. It appears that action is tied not only to phenomena such as belief and desire, but also to various semantical features of language, such as meaning, reference and truth. In the absence of such phenomena, it is not clear how beings of the sort *reflective* creatures are could act. Their use of the language of spiking frequencies could not do the job FP does because the language of spiking frequencies does not include the mental states and linguistic phenomena which appear to be necessary for action. It thus appears that the literal and total rejection of FP would produce a creature incapable of action and so incapable of survival.

But perhaps this conclusion is too extreme; perhaps the language of spiking frequencies could provide the elements necessary for action. To be sure, the creature so speaking and acting would be scarcely recognizable to us; but lack of recognition is not equivalent to impossibility. However, while some sort of conceivability is present here, those who champion it must provide at least some of the explanatory details of what would be involved. And such explanatory detail must allow for the production of action, not just mechanical behavior or reaction. Personally, I am not confident that anything of the sort could be provided. Rather, I suspect that in order to tie the language of spiking frequencies sensibly to action, the former would have to incorporate, though perhaps in somewhat different forms, the very mental states and semantics previously contained in FP. If, however, this were the case, the very same problems which led to the call for the elimination of FP would be present within the new language of neuroscience.

The eliminative materialist thus seems to be confronted by a dilemma: either there is a genuine elimination of the elements and language of FP; or those elements are incorporated within the new, emerging language of neuroscience. If the former occurs, we no longer have a recognizably reflective, somewhat self-directing creature, for the elimination of belief, desire, and the like, as well as the semantical properties of language, seem to eliminate the possibility of acting in the way that is characteristic of reflective creatures. If, however, the latter occurs and the elements of FP which enable action are absorbed into the language of neuroscience, the exact problems which suggested the elimination of FP would simply be reproduced in the new language.

My sense here is that the kind of elimination which is being suggested for FP is just not possible, that any alteration would itself be an elaboration of FP and, perhaps most importantly, constructive alteration would itself have to come from within FP. This last remark suggests a significant area of agreement between the views presently being put forth and those of the eliminative materialist. As the latter suggests, FP is indeed defective, perhaps even radically defective, and so needs to be modified. But whereas the eliminativist suggests elimination, my suggestion is that the changes must come from within FP and so must be modifications of FP and not a move to something entirely different.

But how, it may be asked, can change be accomplished from within FP? Although this is one of the main topics of these writings and will be treated in a number of contexts as we proceed, a few brief and general comments are now appropriate. One aspect of accomplishing desirable change would involve becoming aware, patiently, over time, of how we experience ourselves and the world by means of the categories and the assumptions of FP. If these are constitutive of consciousness and so of our experience of life, then, collectively and individually, we need to see just how and to what degree these elements provide both a structure for, and the content of, experience. That is, we must openly and at depth become aware of how we experience life and the world via these elements. As we become more and more aware of the various dimensions which are constitutively structured by FP, we will enlarge our understanding of how we see things and, hopefully, be in a position to create a more realistic and fulfilling way of experiencing ourselves and the world.

These remarks imply that it is quite legitimate to see philosophy of mind as including within its scope topics such as fragmentation, alienation, integration and the living of the good and fulfilled life. Typically, however, such topics are *not* treated within contemporary Anglo-American philosophy of mind. The reasons for such exclusions are complex and deep, but at one level they are related to the focus on the ontology of the mental, its relation to the physical, and the problem of personal identity. Such concerns are abstract and impersonal and so relate to particular instances only insofar as these instances exemplify the features of the abstract, impersonal case. There is, of course, a similar abstract/particular contrast involved in discussions of fragmentation, integration and the like. We do want to achieve adequate abstract and general characterizations of these phenomena, but such achievement, I will argue, is dependent on some degree at least of actual experiential understanding of these states by the inquiring individual. Explicating the ontology of the mental or the concept of personal identity does not involve this sort of experiential understanding, though of course such work does unfold against the background of one's awareness that one is a particular conscious being. Explicating fragmentation, integration, and the like, involves a grasp of the *particular ways* one is a particular conscious being; and this demands a level of experiential awareness and attention that is not needed in the other analyses.

Although the above approach has a very different foundation and points to very different outcomes than does eliminative materialism, there is yet an additional affinity between the two approaches. For both are suggesting that a clearer and more adequate understanding of our lives — and so a more fulfilling existence — will emerge if we properly understand the nature and workings of our minds. This stress on quality of life or how one lives is, I think, crucial and I see no reason why philosophy of mind cannot be understood so as to include such topics. Indeed, why study the mind at all, if it does not, at least at some points, become a study of the most propitious manner (or manners) in which the mind can operate within life experience. And if this is allowed as legitimate, so also is it legitimate to see how the particular mind we call "our own" can come to operate in this propitious manner.

III

If integration and fulfillment involve working through the elements which comprise FP and which structure our experience of life and the world, there must be some available manner by which these elements can be identified. If they cannot be identified, we cannot get at how we actually see and experience the world and so we will remain unaware within these perspectives.

If, for a moment, we focus on integration and fulfillment, there are three significant implications of the above remarks. I will briefly mention these now and treat them in greater detail later. First, integration and fulfillment are not simply given. They are not automatic properties of creatures who are reflectively conscious; rather, they are phenomena which, if existing at all, have been attained. Second, these phenomena consist of *being in certain mental states* which, in ways to be explained, cohere with the objective nature of the world, one's organism and one's distinctive mode of being. That is, on both a concrete, specific level, and a more general level, one experiences life, lives life, in certain ways. Although these topics can only be touched on at this point, one lives within the moment, spontaneously experiencing and reacting to the situation as it is; more generally, one lives within a realistic understanding and acceptance of one's larger life situation, taking responsibility for the focus and direction of one's energies. Such a life, uniquely possible for reflective creatures, involves absorption within the moment, but with the moment experienced as involving past "determination" and future unfolding. It is thus not a narrow preoccupation with various disconnected and arbitrary demands of the moment.

Third, following from the second point, and modifying the first point, these phenomena are not simply a matter of having correct beliefs or adequate theories. Integration and fulfillment are phenomena involving the internal distributional lay of the entire organism; they are not phenomena generated by one aspect of the organism — reason — adopting views which may not flow coherently from the totality of the organism and which are then externally imposed on the organism.

Integration and fulfillment involve psychic and emotional movement of the sort which require identification of the mental states we undergo at various times, as well as knowledge of why we are undergoing them at that time, what are their causes at various levels, and with what other mental states they are connected. Such probings deepen our understanding of ourselves, for from them there emerges a *felt awareness* that is sharper and wider than previously existed. But such probings also deepen our understanding of the world, for in becoming more aware of ourselves, we become more aware of the beliefs, desires, wishes, fears etc. which we bring with us to experience. Being aware of these, we can then begin to separate out our own reactions to situations from those situations themselves. This, in turn, provides one with an awareness of alternatives to one's dominant perceptions of oneself, others and the world. Finally, such awareness is a step toward positive alteration or modification of how one sees and experiences life and the world. From this perspective, integration and fulfillment involve a transformation of one's fundamental ways of being in the world.

But if this is so, we are again back — though this time with greater urgency — to the problem of identifying our actual mental states. Although beset with numerous difficulties, the method which I think we must employ is identification through phenomenology. The reason why phenomenology is central to the enterprise is relatively clear: since integration and fulfillment are actual states of the individual, they involve experiencing certain mental states. These states must supplant[8] the pre-integrative states of the individual and for this to occur the latter must be identified. Given that the pre-integrative states are the experience of the moment, focusing on the experience, *feeling* it in its full range and at various levels of depth, will reveal the elements which constitute the experience.

The method of phenomenological identification, however, is beset with at least three major difficulties. First, there is the obvious point that at least sometimes we do not know what mental state or states we are experiencing. Assuming the mental state in question has a phenomenology, we can cover over this phenomenology either by failing or refusing to assign it its proper name. Innocently, we may be genuinely confused, uncertain of just what we are feeling; more ominously, we may not want to know what we are feeling. In the latter case, we may believe or think or convince ourselves that we are experiencing **x**, while in actuality we are experiencing **y**. For example, one may be angry, but simply deny it and insist one is indifferent. Here, a present phenomenology and so its mental state, anger, is simply misnamed; but, in a more complex fashion, the actual phenomenology may to various degrees be concealed by a manufactured, but not actually functioning, phenomenology of a different, also non-functioning, mental state, in this case, indifference.[9] Thus, actual, though unacknowledged phenomenologies and their interconnected mental states can in various ways be distorted, misnamed and hidden. As a result, phenomenological identification cannot simply function as a magical entrance into our actual mental states.

But however powerful this objection is, it is not an objection against the method of phenomenological identification; rather it is an objection against an overly simple use of that method. What the objection reveals is that the mechanisms of consciousness are such that phenomenologies and their intrinsic mental states can, in a variety of ways, be masked, covered over, or hidden by other activities and aspects of consciousness. The way out of this difficulty is not a rejection of phenomenological identification, but an awareness of the pitfalls of the method and so a more careful and judicious use of it. Briefly, this would involve the cultivation of the ability to trustingly relax into one's experiences so that their various dimensions will reveal or manifest themselves to explicit awareness. Such manifestations will be a complex of felt aspects of the experience — and these aspects will either have a distinctive phenomenology or will be internally connected to an aspect (or aspects) of the experience which does have a phenomenology.

These identifications and associations enable us to move more deeply into our inner lives and, since we are parts or aspects of the larger world process, into the way the world is as well. As suggested previously, it is through such movement that integration and fulfillment become possible. The method of phenomenological identification is as crucial as it is, for it enables us to be in touch with the felt quality of our lives. If integration and fulfillment are, to a significant degree, matters of the felt quality of our lives, we must work through the felt quality of our lives to attain them.

A second objection to the identification of mental states by phenomenology involves the claim that a large number of mental states do not have a phenomenology. Propositional attitudes, and especially beliefs and desires, often are said not to have any phenomenology at all. This, of course, is a large topic and I will have something to say about it when I discuss desire and belief (in Chapters 6 and 7, respectively). For now, although I think this is a significant problem, I do not think it is an overwhelming one. In many cases, perhaps all, what is crucial is how these phenomena are treated. If they are treated either as pure abstractions, isolable from any and all mental complexes, or as logical abstractions from particular mental states, or both, the temptation is indeed to say they have no phenomenology. If, however, they are treated as modifications of consciousness, inherently interconnected with a larger network of mental states, it is more likely that we will see (and experience) them as having a phenomenology or at least as directly tied to elements of the mental complex which do have a phenomenology. My inclination is to treat them in the latter fashion. But these are complex matters and I will return to them later.

The third objection to identification of mental states by phenomenology has affinities to the first objection, but also has a significantly different source and focus. This objection is especially powerful for those whose primary concern is not with integration and fulfillment, but is with the ontological status of mental states, especially when these are conceived of functionally and/or physically. If, as many materialists suggest, mental states are brain states and/or functional states, the phenomenology of a mental state, assuming it is even acknowledged, is not essential to the typing of that state. What is essential would be the brain and/or functional state which the mental state is alleged to *be*. On this view, we determine what type of mental state some particular mental state is not by its feel or phenomenology, but by discovering what brain state it is and/or by discovering how it functions within the larger mental/behavioral economy of the subject.

This is, of course, an interesting and important claim. But as suggested previously, it cannot by itself eliminate the lived dimension of mental states. Whatever the ontology of such states, there is still the need to determine how to live and so the inescapable need to focus on consciousness and its various phenomenologies.

There is, however, a consequence of this objection which does need attention at this point, for it is undeniable that mental states can be produced, not only through interaction with environmental situations, but also by direct stimulation of the physiological features of the organism which are the physical foundation of that type of mental state. But if this is so, it would seem that phenomenology — at least sometimes — is not relevant to the determination of the individual's life situation and so cannot be assigned the status of being universally relevant to the attaining of integration. This is, I think, correct, for while in one sense attention to an induced phenomenology reveals what an individual is experiencing — after all, that is what is being experienced — in another sense, this is not what is revealed at all. That is, the induced phenomenology does not flow from the individual's self-directed, continuous, organic involvement in experience; it is not connected to what, in the broader sense, the individual is *living through*. Since phenomenologies and their intrinsic mental states can only be indicative of the deeper and more general psychological mode of being of the individual when they arise from continuous, organic involvement in experience, artificially induced mental states and their phenomenologies could not be indicative of such modes. Having been artificially induced, they are isolated and discrete, not organically and coherently tied to the individual's more general mode of, or relationship to, existence.[10] In such cases, phenomenology cannot be taken as revelatory either of the mental state one is *living* through or of one's more general and deeper psychological way of being.

The conclusions reached in response to the first and third objections are somewhat similar. In both cases, it was acknowledged that identification of mental states by phenomenology is not only fallible, but that since phenomenologies can be manipulated or induced in a variety of ways, such identifications are not transparent, unproblematic entrances into one's genuine psychic life. With respect to the first objection, it was possible to claim that a more careful and judicious use of the method would tend to yield knowledge both of particular mental states and one's more general psychological way of being. This, however, is not possible to do in response to the third objection, for on that claim the source of error identification is found not in unawareness or self-deception, but in the different kind of thing a mental state is. And this, in turn, creates the problem of inducement of mental states through physiological stimulation.

The third objection, then, presents a difficult complication for the method of identification of mental states by phenomenology. Since mental states can be induced by stimulating appropriate physiological factors, it not only follows, once again, that phenomenology is not always indicative of what is actually being experienced or lived through; it also follows, uniquely, that reliance on phenomenology limits the class of mental states which are relevant to an exploration of the inner life and so the attainment of integration and fulfillment. Consequently, it becomes necessary to provide a non-arbitrary distinction between those mental states whose phenomenologies are relevant to grasping the inner life and those which are not. The obvious candidate here is a distinction between those mental states which are produced artifically and those which are not. The difficulty is in providing a reasonable content for the terms of the distinction. Clearly, mental states which are produced by the direct application of instrumentation or chemicals to the appropriate physiological areas can be said to be artificial. But a problem arises when we seek to limit artificially induced mental states to such cases, for there are a variety of additional ways in which mental states can be induced artificially, e.g., mind altering drugs, various chemicals in food and the environment, and, most generally, interacting with an environment which is artificial in the sense of not being original.

These last remarks lead to a much larger problem concerning the relationship of the notions of artificial and non-artificial to civilization or the world of the reflective creature. If "non-artificial" means "original" or "not made by human beings," then of course civilization, not being original, is artificial. Indeed, as we shall see in the coming chapters, it is the lot of reflective creatures to create a significantly new form of existence in the light of their need to direct their behavior in a relatively self-aware fashion. Within this situation, mental states arise through complex interactions with an environment which is not entirely original or natural, but has, in part, been produced by the efforts of reflective creatures. Whether one can precisely draw the distinction between what is and what is not artificial in such a context is, for a number of reasons, not clear. But lack of clarity at this level does not mitigate against providing, at another level, content for the needed distinction. From the fact that there is a sense in which much of civilization is artificial, i.e., not original, it does not follow that we can't, within that situation, make a qualitative distinction between types of artificiality. And that is what I wish to do, omitting from consideration those mental states which are produced by the direct application of instrumentation or chemicals. If it is integration and fulfillment we are concerned with and we see phenomenological identification of mental states as necessary to the attainment of such modes of being, the fact that phenomenologies can be artificially produced and so not be expressions of one's actual mode of being is simply irrelevant to the matter at hand.

Again, my concern is with integration and fulfillment, not with providing a comprehensive theory of the nature and ontology of the mental. If one's concern is with the former, it is those mental states which arise in the flow of the life situation which make up the subject matter of the investigation.

When we talk about mental states in what is to come, we will be talking only about mental states generated in interaction with the environment. No doubt such states are not only products of a long evolutionary development, a development to which reflective creatures have contributed, but they also have physiological causes or correlates. However, they will not be artificially produced, but will be seen as occurring within the ebb and flow of non-artificial, concrete, lived experience. The fact that such states are in part the outcome of a process of development does not detract from their role in the lived experience of the individual; nor does the fact that they are tied to a definite physiology detract from their psychological dimension. In short, the fact that mental states occur in interaction with an environment which is in part created, and also have a physiological base does not deprive them of their central place in the kind and quality of life being led by the creature who experiences them.

There is, however, one version of the problem generated by this third objection which would detract from the relevance of mental states *qua* mental states to the attainment of integration and fulfillment. This would be a finding that mental states were never caused directly by interaction within the environment, but were rather always caused directly by physical/chemical processes in the brain. This view would allow that environmental situations could trigger the physical/chemical processes, but it would not allow a separate causal role to the manner in which the individual psychologically experiences and reacts to the environmental situation.

Periodically, this sort of claim is made for certain kinds of mental states, especially "abnormal" ones such as depression. It is said that depression is not an outcome of how an individual is relating and responding to various life situations, but is the outcome of some sort of internal chemical imbalance. If such is the case, alleviation of depression would be a matter of providing the individual with the proper chemical balance, not a matter of identifying, through their phenomenologies, the various elements of depression so they might be adequately experienced and explored.

While this may be appropriate with some instances of depression, it does not follow that it is appropriate with all instances of depression. And further even in those cases in which there is a chemical imbalance, it does not follow that the imbalance was original and caused the depression. At the relevant level, it is possible that the depression in its psychological mode was original and caused the chemical imbalance. No doubt such a possibility wreaks havoc with certain notions of causality; but it cannot simply for that reason be dismissed.

Finally, while the chemical causes of mental states thesis has been held for various abnormal states, it has not, so far as I know, been held in that specific fashion for the whole range of mental states. The range of mental states which have an existence as psychological states is immense and so long as this is so, it is those states which constitute our sense of ourselves, others and the world. As such, they are our levers in the attempt to accomplish constructive, meaningful and fulfilling change — i.e., to establish creative alignment and connection to and within the process of which we are a part.

Conceptual Understanding and Personal Integration

Chapter Two

I

As suggested in the previous chapter, my primary concern is with personal integration. But this concern expresses itself in two interconnected dimensions: as a lived existential phenomenon and as a concept calling for conceptual analysis. This two-dimensional emphasis entails a more general concern, namely, the relationship, if any, between conceptual or analytic understanding of "integration," "self," "consciousness" and "self-awareness," on the one hand, and the phenomenon of personal integration on the other.

Crucially related to those issues is the problem mentioned in Chapter 1, of the nature of our awareness and knowledge of our particular psychological states, including sensations, perceptions, desires, beliefs, attitudes, and emotions. Since in my view integration is not something given, but attained, it is possible — indeed likely — that one's particular psychological states will not be an expression of an integrated self. In order to achieve integration, one would have to become aware of those particular states, understanding that they are not integrated into a coherent psychic order, as well as the factors which are producing the fragmentation and, in light of this awareness, create unity. Thus, the need for accurate awareness of one's psychological states is evident.

Given my concern with both the experience of integration and its proper conceptualization, the question emerges as to the relationship between these. For example, can one *be* an integrated person without having conceptual understanding of such integration? The answer to this seems to be a clear "yes." Integration has to do with how one experiences and acts within life situations, and this can be done in an integrated fashion with little or no analytic understanding of integration.

But, conversely, will a correct analysis of integration and the relevant connected concepts increase or produce such integration? This is complex, for while I think conceptual analysis can have a positive impact on integration, this has to be understood and explained within the context of a response to another question, namely, can one provide an adequate conceptualization of personal integration without being an integrated person? My tentative response to this question is "no," for in the absence of being integrated, what would ground and/or verify one's analysis? If there were not some degree of personal integration on the part of the analyzer, what would inform one's analysis and how would one ever know it was correct?

If this is so, one could be an integrated person without having an adequate analysis of the concept, but an adequate analysis could only be provided by someone to whom personal integration was to some extent an experiential reality, and not just an abstract concept. But now some puzzles seem to emerge with regard to my claim that integration is something which can be attained. First, if only someone who was already to some degree integrated could provide an adequate analysis of integration, it might be suggested that no one could ever attain integration, since in the absence of an adequate concept, one would not know what to pursue. Second, this might, in turn, also suggest what I have implicitly denied, namely that integration is a fixed and final state.

This latter point brings in a further complication, for seeing some state as fixed and final does not rule out the possibility that it was attained. The state could have been attained once and for all. This, however, is not the sort of attainment which is appropriate to integration. The latter can be attained, but not as a fixed, and final end state. Rather it is a dynamic psychic standpoint — itself always developing — from within which one encounters and deals with life situations; it is not a fixed, static state which dispenses solutions to all problems which arise within those situations. From this standpoint, there is no such thing as the "totally integrated person;" and to pursue such is to misunderstand the process nature of integration[1].

But this doesn't solve our first problem, namely, how, if only the at least somewhat integrated person can supply an adequate analysis of integration, one could become integrated. To attain something one needs to know what to pursue and if only having attained it one knows what it is, how then can one pursue it?

I think I can respond to this by elaborating something I previously said. Doing so will also show how conceptual understanding can have a positive impact on integration. Above, I indicated that one has to have some existential, concrete relationship to personal integration if one's analysis is to be at all satisfactory. On this reading, integration would have to be more than just a concept or an abstraction. One would have to see the concept as rooted in and capable of illuminating concrete, lived experience. Employing the concept from this perspective, or in this fashion, would enable one to expand one's personal grasp of integration by opening up further dimensions of one's concrete experience and exploring conceptually and experientially one's various states in that dimension.

The relationship between experience and concept is complex. There is an interplay: experience generates concept and theory, which is focused back on experience in an attempt at further elucidation of experience. The attempt is assessed in terms of the experience pointed to. As a result, re-conceptualization occurs — for experience has been expanded — and this, in turn, is re-focused back on experience. Out of this dialectical movement comes increased self-understanding and more adequate conceptualization and theory construction.

The following rough example will make these points more concrete. The example will be treated in general terms and is not being presented as a correct, full analysis of any situation. The only claim I am making for it, other than its ability to illustrate the relevant points, is that it is coherent.

Suppose one has been in major conflict through much of one's life concerning actions of type X. One strongly wants to perform such actions; yet one also strongly does not want to perform such actions. Let's assume further that the person has not gained any insight into the nature of these wants and so into the nature of the conflict. This individual is being pulled this way and that by elements of the psyche which have not been acknowledged or understood and so here is an obvious instance of non-integration or fragmentation.

Let us say at this point the individual hears a lecture on personal integration versus fragmentation and becomes interested in these ideas. However, he does not yet apply them to *his* concrete experience. He sees them simply as concepts or abstractions calling for analysis; and having an analytic inclination he starts working on the concepts, seeking to set out the logical and conceptual conditions or structures of "personal integration." But he does not see how the concepts can illuminate his experience or how they grow out of concrete, lived situations. What is the value of the analysis he provides? Can he shed any light on the concepts? These are difficult questions, but it is hard to see how his analysis can shed any light on the content of the concepts, for he is out of touch with those aspects of experience which inform the concepts, provide them with their content.

But suppose at some moment he does make the connection to his own experience and realizes that with regard to X, and other situations, he is not integrated. The concept is now illuminating his experience and provides a focus for investigation. Suppose he now begins to explore this particular instance of non-integration or fragmentation. This will lead him to see more deeply into the nature of his conflicting wants. Suppose he sees that for him, actions of type X represent a certain sort of success. He will then need to explore existentially, that is, emotionally and personally, what this means to him. Suppose he further finds out that there are strong feelings of guilt associated with success as he understands it. He is now in a position to see why he has constantly experienced conflict with regard to actions of type X. This, in turn, can lead him to analyze the concepts of success and guilt as well as to plunge into a deeper existential analysis of what his sense of guilt and success are further connected to within his experience.

In short, the concept of integration focused on concrete experience generates existential data. This focus expands personal awareness which, in its turn, generates more specific conceptual elucidations of experience which are further in turn refocused on the expanded existential awareness.

In our particular case, the outcome is a clearer grasp of the person's specific situation, his particular self, as well as various concepts relating to and including integration. He now has a contrast. The non-understood conflict situation is one of fragmentation; the state of insight into the conflict is the beginning of integration. Indeed, if with more work and insight, as well as courage, the person can see into, explore and assimilate in a coherent fashion the previously hidden elements, he will almost certainly become a more integrated person.

II

There are two points of clarification which need to be made at this point. First, the experiential or existential dimension is in a significant sense more fundamental than the conceptual. This is *not* to claim that the conceptual has no constitutive or modifying influence on the experiential. Nor is it to claim that experience offers an area of infallibility which can serve as a criterion for the assessment of all conceptual and theoretical claims. I do not think there is any such area of infallibility. Yet, I do think that it is experience which is the ultimate generator of all analyses and that, although experience is itself in constant flux, we must come back to it so as to ground our assessments and generate new analyses.

Second, though I am centrally concerned with experience and integration in their concrete existential aspect, the relevant conceptual analyses are abstract and impersonal, providing elucidations which hold — at least ideally — for any human being. The particularities of personal experience are thus irrelevant to these analyses. But the tie to the particular person is maintained as the analyses push the person into deeper and more comprehensive explorations of psychic states. Here, then, in the case of personal integration, we have a clear tie between concept and experience.

Now, the concept/experience of personal integration seems to be subsumed within the concept/experience of self. For it is self which — however at this point we understand that notion — can be said to be either integrated or not. Integration, fragmentation or a mixture of the two are forms which self can take. As such, self appears to be a more fundamental notion/datum than integration or fragmentation and so the analysis of personal integration would seem to call for a more fundamental analysis of self. If the analysis of personal integration implies an analysis of self which would be a continuation of the analysis of personal integration, we should be able to move to a deeper level of analysis and further develop the experience/concept dialectic. And this is indeed what I think is needed. Yet, as indicated previously, there are many thinkers who do not treat self in this fashion at all.

Many analyses of self have the appearance of removing themselves from concrete, personal, lived experience. These analyses are generated by various metaphysical, semantic and epistemological questions, and self is often treated as an abstraction from concrete, lived experience, one which is demanded by how we think and talk about the world. Thus given particular experiences or states, we claim there must be a possesser or owner of these, a subject in which these states inhere. Similarly, we talk about self, have an expression "I" and look for what is thereby referred to.

These are interesting, complex and important matters which reflect a legitimate desire to comprehend the general structural features of the phenomenon and its related concepts. However, such analyses often ignore or downplay the experience of *being* a particular self seeking self-understanding. When this happens the two sorts of analyses — abstract and experiential — seem to bypass each other. They come to occupy different, almost alien, realms. As a result, there is little or no interpenetration of the analyses and two radically different perceptions of self emerge. One of these perceptions of self we can refer to as "abstract," the other as "lived."

A number of questions confront us at this point. First, how and why has this split between perceptions of self developed? And second, can the two perceptions be integrated? Can they be seen as coming together at more fundamental levels? Although a full account of the origins and development of this split is beyond the scope of this work, I will, in a moment, offer some general remarks. What I wish to do now is comment on one apparent aspect of the present situation with the hope of casting some light on the split.[2]

As mentioned above, those interested in self as abstract often start their analyses from general considerations concerning language and the structure of how we think about ourselves and the world. These are analyzed and theories are developed to bring together and expand the various analyses. Such undertakings are, of course, quite legitimate. We do wish to understand the phenomena, and if the preferred analyses and/or theories are correct, they yield a generality of structure which holds for all individuals and do not involve the particularities of any individual's personal experience. In this way, then, there is a sense in which experience, *i.e.*, the phenomenologically given, is irrelevant to the analysis of self. But it does not follow that experience or the phenomenologically given has no relevance whatsoever to abstract analyses and theories of self. What I think is relevant here is the more general but still individual experience of living a life as a self. It is this phenomenon which the abstract analyses and theories must describe and account for.

If there is a discrepancy between the account offered and what is experienced, this is reason to think there is something wrong with the analyses and theories. To be sure, it is possible there is something inadequate in our "grasp" of experience itself; but there is a limit to pushing this kind of problem onto experience. If experience is always "wrong," there is no solace to be found in analysis and theory, for the latter are *always* generated from within experience and are also evaluated by means of experience. That is, experience, inevitably, is both the generator and evaluator of analysis and theory. As such, experience is primary in relation to the latter. If we impugn experience at its most fundamental levels, we are doing the same, but even more radically, to analysis and theory.

Yet, it is understandable that experience or the phenomenologically given are looked at with suspicion. For it is not at all clear what is given. To be sure, experience needs to be looked at, explored, taken apart. But recognizing the need for systematic exploration of experience is far indeed from rejecting the latter as hopelessly confused, distorted, or subjective. If we do reject experience or the phenomenologically given in a wholesale fashion, we reject probably the only phenomenon which can take us to the depth of our lived being. And this can be seen even if we focus on language and the structure of thought, the phenomena which typically motivate the various abstract analyses of self.

What is found in our language, in the structure of thought, emerged in the course of living. These do not pre-exist human life,[3] but are created, no doubt non-consciously, in the process of the development of ways of life, in the response by various peoples to various environments. As such, these flow from some of the deepest and most primordial aspects of experience, precisely those aspects which can be discovered through an exploration of experience or what is phenomenologically given. That is, the phenomenologically given being the surface outcome of these developments, the depth of the given will be the dimensions of experience which the surfaces display. Thus, to get a proper sense of language and the structure of thought, one needs to be attentive to their origins in particular life situations. In this way, it can be argued that analyses and theory construction are most promising when they work through experience or the phenomenologically given.

This leads into our second question: can the two realms of discourse, the two perspectives on self, be integrated? Indeed, I think they can. If language and the structure of thought are developments out of lived experience, analyzing them as aspects of the phenomenologically given will bring us, at sufficient levels of depth, to the experiences, the ways of relating to life, which produce them. If this be so, we can continue our experience/concept dialectic with regard to self, for it is, I think, a certain sort of development in the history of consciousness which has produced the experiential datum out of which the language and metaphysics of self has itself developed. Through the course of time, we have become selves in a certain way and thus we can talk about self, the structure of thought and the metaphysics of self.

But in all of this what remains primordial is *being* a self. There are two interconnected reasons for this. First, self as abstract is itself generated by self as lived. It is out of the experience of living that an attempt is made to account in abstract terms for the phenomenon of living as a self. In addition, it is by means of materials furnished by self as lived that abstract accounts of self are evaluated, *i.e.*, there are no criteria of evaluation other than those provided by self as lived. From such a standpoint, self as lived is *necessarily* primordial and fundamental in relation to self as abstract.

Connected to this is the peculiar self-reflective nature of self. The proper understanding of self includes among other things, an experiential understanding of the uniqueness of self seeking to understand itself. Such an understanding cannot come from description, even accurate and adequate description. Indeed, where else would such a description come from, if not from an adequate experiential grasp of the experience itself? To put the point somewhat differently, an adequate understanding of self must come from the "inside," not the "outside." External, descriptive accounts are secondary and removed. Since "inside" accounts flow from *being* a self, are grounded in being a self, the primordial and fundamental phenomenon is, once again, being a self.

III

What, then, is this "certain way we have become selves?" What I think is involved is the occurrence of a certain sort of separation. Somehow, over the course of evolution, consciousness developed the ability to reflect back on itself, to make its own states objects of attention. Once this move occurs, separation occurs in two fundamental and profound ways. First, consciousness becomes divided within itself, for one aspect of consciousness is now capable of attending to other aspects of consciousness. But, if consciousness can now attend to itself, it can develop a standpoint from which its states "are had" in a new fashion. The creature is no longer exclusively immersed in experience, but is now reflecting on experience, "noticing" that those states are its states. This occurrence is, I think, tantamount to the emergence of self. And with this emergence, there occurs the second form of separation, namely, that between self and "not-self." For, in order to have even a rudimentarily explicit sense of self, one must also have a sense of not-self. Indeed, the relevant sense of self emerges only in terms of a simultaneous awareness that there is other than self.

These remarks suggest a crucial distinction between awareness and reflection. Pre-reflective creatures are certainly aware; they are conscious beings which have a wide range of experiences and can be said, in a somewhat limited sense, to live a life. Being pre-reflective, however, they cannot reflect on those experiences and so they neither have a sense of self in the manner under discussion nor experience the kinds of separation this involves. [4] In the relevant sense, then, pre-reflective consciousness is unified, non-divided.

While reflective creatures display a mode of awareness, *i.e.*, *non*-reflective awareness, which is comparable to, although different from, pre-reflective awareness, they also display reflective awareness or self-reflection, which is a divided state of awareness. The consequences of the development of this mode of awareness are quite significant. Pre-reflective creatures, not capable of self-reflection, stay within pre-reflective awareness, cannot know or conceive of anything else, and so don't find this state or their existence problematic. Reflective creatures, however, reflect on pre-reflective awareness and seek to understand it; but such understanding can be found only in terms of reflecting, analyzing, and commenting on the pre-reflective state; and this is something of a different order.

Indeed, given the emergence of reflection, pre-reflection vanishes as a state of the organism and is replaced by non-reflection. Pre-reflection is a state of creatures who do not ever reflect; non-reflection is a state of creatures who do reflect, but are not at the moment reflecting. The non-reflective state is different from the pre-reflective state in that the former, but not the latter, becomes permeated by the products of reflection and so is altered and expanded.

Thus, while reflective awareness provides a startling new development in the movement of consciousness and enables the emergence of the distinctively human world, it can come to obscure and corrupt the direct immersion in experience that was pre-reflective experience.

Given this, a number of large and difficult questions emerge. At this point, I wish to state them and offer a few general comments. I will return to these topics in later chapters, especially Chapter 3. First, to what degree, if at all, can non-reflective awareness — the fruit of reflection — be a direct immersion in experience? Does the shift from pre-reflective to non-reflective immersion produce an unbridgeable gap or distance or separation between creature and experience? And with respect to reflection, does the attempt by reflection to understand, or "capture," the non-reflective moment create a still larger gap between experience and the reflective self?

To focus briefly on the last question, it certainly does seem that once reflection emerges as an autonomous activity, it seeks to impose its way of knowing on the whole range of experience. It seeks to grasp non-reflective awareness in its own terms which is one-level removed conceptualization. But no conceptualization, no after-the-fact analysis, can capture the moment of non-reflective awareness, for these are two distinctly different orders of existence. The latter is a non-reflective, non-self-conscious immersion in experience, while the former is a reflective stepping back from experience so that it may be captured in concept and theory. But this cannot be done: while the former involves the *having* of experience, the latter involves not the having of experience, but a commentary, by means of concepts, on the experience. Having an experience, though no doubt involving concepts at a non-reflective level, is not the same as describing an experience, previously had, by means of concepts.

Reflective consciousness, however, is reluctant to accept this conclusion and so typically responds in either of two ways. First, in its attempt to capture non-reflective awareness, it may blur the difference between awareness and reflection and foist onto awareness what is unique to reflection, namely reflection on the awareness. In this way, awareness becomes obscured, indeed perhaps lost, and separation becomes alienation. Alternatively, reflective consciousness may grasp that its reflections miss what is essential to non-reflective awareness and seek to rectify this by elaborating more complex systems of reflection, including reflection on the reflection, etc. As these systems of reflection multiply, we get farther and farther away from non-reflective awareness and in this way, too, separation becomes alienation.

I am not suggesting that post-reflective awareness can be the same as pre-reflective awareness. Once reflective consciousness emerges, consciousness is irretrievably altered. The original unity of consciousness is broken and awareness is expanded, deepened. This alteration and expansion creates a deep problem for consciousness. For if separation is not overcome and duality becomes permanent or "solidified," alienation is the outcome. Consciousness can get caught up in abstractions, in reflection, and lose its direct tie with lived experience. As a result of these developments, a new unity needs to be created, one which overcomes, among others, the split between reflection and awareness. One way of focusing on this situation is through the concept/experience of integration. From this perspective, the latter can be seen as a personal problem because it is a larger social and, in a significant sense, metaphysical problem.

Separation or reflective awareness seems to be the basic occurrence out of which *all* our questions concerning self emerge. It creates, I think, both of the broad perspectives on self and sets the range of questions associated with each. Just as reflective awareness creates the general problem for the self as lived, *i.e.*, the relation of reflection to awareness, so does it set the general problem for the self as abstract. For with the emergence of reflection, the ability to attend to one's states, one begins to look for the reflector, the attender, the "I" or self which has these states, unifies them. With both perspectives on self, seemingly discrete parts or aspects develop and a sense of wholeness or unity is sought. In both cases, however, it is important to see that such unity does not pre-exist; rather it needs to be developed, created, in the process of living. This is, let us say, *the* contemporary problem of consciousness.

Both perspectives on self—lived and abstract—seem to emerge from the same development and can be understood to seek the same general outcome. Yet, they involve different approaches and surface concerns. In the remainder of this chapter, I would like to explore some of the details of the self as abstract.

IV

If one's concern is with the general considerations that enable us to talk about self or that drive us to talk about self, one will probably first fasten onto the notion of self as owner of particular mental states. There is a distinct oddness to the idea of free floating mental states detached from any greater unity or whole and so it is natural to seek to find a subject for those states, a substance in which they inhere. The naturalness of this model is fortified by the fact that in at least some sense we are aware of particular states and so something—what in this case is suggested by "we"—is aware. What is aware is felt to be other than the observed states and so we now have an observer which is the subject or substance suggested by the previous considerations. This subject we can also call "self." But now we proceed, again naturally, to the next step and seek to observe the observer, so we can know what sort of being it is. But now these seemingly natural steps start producing absurdities and internal whirlwinds. For the observer of the particular states cannot be observed, cannot be grasped. Such a grasp or observation could be accomplished only by something outside the system of consciousness. To observe the observer in the act of observing within the system of consciousness is impossible, for each act of observation includes the observer and so includes as its essential component what is being looked for. There is no state of consciousness which could accomplish this task. Thus the observer or self is systematically and necessarily elusive, not to be known or grasped. Each attempt to find the observer shipwrecks on the realization that one cannot find one's self finding one's self. The finder is not to be found.

Reflections of this sort have led people to deny that there is an internal self or ego, which is the owner of particular states and which can be introspectively known. However, it has not kept people from searching for self in other ways. This is quite understandable, for one of the outcomes of the ability to self-reflect is the sense of "mineness" which emerges not only in relation to the introspected states, but also to the body in which self is sometimes thought of as being encased. There is indeed a sense of unity and however we ultimately decide to characterize it, it is foolhardy to deny this.

One suggestion sometimes offered is that the self is the body. But difficulties develop here, for by "body" does one mean "the whole body?" Hardly, for I can remove virtually any part of my body — say my left foot, right ear, etc. — and still be me. To be sure, if I remove certain parts or enough of certain parts, I will no longer be alive. But if this implies — as it surely should — that I will no longer be a self, then, if the body is self, it must be a live body. That is, a body having parts in a certain relationship to other parts, the outcome of which is animation of a certain sort. Similarly, even if we decide that there is a part of the body, say, the heart or brain, which is essential to a live body, this part by itself would not be the self, for it would have no relationships or connections to other parts which animate the body and make it a personified body. So fastening on the body as the self won't do. It is not the body as body which can be self, but only body which involves certain internal relationships and is capable of generating certain sorts of behavior. If those dimensions of body are not included in our notion of self, virtually any objects — even inanimate ones — could be thought of as a self. Given that not all bodies are selves, we need differentia in terms of which this body is a self and that body is not.

A more likely candidate for self would be the person, the spiritualized body — or, so as not to beg the question against materialism, the properly wired or encoded body. But then our question would be: what is it that transforms a body into a person? And I think what must be the reply here is the ability to self-reflect. But now we seem to have come full circle. We are back with the development, i.e., the split within consciousness, which creates a sense of self which in turn sets off the search for the nature of this self, and if we proceed as before, we will travel the same route and finish again where we are now.

In all of this, the elusive sense of unity is sought by finding something, identifying something as self. Perhaps as inevitable as this approach seems, there is something deeply misleading about it. Perhaps it even solidifies and exacerbates the original problem, namely, the division of consciousness created by the ability to self-reflect.

V

The overall approach we've been discussing is subtle and opaque. Finding its deeper assumptions, bringing them to the surface and providing evaluation is no easy matter. Yet within this approach, some of its ways are more obvious and more easily detectable than others. The search for a Cartesian ego is, I think, an instance of the former. The discussions by John Perry and David Lewis concerning Hume, the mad Heimson and assorted amnesiacs is, I think, an example of the latter.[5] With regard to Hume-Heimson, Perry and Lewis's analyses seem to suggest that in saying or thinking "I believe I am Hume," there is a significant sense in which both Hume and Heimson are saying or thinking the same thing—not just uttering or thinking the same words — so that this locution is equally coherent for both. In a complicated and not obvious manner, I think their claim is an outcome of the larger problem of separation we have been considering.

If I understand the matter, the general problem arises, in part, from the fact that no set of descriptions can substitute for direct self-ascription; or, non-linguistically, that no set of descriptions can substitute for the direct awareness that is involved in self-ascription. Thus, knowing oneself, that is, referring to oneself, under a description is not genuine self-knowing or self-referring unless one knows that the description applies to oneself. In this way a wedge is driven between the direct non-reflective awareness of oneself, *the awareness of immersion in experience,* and various aspects of oneself which one is not directly aware of. Now, this is a situation which is obviously true of all of us all the time. Any number of true descriptions can be found concerning me about which I am unaware. Thus, I may talk about myself and not know I am doing so; I may hear others talk of me and not know they are referring to me; and others may talk of me and not know they are referring to me. In each case, it may not be known that the descriptions employed refer to me.

For example, if I am the five-thousandth person to buy a certain product in the last ten years, and the person who is the five-thousandth person is to receive a gift, then I and someone else, both of whom do not know I am this person, can discuss together who won the prize and not know we are referring to me, though we are both speaking of me.

This is a typical feature — indeed a necessary feature — of everyday life, one which exists given the ability of consciousness to self-reflect. Indeed, as consciousness becomes more and more reflective, making more and more distinctions, separating out more and more actual and possible states and relationships, there will be more and more descriptions of me which I do not recognize. Each time I become aware of one of these, I gain some new piece of *information* about myself. What was unknown, unassimilated, is now no longer so; but it is known as a fact about me.

This, then, is everyday mundane reality, an aspect of self-reflective consciousness and, typically, gets little mention. However, even though we do constantly talk about the self and its states and what it owns, there is a deeper core of self-unity and self-awareness which it is inappropriate to treat in this fashion. This core involves the level of sheer non-reflective awareness. Such awareness, or the absorption in experience which it is, is not something about which I gain information. Indeed, it is not something separate from me about which I could gain information; it is rather the very configuration which my existence takes.

I can, of course, obtain information about the contents or particularities of such awareness; but I do not obtain information about the awareness itself. I non-mediately experience it; the awareness *is* my mode of existence. At the relevant level, I can no more be separated from it, than a knife can be separated from its edge.

It is this non-reflective awareness or absorption in experience which, through the ability to self-reflect, I come at another level of complexity to know of, that is, experience as my particular existence. I am given or take a name and I apply it to this awareness in its various ranges of development. Because I do apply a name to the "stream of life," it is possible, under certain circumstances, for the name to become separated from what it refers to. But the sheer "stream of life" does not itself contain this sort of separation; it rather involves living, non-reflectively, the life of the person one has reflectively come to know one is. In the standard case, I live the life of N.R.; I don't believe either that I am living the life of N.R. or that I am N.R.

As indicated, however, there are cases in which the name becomes separated from its referent. For example, this occurs in various forms of unconsciousness such as sleep or being knocked out. In such cases, a whole range of awareness does not exist and on waking up or "coming to," one can acknowledge that one is a particular person. Thus, there are cases in which our sense that we are the particular person we are is at least temporarily lost. These, however, are cases in which the previously developed reflective sense of self, in its turn absorbed into non-reflection, is lost due to possibilities of consciousness additional to the previous developments. Thus, falling asleep or getting knocked out create situations in which the knowledge/awareness one has developed that one is the person living this life is temporarily lost. On awakening or "coming to" one can regain that knowledge/awareness. But notice, this way of treating the matter presupposes a knowledge/awareness that one is the person one is. In the absence of this, one could not regain it. Moreover, such knowledge/awareness is had only because of the more fundamental absorption or immersion in experience which is not itself reflective; and it is this level of experience which is equivalent to being N.R. or living the life of N.R.

I am suggesting that absorption in experience is knowledge or awareness, but knowledge or awareness which does not involve anything resembling explicit belief. If this is so, my knowledge that I am N.R. or I am living the life of N.R. is direct and non-propositional, although having this knowledge allows me, in certain circumstances, to make it indirect and propositional.

It is, I think, from this perspective that we ought to treat the problems generated by a consideration of amnesiacs and Hume/Heimson. An amnesiac, not knowing who he is, treats every item he gathers in his search for his identity as a piece of information; and then, if these bits of information add up so that he knows who he is, he will treat that knowledge as simply the largest bit of information. In such cases, it is indeed appropriate to say "I believe I am (proper name)."

Similarly with Hume and Heimson. The latter is mad and wishes to think of himself as Hume. Thus, when he says "I believe I am Hume," his claim is intelligible. What makes it intelligible is the falsity of his claim that he is Hume, that he is the person living the life of Hume. This is a piece of misinformation and should be compared to Hume's saying "I was born in Bombay," another piece of misinformation. In contrast, "I believe I am Hume," uttered or thought by Hume in the absence of special circumstances such as amnesia, is not intelligible. For being Hume is not a comment on living the life of Hume; it is rather the absorption in the life flow that the person called Hume experiences. In the absence of special circumstances the only way "I believe I am Hume" is intelligible is if it is assimilated to the gaining of information about ourselves — a model which I am suggesting is quite misleading.

Let's look at this a bit more closely. "I believe I am Hume" could mean: a) "I believe I am the person named Hume;" or it could mean: b) "I believe I am the person living the life of Hume." If a), in turn, means "I believe my name is Hume," then of course it is intelligible, though it is irrelevant to the issue at hand. When Perry/Lewis talk about the amnesiac searching for identity, or Heimson insisting he is Hume, or Hume allegedly believing he is Hume, they are not simply talking about discovering and/or believing what one's name is. They are rather talking about an awareness or knowledge of living a particular life with a particular content. Thus b), or something like it, is the proper interpretation of "I believe I am Hume." But if this is so, there are problems. First, there is the implication that "I" and "Hume" may not be the same. This is, of course, possible for the amnesiac, but I am suggesting it is misleading to think of the standard case in this fashion. Directly related to this is a second problem. If "I believe I am Hume" is interpreted as "I believe I am the person living the life of Hume," and "I" and "Hume" can be imagined as distinct, then the latter sentence should be taken as providing a contrast to "I believe I am the person living the life of Leibniz" — or Descartes or anyone else for that matter. In the standard case — though admittedly not in the amnesiac case — "I" and the life being led do not come apart so readily. It is not that "I" could have been X or Y or Z, and it just so happens that I is N.R. Rather, in the absence of special circumstances, there is no I other than the I which is N.R. Treating the standard case as if it were significantly like the amnesiac case is to imply that such a treatment is not only intelligible, but perhaps adequate. But this, I suggest, is to distort the standard case.

Probably at no point in his life did Hume — or do any of us in our lives — have occasion to say or think "I believe I am Hume" — or "I believe I am (proper name)." This is because we do not, at the relevant level, have a relationship to ourselves; we simply are who we are; this is direct and non-reflective, does not involve separation. That this directness can come apart to some degree (I say "to some degree" since the amnesiac does not forget he exists) is no reason to treat the standard case from the standpdoint of the non-standard. It does not follow from the fact that, though amnesiacs may have occasion to say or think "I believe I am (proper name)," there is ever any occasion for non-amnesiacs to say or think a similar thing. And this is not a point about the conversational appropriateness of certain expressions; it is rather a point about how we live and experience life. To suggest that in the absence of special circumstances it is appropriate for Hume to say or think "I believe I am Hume," is to suggest that in the standard case it is intelligible to think of Hume's awareness that he is Hume as an informational item, an external contingent, happenstance appropriation of what is in reality directly and non-reflectively given or manifest.

Perhaps what is ultimately going on here is a conflation of reflection with what I have previously called "awareness." "I am the person living the life of N.R." This is *one* datum; it is direct, non-reflective. It is only through reflection, *i.e.*, self-consciousness, that I can say or think this sentence. This and other acts of reflection create a separation which *can* become solidified. To foist this standpoint onto the standard case is to read into the latter what is not necessarily there and so to distort the core of the experience. It is to impose the demands of reflection on non-reflective awareness and so pull one farther away from that direct immersion in experience which appears to be vital to integrated living.

There is a sense in which my remarks are not just descriptive, but are normative. Of course I recognize, though lament, the possibility, indeed often the actuality, of self-separation or alienation. Indeed, the more the reality of the latter, the more the appropriateness of "I believe (or know) I am (proper name)." Reflection is a necessary condition for this. My claim is that in the presence of reflection, we need to create a richer, expanded tie to lived experience. I suggest that this tie (or absorption) exists in our awareness of (or immersion in) living a life. Though extremely general and lacking in content, this is direct, not mediated by belief or knowing. Though we can and *must* develop the perspective of reflection — and so reflective belief and knowing — we must not do so at the expense of direct, non-reflective awareness. To do so is to distort what is probably most primordial in existence and so to create what very well might be an insurmountable problem.

Consciousness and Personal Integration

Chapter Three

I

I have suggested that self as abstract arises through the development of the ability to reflect, to make felt experience the objection of attention. I have also suggested that this ability can be developed in such a way that it clashes with and comes to obscure felt experience. When this occurs, we have separation "gone bad," or what is commonly called "alienation." But this possibility, however troublesome, is the other side of the coin of the development of the distinctively human world, which involves the emergence and creation of a "center," or "focus," or self to direct action. But while the reality of human life does lead us to talk in this fashion, such talk does not necessarily point to the existence of a Cartesian Ego or an entity of any sort. Rather, terms such as center, focus, and self express the sense of "mineness" which emerges from the ability to reflect and is tied to the experience of self-directed action.

Once an organism is no longer primarily governed by its pre-reflective instincts, it needs in part to determine how to interact with its environment so that what is needed for survival may be attained. Behavior, that is, must be directed in a fruitful fashion; and, for this to occur, there must be a coherent, ordered center or self. To be effective, such a self must be in direct contact with the residual instincts, the at least surface physiology of the organism, and the environment. The less behavior reflects such contact or connection, the less productive will the behavior be for the organism.

The loosening of the direct, essentially univocal connection between instinct and behavior enables a variety of forces — primarily, but not exclusively, physiological — to compete for expression in behavior. This places a large burden on the center or self for, within limits, it is this center which must determine which of these forces is to be given expression. In order to do this successfully, self must be able to distinguish, in any particular case, those forces which are worthy of expression from those which are not. Minimally, then, self must be in direct contact with both the relevant forces and the nature of the environment, as well as have a sense of what outcome is worth having. This is obviously no small accomplishment. Indeed, it is no exaggeration to say that the need — and thus the task — of humanity is to create this essentially new way of existing.

The development of self, and so the process of reflection and choice, is itself a historical one, ranging from primitive and rudimentary versions of the relevant forces at the beginnings of reflection to more sophisticated versions as the process complicates itself. Complications proceed by means of the introduction of expanded or new elements into consciousness. These include items of information concerning physiology and the environment, as well as items peculiar to the development of consciousness itself. Thus, belief, desire, want, need, and particular emotions either come into existence or are expanded out of similar but significantly less developed aspects of consciousness. In addition, and with far-reaching consequences, the ability is developed not only to reflect on the choices made and the items involved in the choices, but also on the reflection itself.

Due to the complexity and obscurity of the task of self-direction in the world, the center or self is in constant danger of not achieving a unified standpoint or, if achieved in some instances, coming apart or fragmenting in others. For example, one force among others may gain ascendency because of a failure to recognize or acknowledge its operation; or a force may be recognized, but its appropriateness to the circumstance misjudged; or an aspect of the environment may be misunderstood or distorted; or the value of an outcome may be misevaluated, and so on. There is thus a need to integrate the center or self with regard both to its "internal" components and its relationship to "external" not-self.

But now we have a series of problems, not the least of which is a conceptual one. Integration can be taken exclusively as a descriptive term. As such, it refers essentially to unity or wholeness, non-fragmentation. This use, however, says nothing about the content of unity or wholeness. For example, someone who engages in willfully destructive or evil action may be perfectly integrated in feeling, intent and action. If this is so, then on a purely descriptive level integration is compatible with destructiveness and evil. This, however, is incomplete, for in addition to having a descriptive meaning, integration also has a normative meaning; and this latter meaning is not to be understood entirely in terms of the agent's ability to achieve his intent in action. If we fail to acknowledge such a normative meaning, the individual of destructive or evil intent who was not able to achieve his goal either because of an internal conflict concerning intent or goal, or a failure in executing the intent, would not be integrated, while an individual with the same intent who had neither a conflict nor a failure of execution would be an integrated person.

In contrast, I am suggesting there are levels of integration and that the normative use of integration reflects more deeply the way the individual relates both to the forces within him, and to others and the larger environment. Most generally and fundamentally, integration has to do with the way these forces and aspects of existence are or are not aligned. Unity is integration; disunity or fragmentation is non-integration or alienation. From this standpoint, someone who is integrated at the level of destructive or evil action is not integrated at more fundamental levels, for the interconnected emotions, intentions and actions display a disunity with the deeper elements of existence.

If we look at integration in this fashion, we see that it is interconnected with other terms, such as "happiness" and "fulfillment," which are normative in the same fashion. Understanding these and like terms within the metaphysical perspective of awareness, reflection, separation and the overcoming of separation yields a vision or ideal of life as involving creative integration. It is the emergence of a self or center which is productive of action that necessitates that we treat these notions in such a manner; for without them so functioning, we cannot create the new form of life demanded by the loosening of instinct and the emergence of self awareness. That is, in the absence of normative or value perspectives, the self or center cannot perform the functions which must be performed if survival and flourishing are to be attained.

II

These are large and controversial claims which I will return to as we proceed. For now, I wish to emphasize that the route to the achievement of degrees of integration is through lived experience, or what in the last chapter I referred to as "self as lived." In addition, I wish to add a further word on the place of self as abstract in this process.

Since integration is a concrete, lived phenomenon of human existence, it will emerge only by means of contact with various elements of concrete, lived experience. In the absence of such contact, one may develop new ideas or concepts, but one's deeper emotional life will remain largely, perhaps entirely, untouched. This perspective on integration requires that we treat self as lived, not abstract; but it does not call for the rejection of self as abstract. With the advent of reflection, especially advanced reflection, self as abstract becomes both an integral and helpful aspect of human existence. Having such a notion enables us to gain at least some abstract understanding of reflective consciousness and to develop an increased sense of how best to relate to the various aspects of existence. That such abstract analysis must be grounded in and evaluated within the structure of concrete, lived experience does not detract from the importance of developing coherent abstract analyses of the phenomena. Indeed, what is needed is an understanding that the dichotomy "self as abstract/self as lived" is a false dichotomy and that both notions are encompassed within a broader perspective in which the ability to reflect flows out of concrete, lived experience and expands lived experience to such an extent that the individual (and the species) become socially self-aware (partial) directors of life.

If this is so, a very interesting and important point seems to follow. If lived experience is primordial, then any state of consciousness including any abstract view of experience or the world or self is itself an instance or expression of lived experience. However remote or non-existent the tie to lived experience may appear, it yet remains, and all elaborations of consciousness are variations of lived experience. This suggests that while the connection of consciousness to lived experience may become attenuated, distorted, obscured, or even lost both to awareness and reflection, it is nonetheless ineradicable. One's state of consciousness, one's ideas, concepts and theories, may seem to populate a world divorced from lived experience. This, however, is not so; it is just that the connection to the forces operating within lived experience is lost sight of, not recognized. But whether recognized or not, these forces retain their constitutive and causal power. Indeed, it is often the case that the less they are recognized, the more potent is their constitutive and causal efficacy. In such circumstances, we remain tied to lived experience, but in an unaware, unconscious fashion. In a word, we become alienated, for we are out of touch with, unaware of, the elements in lived experience which are effectively operating on us.

This situation has dire consequences. Having lost its deeper and actual tie to the flow of experience and the dimensions of feeling, expectation and desire involved at that level, reflective consciousness creates its own repertoire of feeling and belief to handle the demands of everyday existence. Unhappily, however, as a result of such a move surface behavior expresses fragmentation in two interconnected ways: behavior becomes fragmented both within itself and with regard to the deeper sources of its creation. Not being aware of the deeper sources of behavior, one is disconnected—and so alienated—from these sources. As a result there is a split or fragmentation between surface behavior and its explanation, on the one hand, and the depth of lived experience on the other. This, in turn, is connected both as cause and effect to the dynamics of surface behavior. Since the forces are not assimilated into and directed by an ordered self, they express themselves, willy-nilly, in any number of directions. This creates a series of internal conflicts which are typically resolved by the relative strength of the forces, not by a sense of what is aligned with the objective situation and is worth expressing. Often different constellations of purpose, meaning, belief and desire coalesce, each seeking expression in the same behavioral situation. But since the forces at work are not in such cases available either to awareness or reflection at the moment of operation, they cannot be formed into a coherent order.

The outcome of this complex of processes is the tenuousness of reflective consciousness; and so the latter spends much time seeking to provide a rational, coherent order for these behaviors. This, however, cannot be done in the absence of direct connections to the relevant dimensions of lived experience. And so instead we have the pervasiveness of rationalization, *i.e.*, the providing of "acceptable," but non-functioning, reasons for patterns of behavior that would otherwise be unintelligible and unacceptable. Rather than alleviate the difficulties of the situation, the providing of non-functioning reasons adds to them and becomes an integral part of one's alienation from the flow of experience.

A special complexity which exacerbates the situation is that the tie to lived experience, the flow of life, has to be both maintained and created anew. There are a number of reasons for this. First, the perspective of reflection necessarily removes us from the pre-reflective immersion in lived experience instinct affords. Second, as awareness and reflection develop, they add further and distinctive elements of change to an environmental situation which, through the various forces acting on it, has an independent source of change and development. Consequently, both the flow of experience and the tie to the flow are ever developing, ever changing. In such a situation, the standpoint of reflection, or self, is unsure of itself, both in terms of its own states and its relation to not-self.

This uncertainty can be seen more clearly if we expand our perspective beyond the individual. Indeed, such an expansion is appropriate, for the problems we are discussing have a larger and more fundamental dimension. As indicated previously, the problems of separation and integration are problems of the species. Since reflection, and what it brings with it, emerges in the historical development of consciousness, it involves the species as a whole. Seeing matters in such a fashion makes us aware that there is a specific social dimension to these problems; for once reflection — and thus the individual — emerges, original, pre-reflective sociality is altered. The individual, now aware of himself as an individual, can imagine himself separate from the social whole. This can and has given rise to the sense that the individual is a self-contained, self-sufficient entity; that social existence is one form of existence, individual existence another and the tie between them merely contingent. This is, I think, an example of deep social alienation, for individualism, I would argue, emerges only through the process of socialization. The emergence of individualism does not cancel sociality, but creates the simultaneous duality of individual and collective existence and so poses the problem of the integration of the two dimensions of existence. It is this situation which adds to and deepens the uncertainty of the reflective standpoint or self.

But while sociality precedes and is more fundamental than the individual, we must nevertheless face our problems from the standpoint of the individual. Given the development of consciousness, it is the standpoint of the self-aware individual which is pre-eminent. This is the channel to the worlds of both objective, external fact and the flow of lived experience. In addition, since the emergence of reflection and self-awareness has created the need for the directive standpoint and integration, it is the very perspective of reflection and self-awareness which must engage our attention. That this may limit our ability to grasp the phenomena (since the perspective of reflection will be seeking to understand itself) is something we will have to face as we proceed. But any attempt to bypass or start outside of consciousness will virtually insure that the problems of the reflective standpoint will be projected onto that starting point. Thus, the focus on both self as lived and personal integration.

III

From the standpoint being developed, the distinction between awareness or consciousness on the one hand, and reflection on the other, is central and crucial and so calls for further clarification. In its turn, this discussion will lead to a discussion of different dimensions of consciousness.

There is, first of all, the question of awareness itself. What is it? How, if at all, can it be characterized or described? As suggested earlier, my inclination is that sheer awareness cannot itself be characterized; it is a felt phenomenon, knowledge and understanding of which consists simply and entirely in *being* aware or immersed — non-reflectively — in the flow of experience. We can, of course, step back from such awareness and seek to characterize it in one way or another. But such attempts seem necessarily to omit the dimension which is essential to awareness as I am speaking about it, namely, the awareness itself.

But though awareness itself may not be susceptible to characterization, we can say more about consciousness and its operation if we focus on the presence or absence of the capacity to reflect. A brief, preliminary look at how the presence or absence of this capacity determines the sorts of belief different kinds of consciousness are capable of having should prove helpful.

Awareness or consciousness is something a creature may be capable of though it is not capable of reflection or self-consciousness. Thus, animals are aware, or conscious. So far as we know, however, animals do not reflect on their awareness and so are not capable of taking up attitudes toward this awareness. Yet, the higher animals clearly seem not to be limited to the having of sensations. So what does their awareness come to?

Obviously, animals are aware in that they are immersed in the flow of events; they feel or have sensation. But the complexity of their organism is such that in addition felt experience somehow expresses a limited standpoint or point of view. This standpoint, however, appears to be neither available to inspection nor, even in part, created by the creature in an active fashion. It is rather the outcome of the interplay of instinct or physiology and the environment. Animal immersion in experience involves sensation, pre-reflective awareness of the environment and desire. But given the existence of a standpoint — limited though it is — and a capacity to act, does it also involve belief?

This is a crucial matter, for belief straddles the distinction between awareness and reflection in a complex fashion. As a result, if we are not clear on how belief does and can function within a creature's consciousness, we are apt to misunderstand the nature of — and the possibilities for — that creature's experience.

Clearly, it is only a reflective creature which can develop the *concept* of belief, as well as entertain, weigh and hold beliefs. Since these activities involve reflection and animals appear to be incapable of reflection, animal awareness cannot involve belief in the sense that involves these activities.

Yet, there seems to be a clear sense in which it is necessary to say animal awareness does involve a capacity to distinguish and so, in a somewhat limited sense, a capacity to categorize. The cat is aware of the dog as that type of animal rather than some other type; and, as a result of this awareness, acts accordingly. Does this imply that the cat has beliefs? In some sense it does, for to act in one way rather than another, a creature has to see its situation as of a particular sort and not as another sort. This involves a distinction producing apparatus and, so in a limited sense, belief. We seem to have to say that the cat acts as if it has at least something like beliefs. And the reason we are likely to say the cat has beliefs, while a machine which also can make distinctions does not, is because we believe that the cat is conscious, is aware, and the machine is not.

But here is where problems can develop. For once we assign beliefs to cats even in a limited sense, we become prone to forgetting crucial distinctions. The cat clearly does not treat its belief as an entity or datum over and above the concrete situation; does not state it or reflect on it. The cat is immersed in a situation and acts essentially according to instinct. However, it may be helpful to say that the cat has a belief; but one which is inherently and indistinguishably — to the cat — *part of* the experience.

Human beings, *i.e.*, reflective creatures, have beliefs of a sort similar to these — beliefs which occur at the level of non-reflective awareness. But this is not the typical sense "belief" takes for reflective creatures. Since reflective creatures do not rely exclusively on instinct for survival, they need to develop a guiding center — or self — to determine optimum behavior. A crucial component of such relatively self-directing behavior must be belief. These must be formulated, weighed and expanded. In order for this to occur, they must be made into objects of attention, *i.e.*, involve reflection.

This is the distinctively human model of belief. If we foist this model onto the behavior of animals such as cats, we obviously make a mistake. But I think we make a similar mistake if we foist this model onto non-reflective human awareness. Like animals, humans are often immersed in experience. To be sure, this immersion is richer and deeper for humans, for such awareness has absorbed many of the expansions and extensions afforded by reflection. But non-reflective awareness does not involve belief in the same fashion that reflection does. If I am absorbed in some activity, the latter implies belief, but only in the way belief is implied for the activity of animals. I need not be conscious of the belief, directed by the belief or in any way separated from the action or situation by the belief. For example, if I am looking at a multi-colored sunset, I see it as a multi-colored sunset. This implies a number of beliefs, but these are extracted from the experience; they are implied by the experience; they are not states over and above or in any way separate from the experience. When I see a sunset, assuming I am immersed in the experience and not reflecting on it, that is what I am doing — seeing a sunset. I am *not* believing I see a sunset, taking belief as a state additional to seeing a sunset. The most that can be said is that my seeing implies that I believe I see a sunset. But this, in terms of what is involved in the experience, is equivalent simply to seeing a sunset.

IV

This brief focus on the phenomenon of belief reveals one crucial instance in which the presence of reflection alters the very nature of consciousness. Given these alterations and especially the *nature* of the alterations, *i.e.*, the ability of consciousness to become self reflectively aware of itself and so create further alterations of itself, it becomes vital, as a continuation of the ability to reflect, to sort out various modes of consciousness.

In its simpler form, consciousness is pre-reflective immersion in experience, the flow of events. Reflection, which is an outgrowth or expansion of pre-reflective awareness, creates an enlarged sense of "consciousness," which includes pre-reflective awareness, non-reflective awareness and reflection itself. But this enlargement of consciousness also brings with it an entirely new dimension, a new kind of *un*awareness which we can call — without making any commitment concerning structure or ontology — "unconsciousness." The terminology and understanding here, however, are far from clear, in part creating and in part expressing confusions about consciousness in its various aspects.

The first distinction that needs to be made is between non-consciousness and consciousness. Rocks are non-conscious; dogs and people are conscious. But while paradigms are available to instantiate the distinction, it is not clear just how to make the distinction. One clearly unsuccessful way would be in terms of the inanimate/animate distinction, for plants are animate, though almost certainly not conscious.

A further difficulty is that what justifies calling rocks "non-conscious," their exclusively mechanical physicality, is also to be found as an aspect of those beings we call "conscious." With the latter, there is "something" or some series of "things," or some additional configuration, in terms of which they are conscious;[1] but it still remains the case that they are also non-conscious, physical entities. Although the domain of non-consciousness slowly diminishes as consciousness expands, and diminishes still further as reflective consciousness develops, there are dimensions of a reflective creature's existence — both physical and "non-physical" — which always remain non-conscious. It is, of course, not clear what the limits are here.

An additional point, made by Colin McGinn, is that the inanimate/animate distinction is one of degree, while the non-conscious/conscious distinction is not.[2] While animation or life can be seen as gradual in development, allowing for intermediate stages between the inanimate and animate, consciousness cannot and must be envisaged on the model of "a sudden switching on of a light."[3]

McGinn's point about consciousness seems correct; any degree of consciousness would itself be consciousness and so talk about degrees of the very phenomenon of consciousness or sheer awareness seems not to be possible. But there is a very interesting sidelight to McGinn's claim. I have claimed that the development of consciousness is historical, both in its original emergence and its development subsequent to emergence. In light of McGinn's claim, there are no new difficulties or puzzles concerning development subsequent to emergence, but there are special and new difficulties concerning original emergence.

There is, of course, a long standing immense puzzle about how consciousness can arise from non-consciousness. McGinn's claim which suggests such emergence has occurred — for there was a "moment" prior to the switching on of the light — is vulnerable to this line of difficulty. But it also poses an additional set of puzzles, for if, as seems more than likely, he is correct, emergence has been discontinuous, expressing an alteration not merely of degree, but of kind. If we accept both emergence and discontinuousness, as I am suggesting we should, we are left with massive puzzles concerning the workings of historical development. I mention these problems, not to attempt a response, for I have none, but to spell out a significant and perplexing set of puzzles.

In any case, we still do not have any content for the non-conscious/conscious distinction. Non-awareness/awareness might be a way of providing the needed content, but this is only a bit more informative than the distinction it is attempting to explain. This kind of problem with the non-awareness/awareness distinction, however, puts us back in touch with a point made on several previous occasions, namely, that sheer awareness (or consciousness) cannot adequately be characterized by descriptions or concepts. If this is so, it would present us with a certain asymmetry concerning the non-awareness/awareness distinction, for the inability adequately to conceptualize awareness does not rule out adequate conceptualization of non-awareness or non-consciousness. The latter, being physical in a certain way, could be described by concepts, for in its mode of actuality it does not require self-involved acquaintance as a condition of being known. In its mode of actuality, however, awareness does involve such acquaintance to be known and when the "distance" of description occurs, acquaintance vanishes.

So again, perhaps the consciousness part of the non-conscious/conscious distinction cannot be adequately conceptualized and we have to be content, when communicating, to rely on paradigms and somewhat uninformative explanatory terms like "awareness" or "immersion in experience," believing that each of us has acquaintance with the phenomenon and so can experience and understand what is being discussed.

But there is a different sort of problem with accounting for the non-conscious/conscious distinction by means of the non-awareness/awareness distinction. If "non-conscious" refers to what is not conscious because it is purely physical, then some other term must be employed to refer to the non-consciousness that occurs within the realm of consciousness. That is, with the emergence of consciousness, "non-consciousness" no longer refers exclusively to a physical state, but can also refer to a psychological state, the state of not being conscious of something or other. This problem first emerges with the emergence of consciousness in pre-reflective creatures; but it does not reach full bloom until the emergence of reflective creatures.

It is not at all clear to me what the state of psychological non-consciousness is for a pre-reflective creature. But whatever analysis we give here, it is clear that the psychological non-consciousness of *reflective* creatures cannot in all instances be the same as the psychological non-consciousness of pre-reflective creatures. With the advent of reflection, aspects of consciousness become available to itself. But what is or was available may become unavailable; and this unavailability is not simply equivalent to the non-consciousness of the pre-reflective creature. The presence of reflection creates a new sense of psychological non-consciousness which cannot be accounted for by the non-awareness/awareness distinction as it applies to pre-reflective creatures.

With the emergence of reflection, there is, besides simple awareness or consciousness, reflective awareness or consciousness. Some term is therefore needed to refer both to what was available to awareness or reflection and no longer is, and to what could be available to awareness or reflection, but is not. Given the ability of consciousness to reflect, as well as the need for a "center" to direct behavior, instances of awareness and, at various levels of sophistication, instances of reflection, become available to reflection or the center. But not all that could be the object of awareness or reflection, at any moment, is. Some "items," once the object of awareness or reflection, no longer are; they've been repressed, forgotten, or the like, whereas other items capable of being objects of awareness or reflection, simply aren't — attention is elsewhere or fuzzy.

The essential aspect of this claim, namely, that items once the object of awareness or reflection can again become objects of awareness or reflection due to the presence of the capacity to reflect, separates these phenomena from the life situation of pre-reflective creatures. Given this, it would be very misleading to employ the same term both for this non-awareness and the non-awareness of pre-reflective creatures. I suggest we call the non-awareness which arises from the capacity to reflect "unconsciousness" (or "unawareness"), not "non-consciousness" (or "non-awareness"), and to differentiate such unconsciousness both from the non-consciousness of physical things and the non-consciousness of pre-reflective creatures.

Although the notion of unconsciousness needs much analysis and elaboration, I wish to postpone this for now. But what can't be postponed is my claim that unconsciousness is not a concept that applies to pre-reflective creatures, e.g., cats. Is it legitimate to draw so sharp a distinction between the consciousness of humans and the consciousness of cats? There is, after all, a sense in which cats have beliefs; and beliefs are propositional attitudes which, apparently unlike sensations, can be either conscious or unconscious.

While I have suggested there is a sense in which cats have beliefs, and while beliefs are propositional attitudes, the sense in which cats have beliefs appears to be so limited, I do not think we can call such beliefs propositional attitudes. Since cats are not reflective beings, their beliefs are not aspects of their consciousness which can either be looked at or not looked at — by cats! These beliefs are not — and as cats are now, necessarily not — available to reflection; and since the concept of propositional attitude is one which has been introduced to account for a dimension of the peculiar way reflective creatures relate to experience, it cannot be applied to a creature which cannot relate to its experience in that fashion. The notion of a propositional attitude seems to include the notion of at least possible availability to reflection. Since such availability is not present for cats, they cannot be said to have propositional attitudes.

In sum, the conscious/unconscious distinction occurs within the broader non-conscious/conscious distinction. Within the class of conscious beings designated by the latter distinction, there are some creatures, namely reflective ones, to which the conscious/unconscious distinction applies.

The concept of unconsciousness is crucial for proper understanding of the problem of personal integration. Since it is only reflective creatures which confront this problem, and since it is reflection which makes unconsciousness possible, personal integration must reflect an awareness of and relationship to unconsciousness. Pre-reflective creatures have the unity or integration of instinct; and since the workings of instinct are non-conscious, what is in this way not known to the creature is not a threat to the creature's unity. But a reflective creature is one which must direct its life. To do so, it needs to become aware — reflectively aware — of the sources of its attitudes and behavior and in light of this awareness create internal and external harmonies.

Such awareness, however, is radically limited. Much is unconscious, not at the moment available to awareness or reflection. And what is not available *can* become solidly separate or isolated, producing fragmentation or alienation. Such separation, however, does not typically diminish the influence of these factors on mood, emotion, belief, behavior, and so forth. So, again, the quest for integration involves bringing to awareness elements of the psyche which would otherwise be unconscious.

There is a bit more terminology which needs attention. Although at times I have used "reflection" and "self-reflection" interchangeably, this is misleading, for they are not identical. Indeed, I think self-reflection grows out of reflection. Reflection refers to the ability to focus on, attend to, various aspects of consciousness. Self-reflection is a more specific and complex form of reflection, involving attention to the reflective process itself, including both the alleged reflector and particular instances of reflection.

Finally, sometimes self-consciousness is taken as equivalent to self-reflection. This, too, can be misleading, for the former can refer to an uneasy preoccupation with one's person, especially in the presence of others. Although self-consciousness in this sense is relevant to the problem of alienation and integration, this is not the sense that expression is taking in this context. Here, self-consciousness is to be understood as equivalent to self-reflection, as explained above.

V

In Chapter 2, I argued against conceiving "self" as any sort of ongoing entity or substance. Yet recently I have been talking about a center or focus or, indeed, self as a partial director of one's life. How, it may be asked, is such talk any different from talk of self as an entity or substance?

This is a crucial matter, for in dealing with reflective consciousness two general claims seem simultaneously to be true, and it is not clear how, if at all, they can simultaneously be true. The first is that there is no ongoing entity or substance called self. The second is that there is a felt sense of "mineness" which is somehow included as part of many states of consciousness. This felt sense of mineness at a particular time seems to be involved in one's sense of identity at a particular time. Additionally, this felt sense of mineness seems to attach to a range of states of consciousness and various aspects of one's being over time, producing a sense of continuity or identity over time. Related to this is the sense that a life — mine — is being lived; or, in the active voice, that I am living a life. What is this felt sense of mineness, how does it develop and how is it different from a Cartesian Ego?

My suggestion is that anything beyond the brute registering of perceptual and organic sensation, the sense of mineness involved in seeing an object or feeling a sensation, is tied to reflection. Pre-reflective creatures certainly experience perceptions and sensations as theirs. They see the object and suffer the pain or enjoy the pleasure. In a word, they undergo or have the experience. But this is simply the brute perception or felt sensation of the moment. The mineness is pre-reflectively involved in the experience; there is no sense of mineness beyond the having of the experience.

This level of brute, felt experience obviously exists also for reflective creatures. But such creatures have the additional ability to reflect upon or, at another level, become aware of felt experience; and with this ability there arises a standpoint which is, I think, tantamount to the emergence of a fuller sense of mineness. Once a creature is able not merely to feel a subjective state, but also, from another vantage point, to focus on the state, and become aware of the state, we have at least the beginnings of an expanded sense of mineness.

This standpoint is simply another aspect of consciousness. It is consciousness, expanded, filled out from the simpler, sheer awareness of pre-reflective consciousness. As this standpoint becomes more and more of an observer of and commentator upon aspects of consciousness and the world, memory takes on a new dimension, enabling the recall of past experiences and thus their linkage to present, and other past experiences; consequently, a still larger sense of self or mineness develops, the one involved with living my life.[4]

The sense of mineness, then, originally involves the felt or subjective registering of various experiences. The expanded sense of mineness involves the attainment of a perspective which is tied directly to the experiences, yet is not identical with them and so can, in a somewhat detached manner, focus on them. It is as if a standpoint is being constructed by assembling into a somewhat unified whole items of felt experience and the reflective awareness of those items. Doing this makes one aware — both reflectively and non-reflectively — that one is leading this particular life. This construction, moving to and fro, in constant process, is what I am referring to by standpoint or focus or self. So conceived, it is not an entity or substance.

If this is correct, the sense of mineness is inherent to consciousness itself; it is neither all of consciousness, nor something separate from consciousness; it is simply a developmental aspect of consciousness. The sense of mineness, conceived in this fashion, necessarily implies some degree of unity. For in the absence of any sense of unity, there would be no sense of mineness beyond the felt experience of the moment. This unity, however, can occur to various degrees. Indeed, in the case of the amnesiac, it may be almost entirely non-existent. But in less extreme instances, it can range from connecting to and identifying with some few, vague memories and aspects of the present to a much fuller owning of various ranges of one's past and present experiences, motives, emotions, desires, and so on. From this perspective, the notion of owning, or accepting, or taking on aspects of consciousness is crucial both to the very idea of reflective mineness and, more specifically, to the way particular minenesses, *i.e.*, particular lives, are worked out. The possibility of owning or accepting states of consciousness, when treated abstractly and impersonally, connects to the metaphysics of reflective mineness, providing one aspect of what makes such mineness possible. When owning and accepting states of consciousness — and their paired opposites, disowning and rejecting — are treated concretely, personally and psychologically, they are connected to the particular way we live the lives we call our own. As such, they are deeply and essentially connected to the main topics of this study, integration and alienation.

A corollary to the expanded or reflective sense of mineness is a new level awareness that I am experiencing this or that; that an experience of the moment is mine in a way that it is not anyone else's. This phenomenon, which we can call "interiority" or "privacy" or "subjectivity," is contingent on the development of reflection; for without the latter, there is no capacity to be aware of the experiences in the fashion needed to have a sense of interiority, etc. Thus, while pre-reflective creatures undergo experiences and in that sense can be said to have interior experiences, they do not — from their standpoint — have such experiences as *that sort* of experience and so cannot contrast them with other, different sorts of experience. Since it is necessary to have a contrast between interior-exterior, private-public, subjective-objective in order to have a sense of interiority or privacy or subjectivity in the manner I am speaking of, pre-reflective creatures, who have no such contrasts, cannot have such a sense.

In light of this, interiority, etc. is not any kind of problem until there is reflective awareness of items of consciousness. In the absence of such reflective awareness, there is no possibility of a grasp of items of consciousness *as* items of consciousness and so no possibility of a contrast with what is other, *i.e.*, other than items of consciousness. Interiority, in the absence of reflection, is simply the brute, subjective immersion in experience which is the lot of pre-reflective creatures. As such, interiority or privacy pose no difficulties of understanding, communication or behavior among such creatures, for there is no articulated or grasped sense of what is non-interior or public and so no alternative with which interiority can be contrasted and compared.

The concept of the public, exterior or objective world is dependent for its development on the emergence of reflective awareness, for one dimension of the latter is awareness of the private, interior or subjective. Without reflective awareness of the private, there is no grasp of the public. However, it is not that the concept of the private precedes and enables the development of the concept of the public; rather, both concepts and the modes of existence which they represent come into being simultaneously. Grasp of the private is simultaneously grasp of the public. But while the concepts, and so the graspable reality, of private and public emerge simultaneously, ontologically the public or exterior both precedes and is the necessary foundation for the private or interior. It is a certain development of the public or exterior — including consciousness in its pre-reflective or non-self-aware state — which issues in interiority or privacy.

As previously suggested, the public or exterior is originally non-conscious, purely physical and so mute. The emergence of pre-reflective consciousness alters this muteness, but does not yet allow for an articulated sense of private/public. The latter becomes articulated with the emergence of reflection. But the startling and revolutionary nature of the emergence of interiority or privacy as a graspable reality has led many thinkers, over an extended period of time, to see interiority as original, independent, self-sustaining, and the like.[5] Indeed, we not only have intellectual claims to this effect, but more ominously, the emergence of a sense or feeling on the part of many that interiority is most fundamentally self-sustaining and real. As a result, many people live their lives as if this, or something very much like it, is true.

When interiority is seen — intellectually and/or experientially — in this fashion, it has no necessary developmental connection to what is exterior, to the world flow or the public, exterior world. But this, I suggest, is to make interiority unintelligible, for it is to treat it as inherently divorced from the ground out of which it emerges and to which it must relate in a certain way if it is adequately to grasp its experiential situation and options.

It is, of course, possible both to think of interiority as prior to and separate from exteriority and to attempt to live one's life as if this were so. Indeed, this is part of the problem, for one major outcome of interiority — individualism, interpreted and experienced in a certain way — has led to a situation in which such perspectives are commonplace and seem entirely intelligible. My suggestion, however, is that much of this is precisely the problem of alienation. Having emerged from pre-reflective absorption in experience and so articulated the interiority/exteriority distinction, we have separated out interiority from its ground to such an extent that, typically, we have become thoroughly disconnected—and so alienated—from this ground.

As the source of articulated privacy, reflection creates the possibility of alienation, but it also creates the distinctively human world and, so among other things, the possibility of constructive individuality and freedom. But for the latter to be achieved a radically new mode of understanding and activity must develop. Reflection is indeed a two-edged sword.

VI

Privacy or interiority involves the ability to focus on items of one's consciousness, treat them as one's own, and so separate them and the "space" in which they occur from what is not one's own, what is public and occurs in public space. In a way, privacy involves the creation of an individual world to which one has apparently privileged access and from which everyone else can apparently be excluded. There is no doubt that one can choose either to reveal or not to reveal to others particular thoughts, feelings, fantasies, and the like which one knows one has; and similarly that one can deceive others by telling them one has thoughts, etc., which one knows one does not have.

These are facts; but they produce countless puzzles and problems on both a metaphysical and a social level. Metaphysically, the puzzles are legion. The phenomenon of reflection — and its subphenomenon, introspection — requires an analysis of what, if anything, is reflecting, what the objects of reflection are, how reflection is occurring and in what medium. The easiest way to conceptualize this is on the model of visual perception. There is a perceiving entity (the self), perceiving objects of perception (mental states), by looking or scanning within some non-physical space. But this won't do, for every item on this model is treated on analogy with the items involved in visual perception and the latter are sufficiently dissimilar to the former to insure the almost immediate breakdown of the analogy. Whereas in visual perception there is a human being with a visual apparatus perceiving physical objects in physical space, introspective awareness is said to take place in non-physical space and involve a non-physical self and non-physical mental states. Everything, as it were, becomes metaphor and in place of explanation and understanding, we get suggestive and misleading pictures.

My estimate is that so long as we do not adequately understand consciousness, any model of interiority or self-knowledge will involve structural difficulties at least related to those just mentioned. However, the model presented above, which I will call "introspection by observation," has in addition structural difficulties of a different kind. It is a faulty model which is nevertheless commonly employed both as a partial model of how consciousness works and of how we attain self-knowledge. The way out of this added difficulty is not a reconstruction or proper explanation of the model, but insight into the way the model distorts our understanding of consciousness and self knowledge and, in addition, creation of a model which more adequately presents the workings of consciousness and the achievement of self-knowledge.

Introspection is a significant mode of reflection. It is not, however, the whole of reflection, for one can reflect upon, pay attention to, any number of phenomena which are not states of one's consciousness. One can think about numbers, books, people, yesterday, tomorrow, China, etc. To be sure, such thinking involves concepts, mental components of some sort, and in that sense involves components of consciousness; but such reflection does not, typically, involve direct attention to the components of consciousness. The reflection that is involved here is non-introspective, but is nonetheless unique to reflective creatures, for it does involve the use of a symbol system, creation of which is contingent on the ability to step back from simple and complete immersion in experience.

But reflection often does take the form of introspection, that is, observing or attending to states of consciousness, whether these be simple or complex. And when it does, a variety of problems come to the fore. The first suggestion I wish to make here is that while introspection does sometimes take the form of some sort of observation of states of consciousness, this is not its typical mode of operation. More often, much more often, introspection is not observation, but is the self-revelation of a particular state of consciousness. That is, coming to know what mental states one is undergoing is not always or even usually a matter of observing or looking at them, but is rather a matter of non-observationally experiencing them more fully and directly, without distraction. I often come to know what I am feeling, not by locating and looking at the feeling, but by removing any separation there is between my ability to register feeling and the feeling itself.

Introspection, conceived exclusively on the lines of observation or looking, produces a separation or gap between the observing — including the elements involved in the observing — and what is being observed. As such, its reliability is quite suspect. Introspection, conceived as the self-revelation of states of consciousness, does not involve this sort of gap and so does not have this source of unreliability. Its source of unreliability — a point I will come to in various ways as we proceed — is essentially limited, I think, to the conceptual and reflective schema in terms of which we grasp what is revealed.

However we conceive introspection, it is obviously directly related to self-knowledge and so intimately connected to the attainment of personal integration. Of the two modes of introspection I have mentioned, introspection as revelation is the favored notion. As such, it calls for considerable and extended clarification and I will try to provide this both directly and indirectly as I proceed. However, there is still introspection as observation and while this is not the method which most readily provides self-knowledge, it is real and at least appears in many cases to provide genuine self-knowledge. So, when do we introspect in this fashion and how does such introspection work?

Obviously enough, introspection as observation occurs when we wish to know some aspect of our state of consciousness which, in the absence of such observation, we do not know. For example, I may have a strange, unclear disquieting feeling, and so may attempt to isolate and observe it to see what it and its components are. By means of such introspective observation, I may locate a belief that such and such is the case, a desire to avoid the situation and a fear of the situation. This, of course, is introspection as observation at its very best; but even here there are significant questions to raise. For it is not clear that *observing* beliefs, desires and fears is quite the same as having self-knowledge of them. To know one believes x is not, I think, equivalent to believing x; nor is knowing one desires x or fears x equivalent to desiring or fearing x. To be sure, one can only know one believes or desires or fears x if, in fact, one believes or desires or fears x. But the believing or desiring or fearing x is not necessarily the same psychical state as knowing one believes or desires or fears x.

One general reason for separating these states is that one can believe or desire or fear x and not know that one does so — one may dissociate from, or refuse to acknowledge, these states. But this consideration, though valid, does not get to the heart of the matter in this circumstance. For if we say introspection as observation provides knowledge of a belief or a desire or a fear, then the knowledge must arise from having direct contact with the belief or desire or fear. But here is the rub, for the kind of contact which is needed to provide such knowledge is not provided by observation or looking; it is rather provided by directly experiencing the relevant phenomenon; and this occurs only when introspection is functioning as revelation.

In the absence of revelation, introspection can yield at most the edges of the state being observed, that is, the bare surface of the belief, desire or fear. And even here introspection as revelation appears to be functioning, for how else would one know these were the edges of the specific belief, desire and fear presumably introspected? What causes confusion here, I suspect, is that the items said to be observed by introspection are rather inferred from other aspects of the mental complex. We felt uneasy so we must have a certain kind of belief, an adversive desire and some fear. But such inferences, even when more specific *and* correct, are far indeed from the kind of self-knowledge one attains by directly experiencing the relevant states.

These remarks suggest there are severe limitations to introspection as observation. But they also suggest something quite interesting and I suspect quite controversial, namely, that we employ introspection as observation when we are either not in general aware of (or, in particular cases, capable of operating) introspection as revelation.[6] We are essentially disconnected from some aspect of consciousness and so we try to reconnect to that aspect, restore unity by employing that capacity of consciousness which is capable of looking inwardly. However, what we don't realize is that we reconnect, the unity is restored, not by looking, but by sinking into the somewhat, but not completely, disconnected part of consciousness.

The above remarks relate to one aspect of the metaphysical problem produced by the phenomenon of interiority; but, as suggested above, interiority also produces significant problems on a social level. In a complicated fashion, these problems cluster around the capacity—and willingness—to communicate. The emergence of a private self, with thoughts, emotions, desires, fantasies, and the like, particular in their felt quality to that self, produces a situation in which one is often unwilling to reveal these elements to others. The uncertainty and lack of clarity concerning these elements, their relationship to the life flow, the status of self, and one's relationship to others, creates a vulnerability of self which strongly mitigates against the revelation of such phenomena. As a result, there is a question concerning the ability of others to know one. The question arises not only from the inability of others to experience directly what one is experiencing, but also from their knowledge that one may not honestly be communicating what one is experiencing. This creates a problem of trust. Each of us knows the other has a private, relatively inaccessible, life and so knows the other may not be forthcoming. And obviously, the problem exists not only from the standpoint of self, but also from the standpoint of other. It is in this context that there is a groping towards revealing our private self to others and being receptive to and trusting of the revelations of others. These can be accomplished with different degrees of success; but the less they are accomplished successfully, the less there is genuine communication and the more there is alienation among people.

But there is another, deeply troublesome and complicating factor involved. My above remarks can perhaps be interpreted as suggesting that each individual has accurate knowledge of his private self and it is simply a matter of revealing this to others and trusting their revelation of their private self about which they also have accurate and adequate knowledge. But this would be mistaken, for I do not think that, typically, we have accurate and adequate knowledge of our "interior world."

The reasons for this are many and varied and as we proceed I will touch on the kinds of possible errors which attach to different types of states of consciousness in light of the capacity to reflect. For now, let it suffice to say that one deep reason — perhaps the deepest reason — for the lack of self-knowledge involves the process nature of experience. Within the flow of experience, there emerges reflective consciousness whose impulse and task is to grasp experience by means of names and concepts. The constructive and ongoing nature of this activity reflects the impermanence and non-absolute character of modes of consciousness; yet the activity is operated so as to gain some more or less fixed grasp of the phenomena. But these bits of fixity, while necessary and helpful up to a point, can also be very misleading, especially when they appear to obliterate the developmental nature of experience and consciousness. From this standpoint, the very question of the possibility of accurate and adequate knowledge of one's private self[7] is raised in a new and radical fashion. And this in the absence of any of the more surface and specific reasons for claiming that self knowledge is often not present.

What we see, then, is that besides the possibility of alienation from others, interiority or privacy also creates the possibility of a deeper form of alienation, namely, that involving disconnection from aspects of one's interior world, one's states of consciousness.

VII

Before proceeding on to the details of the sorts of errors reflective consciousness is susceptible to, I wish to spend some time discussing solipsism. There are two reasons for this: 1) solipsism appears to be the final and extreme stage of interiority or privacy; and 2) while being a difficult and disturbing view, it is also very instructive for what it reveals about the development of reflective consciousness and how such consciousness sees itself.

On the one hand, solipsism involves the most radical sort of disconnection imaginable, for it suggests either, epistemologically, that one knows only one's mental states or, ontologically, that only one's mental states exist, or both. On the other hand, solipsism, typically, makes an equally extreme claim — though in the opposite direction — namely, that one has certainty concerning both the existence and nature of one's mental states. Both claims flow from the creation of interiority by way of reflection. Having separated self or subjectivity from not-self or the world, reflective consciousness can then get locked within itself, taking its states as solely real and knowable and obliterating knowledge of, and even contact with, what is not-self.

Both positions, however, are radically defective, for they manifest a loss of the natural and original connection and continuity which consciousness has with the flow of experience, *i.e.*, pre-reflective living in the world. To be sure, whatever constructs or positions we develop, the deeper, necessary and ineradicable ties to the flow remain but they nevertheless become, in different degrees, lost to reflection and to conscious (as opposed to unconscious)[8] awareness.

Let's look at this general problem more closely. Solipsism involves a deeply skeptical component, for in its various forms it denies knowledge of the existence and nature of mental states other than one's own. But this skepticism is not carried over to one's own case, to knowledge of one's mental states. Indeed, solipsistic skepticism is often coupled with a claim to infallible knowledge of at least some of one's mental states. This is a very peculiar situation, for it assigns certainty to consciousness in at least some of its reflections on itself while severing it in all cases from knowledgeable commerce with others and the world. This is to see consciousness as a being entire to itself; it is to fail to see, and so to obliterate, the larger public world out of which consciousness flows and to which consciousness always remains — though sometimes obscurely — connected. The world and others get blocked out; and the self or one's consciousness becomes the rock-bottom of reality. But this is to insure that alienation, which is only a possible or potential outcome of the emergence of reflection/interiority, becomes an actuality and indeed an actuality which appears to be all that is possible.

To be sure, solipsism, in this or any other version, is contingent on the development of reflection/interiority — pre-reflective creatures cannot be solipsistic. But solipsism is neither an inevitable outcome of reflection/interiority, nor does it provide the ultimate description of reflective consciousness. Solipsism, rather, is the extreme form of the disconnection which *can* — but need not — develop once reflection/interiority emerges.

From this perspective, solipsism is not a timeless, non-historical theory or position; it is rather a particular and very difficult *life problem* which emerges at a certain stage in the development of reflective consciousness. But solipsism, typically, is treated exclusively as a conceptual or intellectual theory or position. When this happens, the state of mind which is treating solipsism in this fashion gets further disconnected from the forces which make solipsism possible. That is, treating solipsism as a theory or position is an additional step in severing solipsistic consciousness from the forces which produce the state. The very position of solipsism — that nothing is known or real other than one's states of mind — denies what has to be seen — that solipsistic consciousness is one outcome of a variety of factors which are other than solipsistic consciousness — if solipsism is to be understood and provide insight into the nature of knowledge of self and the world.

When solipsism is treated exclusively as a theory or position, it is particularly frustrating to deal with. Since it takes its standpoint as the court of final appeal, it cannot be refuted. There is no manner of refuting solipsism by means of argument to the disconnected standpoint which is itself the initial generator of the problem, for in such a case the position is the outcome, not of argument, but of the deeper movement of consciousness. The only hope is for one to see how the problem emerges, how it is a genuine existential problem, and to come to grips with interiority or privacy in such a manner as to reconnect to the public process, the life flow, out of which interiority develops. This, obviously, is not simply a matter of intellectual conviction; it is rather a matter of self-awareness and insight.

Consciousness, Knowledge and Error

Chapter Four

I

Reflections in the last chapter on "mineness" and interiority and their connection to reflection led to some discussion of introspection, or how the reflective creature comes to know its states of consciousness. But the emergence of the problem of introspective knowledge raises also the larger problem of extrospective knowledge. Not only does the presence of reflection generate the problem of how the reflective capacity knows both other elements of consciousness and itself, but it also generates the problem of how consciousness, now altered and expanded by the capacity to reflect, knows not-self or the world. Both problems, and especially the latter, are extremely pressing for a creature which, at least in part, must direct its behavior in a self-aware manner. If, even in a limited fashion, a creature is to choose how to act then, for its action to be coherent and successful, the creature must have a reasonably accurate sense of the situation within which it is acting. That is, it must have something like knowledge of the situation. In the absence of knowledge, the self-directed behavior will lack alignment with the objective situation and the creature will founder.

This obviously is a problem which is not crucial in the same fashion for pre-reflective creatures. Not having the capacity to reflect, and being guided essentially by instinct, they do not develop a center or self to direct action. They thus do not have to contend with the problem of whether or not, or to what degree, the center or self has knowledge of the situation in which it acts and of the elements of consciousness that are operating in its coming to act. For prereflective creatures, the problem of knowledge is limited to the non-self-directive fitting of instinct to the environment; for the reflective creature, the problem of knowledge is expanded to the post-instinctual, reflective and self-aware capacity of the creature to see how the world is.

Thus, again, reflection adds a startling new dimension to consciousness and the life of the creature which is reflectively conscious. This dimension involves the ability to attend to various states of consciousness and raises the question: what in the way of knowing is produced by such attending? But it also raises the question of how this attention to consciousness alters consciousness itself and so alters the creature's perceptions of the world. I am by no means clear on the developmental sequence of these matters, but the outcome of reflection involves both a new type of awareness of states of consciousness and a battery of elements, derived from reflection, in terms of which we experience the world (and, for that matter, consciousness itself). In light of this, what needs to be looked at is how reflection and the elements produced by reflection affect the reflective creature's ability to know both the world and itself.

Another, perhaps more detailed, way of looking at this is through the phenomenon of interiority/access. All forms of consciousness involve interiority and access, for to be conscious is to have experience; and the having of experience involves interiority and access. From this perspective, interiority and access are simply two sides of the same phenomenon, namely, having experience or being conscious — *i.e.*, feeling some state or aspect of one's organism. But while consciousness universally involves interiority and access, the nature of interiority and access varies depending on the type of consciousness involved. And it is this varying of interiority and access which gives rise to the different kinds of problems of knowledge.

These matters are, I think, best approached through a further specification of the mode of operation of the three forms of consciousness: pre-reflective, non-reflective and reflective.

Let's begin by looking at pre-reflective consciousness which, in many ways, is the simplest case. Pre-reflective consciousness is non-divided consciousness. In the absence of division, there is no standpoint of reflection and so no possibility of reflective or introspective knowledge. This, however, does not imply that pre-reflective creatures do not have knowledge of their consciousness. They do have knowledge, but it is the knowledge of direct awareness, direct immersion in experience, and is not the knowledge provided by introspection.

There is an interesting point of clarification which needs to be made here. In the last chapter, I distinguished "introspection as observation" from "introspection as revelation" and argued that the latter is more readily productive of knowledge than is the former. In light of this, and the remarks of the preceding paragraph, it might be argued that while pre-reflective creatures could not have introspective knowledge, if such knowledge were thought of along the lines of observation, they could indeed have such knowledge, if it were thought of along the lines of revelation. Indeed, it might be argued that the normal, everyday consciousness of pre-reflective creatures is precisely introspection as revelation, for such creatures are immersed in experience, not distracted by the elaborations and pre-occupations of reflective consciousness.

This rendition of the everyday consciousness of pre-reflective creatures is, I think, largely correct. However, this state cannot be equated with introspection as revelation as applied to reflective creatures. We can see this if we notice that with respect to pre-reflective creatures, there is essentially no contrast of revelation with other states of consciousness. Pre-reflective creatures can, of course, be distracted by events in the environment and so lose touch with the previous absorption of the moment; but they cannot be distracted by the various workings of the elements of reflective consciousness, for there are no such elements within their consciousness. With reflective creatures, however, introspection as revelation and the immersion in experience which it involves, does have a contrast and a common one at that, namely, pre-occupation with and attention to various elements of reflective consciousness. What is crucial to see here is that the distinction between introspection as observation and introspection as revelation is a post-reflective distinction and so involves elements and perspectives which are unique to reflective consciousness. So while there are similarities between pre-reflective immersion in experience and introspection as revelation there are also significant differences which must be taken account of. One such difference, that concerning the kinds of error different kinds of consciousness are capable of making, is of great importance and has far reaching consequences.

The absence of the reflective standpoint suggests something quite interesting for pre-reflective creatures, namely, an inability to make certain sorts of mistakes or errors. In the absence of the capacity to reflect, they can make no errors which are contingent on the existence of the capacity to reflect. If we grant what seems reasonably clear, namely, that the development of concepts, perspectives, attitudes, and the like are necessarily tied to the ability to reflect, then pre-reflective creatures cannot develop or have such phenomena and so cannot make errors which stem from these phenomena.

This precludes the possibility both of perceptual error stemming from inadequate concepts, conceptual schemas, perspectives, attitudes and the like and errors relating to what is being immediately experienced. While pre-reflective creatures can make another sort of perceptual error — which I will comment on presently — they cannot make errors concerning immediate experience. Their awareness or consciousness is pre-reflective, unmediated direct acquaintance. As such, it is immune to error and so infallible. But it is vital to see that this is a unique kind of infallibility, for it predates the possibilities of reflective knowing and not knowing, knowing with certainty and knowing with less than certainty. There is a sense, then, in which the awareness of pre-reflective creatures is infallible. But this is *not* the sense in which such awareness and the knowledge it provides is infallible as opposed to fallible. Rather, it is the sense in which the fallible-infallible distinction does not even take hold.

Non-reflective consciousness, on the other hand, is consciousness which is the outcome of the reflective standpoint, but is not (presently) involved in reflection. The awareness which is involved in such consciousness is direct, but is not unmediated by concept and perspective as is pre-reflective consciousness or, at least, is not unmediated to the degree pre-reflective consciousness is. But this importation into non-reflective consciousness of items developed by reflection raises questions concerning the ability of non-reflective consciousness to adequately know the world (and itself).

Let us, for a moment, focus on non-reflective awareness of the world. Just as we can talk about introspection as either observation or revelation, we can talk in somewhat the same manner about extrospection. This may seem strange, for there is a clear sense in which we obviously observe the world — at least if we are talking about vision — and it is not quite clear what we are to contrast this with. But I think there is a contrast available, namely, that between employing elaborate and less than adequate reflective constructs as our means of observing the world and a diminished use of more adequate constructs such that the world can manifest itself, much as we sometimes allow feelings to manifest themselves. Besides being quite vague, this is clearly a relativistic contrast. It is a contrast between the kind and degree of construction reflective consciousness puts on the world; it is not a contrast between constructs and the absence of constructs. But this is an outcome of the very nature of reflective consciousness, for once reflective consciousness emerges, the view or look of the world becomes, *necessarily* becomes, constructed. In order to act, to direct its life and survive, the reflective creature must place a structure, in part of its own making, onto the world. As a result, extrospection — and introspection — must contain a variety of constructs, elements derived from the operation of reflection. Given this, both extrospection and introspection contain possibilities of error which are not to be found in pre-reflective creatures who cannot create such constructs.

The necessary presence of constructs entails that adequate knowledge, if there be such a possibility, is to be found within the constructs and raises the question of the possibility of comparing and choosing between alternative constructs. This is obviously an immense task and needs to be preceded by a detailing of the constructs (and their elements) in terms of which we experience the life flow. Broadly, reflection expands consciousness by means of the construction of concepts, perspectives, attitudes and the elements of these, including, beliefs, desires, wishes, emotions, and so on. These phenomena can be inadequate, incoherent, distorted, biased, and inappropriate. When they are, we again have alienation; integration arises, in degree, when these phenomena are lessened and the constructs in terms of which we experience the life flow are reflective of "the way the world is" and the way or ways reflective consciousness can most fruitfully develop. But whatever we say about such possibilities, once reflection emerges, we no longer experience the life flow—even when it is direct and non-reflective— in the simple, relatively uncomplicated fashion in which the higher animals do. And this must have a significant impact on our ability to know both the world and our own mental states.

Before proceeding to some of the details of these matters, there is an additional outcome of the capacity to reflect which needs to be mentioned. This concerns the reflective creature's knowledge of its mental states. The possibility of knowing one's mental states in a new way arises from the ability to reflect. But this possibility, as previously suggested, leads to a problem, for once we can attend to our states, consciousness is divided. As divided, the problem is: can consciousness know its own states? In light of this, while many have argued that the access consciousness has to itself assures certainty or infallibility concerning its own states, I wish to suggest the reverse, namely, that the emergence of reflective access makes new sorts of errors possible, thereby assuring a significant narrowing, if not a total rejection, of claims to infallibility.

This needs some expansion. Introspection as observation involves two kinds of possible error: those emerging from the distance between the observation and the mental state and those involving the reflective elements in terms of which the observation is being made. Introspection as revelation involves only a variation of the latter sort of error. Since such introspection involves immersion in the state of consciousness, the only possible error is in experiencing the state as this or that state. Given the emergence of the elements of reflection, the non-reflective particularization of the experience can, in various ways, be mistaken or erroneous. This possibility is sufficient to differentiate such experience from that of pre-reflective creatures who, not having developed the elements of reflection, cannot particularize their experience in this manner.

The unique type of access reflective consciousness has to itself—even in the form of non-reflective awareness—is precisely what creates the possibility of not knowing or losing touch with one's mental states. Part of what is involved here is the emergence of an explicit idea of knowing and so also an explicit idea of not knowing. But what is more significantly and fundamentally involved is the possibility of actually making various sorts of errors. So this is not just a conceptual point about the emergence of a new conceptual distinction; it is also an empirical point about the way consciousness is now working.

These, however, are quite complicated matters and I think it best to begin talking in some detail about different categories of mental activity rather than mental activity as such. Let's start with perception.

II

Perception involves both the state of the observer and the purported object of perception. This is true whether we are talking about pre-reflective or reflective creatures. In both cases, it is appropriate to talk about the creature's perceptual experience. This is so even though the reflective creature's immediate experience is richer due to the presence within immediate experience of elements derived from reflection. This difference, however, does not imply that pre-reflective creatures do not perceive objects as of a certain sort. Clearly they do, for in the absence of such an ability, their behavior would be either uniform or random, involving no consistently differential behavior toward different types of situations, objects and creatures. Since their behavior is differential, not uniform or random, we can infer that they do perceive objects, etc., as of a certain sort.

Such differentiation implies that pre-reflective creatures are capable of a certain sort of perceptual error, the kind stemming from physical and/ or physiological factors within the perceptual situation. For example, there may not be sufficient light and so an object or creature may appear to be other than what it is. In this fashion, a feature of the environment conditions a perceptual error. Alternatively, a creature may be of failing health, may not clearly see the object under observation, and so may misidentify it. Here a physiological factor is instrumental in producing perceptual error. Obviously, these two factors, the physical and the physiological, may combine to produce other instances of this sort of error.

In light of these considerations, it is clear that pre-reflective creatures are not immune to perceptual error. However, they are immune to certain kinds of perceptual error, the kind which flow from the ability to reflect and involve inadequate or distorted concepts, biased perspectives, inappropriate attitudes, and the like.

Pre-reflective creatures do have some sort of relatively primitive classificatory system which enables them to perceptually differentiate within classes of situations, objects and beings. But if such creatures can differentiate, they must have available the means for such differentiations; and the means might be said to be concepts. If it is, then, in this instance, it appears that pre-reflective creatures are not different from reflective creatures; for if both perceptually differentiate in terms of concepts, both are susceptible to the kinds of errors which stem from inadequate or distorted concepts.

But even if we allow that in some rudimentary sense of "concept," pre-reflective creatures perceptually differentiate in terms of concepts, this is not the sense of concept in which reflective creatures perceptually differentiate. The concepts of reflective creatures are aspects of a larger reflective system which, among other things, includes perspectives and attitudes. The elements of this system are all intricately interconnected, with concepts influencing and being influenced by perspectives, attitudes and the other elements of the system. It is the presence of this larger system of reflection which accounts for the kind of error which I am suggesting is unique to reflective creatures. Even though there is an overlap between pre-reflective and reflective creatures in that they perceptually differentiate, there is no overlap with respect to the presence of a larger reflective system which includes perspectives, attitudes, and so on.

It might be responded to the above that the distinction being drawn between the standpoint of pre-reflective and reflective creatures is too sharp and absolute; for it can reasonably be said that pre-reflective, like reflective, creatures have a point of view—that it makes sense to talk about "what it would be like to be a . . . ." This, I think, is correct; it does make sense to talk about the point of view of a pre-reflective creature. However, such a point of view is neither reflectively created — even in part — nor is it one

among a variety of possibilities. "Point of view," when applied to pre-reflective creatures, simply refers to the creature's subjective bearing or stance
within the life flow, what I have called "direct immersion in experience." It
clearly does not refer to a self-aware, created standpoint. What we call the
standpoint or point of view of pre-reflective creatures develops and operates spontaneously and non-reflectively in the interaction of creature and
environment.

But, it might be said, don't reflective creatures also interact spontaneously within the environment? And if they do, isn't this fact sufficient to
cast doubt on the sharp distinction being drawn between the standpoints of
pre-reflective and reflective creatures and the claim to a unique kind of error based on this distinction? It is, of course, true that reflective, like pre-
reflective, creatures interact spontaneously with the environment. However,
it is one of the main theses of these writings that such spontaneous interaction is not identical in the two cases, that the presence of the larger reflective
system and its elements comes to permeate non-reflective, spontaneous interaction with the environment so that it becomes significantly different
from pre-reflective immersion in experience and accounts for the unique
sort of error being attributed to reflective creatures. That is, the kind of error
being discussed is internal to the constructed, reflective system itself. Obviously, in the absence of such a system, this sort of error is not possible.

While the general conclusion developed above may be acceptable in
certain sorts of cases, it may be objected that there are a number of other
sorts of cases in which such a conclusion is extravagant. It might, for example, be suggested that it is hard to conceive how the simple seeing of, say,
a tree with green leaves could be infected with any sort of error other than
that stemming from physical and/or physiological factors within the perceptual situation. What kind of conceptual, perspectival or attitudinal inade-
quacy could possibly be involved in such a perception?

It is, of course, true that perceptions of the sort just mentioned are
rarely, if ever, contested from any standpoint other than distorting physical
and/or physiological factors. But the fact that such perceptions are not otherwise contested is not—contrary to what many people suggest—due to the
presence, in such cases, of bare, unmediated perceptions shorn of any elements or constructs contributed by the observer. There are, I think, no such
perceptions to be found. Rather, the non-controversial nature of such perceptions stems, I think, from two factors: 1) we tend to treat such perceptions as discrete, entirely separate from other perceptions and the larger
conceptual system into which they fit; and, as a result of this, 2) the con-

structs involved become isolated and divorced from the basic human needs, desires, attitudes, values, and other factors which permeate the larger conceptual system and with which the individual perception connects. If, for a moment, we take another kind of example, I think we will see how the situation shifts when a perception involves directly experienced human problems, needs, and desires. In such cases, perceptions — and not just evaluations of the perceptions — are vehemently contested. For example, some people observing certain sorts of political protest, see — actually see — the participants as menacing and disruptive. The appearance of the protestors sets off fear and anger. They are not seen as human beings of a certain physical appearance, making certain physical movements, carrying various signs. Rather, the perception is of a menacing and perhaps evil creature, disturbing, at a deep level, the settled framework of the observer's life. To others, the protestors are seen — again, actually seen — as benevolent, committed creatures, attempting to point out and correct past injustices and establish current and future fair practices. In both of these cases, perceptions are guided, indeed structured, by a variety of interconnected concepts, perspectives and attitudes. The presence of these makes possible various sorts of distortion, exaggeration, mistake, and so on, none of which are possible for pre-reflective creatures, and none of which arise from physical and/or physiological factors within the situation.

Let us cite one more similar, though more circumscribed, example. One perceives another person with a certain bearing *as* angry. The observed, however, turns out not to be angry, but a certain sort of excited. Here, the original perception can be mistaken for either of two reasons: 1) the observer's concept of anger is roughly correct, but the excitement was simply misread as anger; or 2) more gravely, the observer's concept of anger is faulty, including such excitement as a component of anger.

These and like examples are typically countered by the suggestion that the perceptions discussed are not pure perceptions at all. This suggestion, however, has two forms, one more radical than the other, though I am inclined to think they slide into each other. The less radical objection insists that the perceptions cited, especially the first, are not neutral perceptions at all, but include substantial value, perspectival and attitudinal contributions from the observer's subjective consciousness. The second, more radical, objection insists on a distinction between sensation and perception, the former referring to raw, unadorned feels, looks, and so on, the latter referring to the constructed totality, including what is given in sensation and what is subjectively added.

Although in somewhat different ways, both objections assume there is a neutral given which is then added to by the observer and that it is these additions which are the source of the sort of distortions and errors under discussion. If, the objection continues, we eliminated these additional elements and limited our perceptions to what is given, we would eliminate this sort of error and the only sorts of possible error remaining would be those flowing from physical and/or physiological factors within the perceptual situation. If this were so, then, in this class of cases, the possibilities of perceptual error of reflective creatures would be identical in type to the possibilities of perceptual error of pre-reflective creatures.

Let us take up these objections, starting with the less radical of the two. The claim that there is a clear and always to be made distinction between factual concepts and value concepts or, more extravagantly, factual realities and value realities cannot, I think, be sustained. To be sure, the world exists independently of us. Taken in itself, independent of and/or prior to any reflective standpoint, it is neither of value nor not of value—it simply is. Without the presence of reflective consciousness, that is, without the presence of a creature who has the ability to and must *make* choices in terms of preferences, there is no value or disvalue. How else, it may be asked, could value come to exist other than through the confrontation of a selecting, choosing creature with an externally existing environment?

But it doesn't follow from the emergence of a fact/value distinction that we can defend a metaphysical distinction between factual reality and value reality. That is, it does not follow that we can, after creating a distinction between fact and value, treat it as pointing to a distinction which exists independently of the reflective standpoint. The development of aspects of reflective consciousness, including language, and more particularly, value language, transforms the world such that it *always* has to be seen as a "consciousness-world" amalgam; and this, given its emergent structure, is a value permeated reality.[1] Reflective consciousness merged with the world— but *not* in the sense there are two things—is inherently value constituted. To make the same point, but from the other way round, in creating the reality of value, reflective consciousness also creates its contrast, namely, fact— but again not in the sense that reflective consciousness creates the world.

The denial, then, of a metaphysical distinction between fact and value is compatible with the recognition of a fact/value distinction within the consciousness-world amalgam and so the recognition of a distinction of degree between instances of language use which can be characterized as purely factual, *e.g.*, "this is a tree with green leaves" and others which are largely, though not exclusively, value laden, *e.g.*, "this is a good tree." As suggested, however, this distinction occurs within the larger value constituted standpoint of reflective consciousness and so does not point to a metaphysical distinction between facts and values. And if there is no such metaphysical distinction, perceptions cannot consist of factual givens which are then distorted by subjectively added values. Rather, the fact/value distinction, itself a creation of reflective consciousness, permeates all of reflective consciousness and so affects all the perceptions of reflective creatures.

Even if this is correct, however, it does not account for certain significant facts, namely, that we do draw a distinction of degree within the reflective standpoint between fact and value, and do, in various degrees of awareness, employ it. How, then, is this distinction drawn and how do we apply it in particular cases?

There is, within language, the presence of largely, though not exclusively, value words, such as "good," "bad," "right," "wrong" and many more. The use of these almost, perhaps, always signals that we are on the value side of the fact/value continuum. But the question is when do we use these and other value words? Roughly, I think, we use value words largely as a function of the degree to which the situation at hand is experienced, or is treated, as affecting human concerns, problems, needs, desires, and so forth. In addition, I think we experience or treat the situation at hand as connected to human concerns the more we experience it as connected with further elements of the life process. That is, the more we isolate a situation and treat it entirely on its own, the more likely we are to see it as "purely factual." Conversely, the less we isolate it and instead experience it as connected to broader concerns, the more we will be led to treat it as value infused.

Thus, "this is a tree with green leaves" is typically taken as purely factual, for it is treated as describing an isolated phenomenon, neither related to any human concerns, nor connected to anything beyond itself. The perception, in short, is treated as separate from the larger reflectively constituted world in which it occurs, and so the elements of the reflective system which condition and provide the structure for and the interconnections with the perceptions are eliminated. As a result, it looks as if we have a discrete, purely neutral description of what is seen.

When we perceive the tree as a good tree, however, we are connecting it both to human concerns and a larger situation. These may include aesthetic appreciation by the observer or functional use by some person or group of persons or participation in the larger ecological system. These latter elements, or others like them in type, minimally lurk in the background of all our purely factual uses of language. When they are touched, there is the emergence—sometimes explicit, sometimes not—of the evaluative elements which are in part constitutive of the reflective standpoint.

My suggestion, then, is that *all* perceptions of reflective creatures contain within them elements drawn from the larger reflective system which conditions them and makes them possible. If this is so, there are two mutually interconnected ways in which constructed value elements permeate perceptions and make them susceptible to error in a fashion not possible for the perceptions of pre-reflective creatures. First, there are the elements of the larger reflective system which set the framework within which any particular perception takes place. Second, there is the particular perception which employs various elements of the larger system. Since both the system as well as particular elements of the system are constructs, they can be inadequate or distorted, and thus any particular perception can be inadequate or distorted.

The upshot of these remarks is that while we must recognize a difference of degree between factual and value language, this is a distinction within the constructed reflective system and does not reflect a distinction within the world. Treating perceptions as purely neutral or factual is thus a way we have of operating within the fact/value distinction created by reflective consciousness and not a reflection of a purely neutral, factual given which is the object of the perception. When treating perceptions as purely neutral and factual, we are simply suspending recognition of the value elements which structure the larger reflective system and at least implicitly infuse the particular perceptions, whatever they are. Finally, *no* perceptions of reflective creatures are immune to the possibility of the unique sort of error which flows from the presence of reflective consciousness.

Before proceeding to the more radical objection to these claims about perceptual error, I wish—for now—briefly to mention and discuss a major difficulty which is emerging from these remarks. This has to do with the sort of skepticism and relativism which can arise from the combination of a denial of a non-constructed given and an insistence that reflective consciousness experiences the word *as* constructed. There are a number of interconnected problems here, but I will mention just a few. If there are only constructs and no experience of what is not a construct, then how can we know if the constructs are adequate to what they are constructs of? Also, if all experience consists of constructs, how can it be other than arbitrary which construct we devise and employ? And, finally, if the world is experienced through constructs, and the constructs vary with time and place of construction, then so will reality vary — reality will become relative to the construct describing it.

These are, of course, monumental questions which also express, in a poignant fashion, one aspect of the plight of reflective creatures. If reflective consciousness must provide some created structure, some grasp of the world, so that it can act in the distinctive way it must to survive — and if the foundation for such creation is not simply externally given, but at least in part is created through the insight and understanding of reflective consciousness — then the reflective creature is pushed back onto its own problematic resources.

While there are clearly genuine and perplexing problems here, they can strike us as more dire than they are if we are taken in by two implicit dichotomies which are often assumed. The first is that either justification is based on some non-constructed, neutral given or that there is no possibility of justification and everything is as good (or as bad) as everything else. The second is that either the world exists as neutrally given, or it is a sheer construct, having no existence other than through the construct. Both of these dichotomies, however, are less than exhaustive. In the absence of foundationally based justifications there are other sorts of justification. Indeed, there are also denials of the need to justify in the manner foundationalists construe justification. Also, to claim that reflective consciousness experiences the world *as* constructed is not to claim that there is no world independent of the construct.

In light of such expanded alternatives, I wish to suggest that even though reflective consciousness experiences the world as constructed, it is possible to identify inadequate and/or distorted aspects of a construct or even of a construct as a whole. One very crucial point here is that we survive or perish, thrive or languish, within a world which exists independently of us. Thus, any reflective system which does not take cognizance of the world — including the biological and psychological aspects of the reflective creature — will produce less than beneficial behavior.

That there is no non-constructed given available to reflective consciousness does not imply that there is no interaction of reflective consciousness with the world; nor does it imply that a reflective system does not have to recognize such interactions. To say that reflective consciousness never has contact with a neutral, non-constructed given is not to say that reflective consciousness has no contact with the world. We do indeed experience the world, but *as* constructed. And it is in terms of such constructions that we fare well or ill in the world.

It might be thought that the above talk about the world is simply a way of smuggling in the reality of a non-constructed given. But this is not so, for the notion of a non-constructed given is itself a creation of reflective consciousness. Like the notion of a factually given, the notion of a non-constructed given is itself a construct of reflective consciousness. So in saying there is interaction between the world and reflective consciousness, we are not re-introducing the notion of the world as a non-constructed given, for such a notion is simply one aspect of a distinction created by reflective consciousness and so does not refer to a reality separate from reflective consciousness. There is, no doubt, a world separate from reflective consciousness, but the world is not a non-constructed given which provides clean data for reflective consciousness.

These remarks, of course, only push the problem one step further back, for, among other things, terms like "thrive," "languish," "beneficial," "fare well," and "fare ill" are themselves aspects of the constructs of reflective consciousness. As such, they too call for examination, exploration and some form of justification. As it were, reflective consciousness creates the very means for the evaluation of its constructs. And the various problems which arise for the original constructs arise also for the evaluative constructs. So again, reflective consciousness is thrown back on its own resources — something, I am suggesting, it cannot avoid. But more of this later.

III

Prior to this brief discussion of skepticism and relativism, I was discussing the claim that perception can be purged of subjective components and can be reduced to some form of neutral presentational or representational phenomenon. This objection did not deny to perception the presence of all constructs, but only non-neutral, evaluative constructs. The more radical objection, which I will now discuss, does, however, seek to purge perception of all constructs, for it wishes to distinguish between the raw given, the feels and looks involved in the having of sensations and anything beyond this. But this is not quite clear, for it is not clear whether the claim is: 1) that there is some thoroughly undifferentiated given, completely lacking in form, and that whatever form is to be found is supplied by the perceiver; or 2) that even the most basic sensations are already "formed," already a sensation of this or that, but that granting this there is still the need to distinguish raw, though particularized and so classified, sensations from larger constructed additions.

It appears that the former view cannot be correct. For, if it were, sensation would be a whirly-gig of chaos. Not only would there not be sensations of trees, rocks and dogs, the standard objects of everyday perception, there apparently would not even be sensations of color, size and shape; for these, too, involve *recognition as* and thus seem to involve at least rudimentary constructs or classifications. If the denial of all constructs to sensations implies the absence even of sensations of color, size and shape, this is probably a *reductio* of the view that sensation involves no constructs whatsoever. Thus whatever we take to be raw sensation, it appears we must say that at least in a minimal sense of construct, all sensation involves constructs.

This concession may be fatal to the notion of a raw, unadorned given, for if the notions of size, shape and color are, as they certainly appear to be, components of a larger reflective system which can in various ways be incoherent, contradictory, inadequate, and distorted, there is the possibility that any particular sensation which involves such notions could itself display such defects. If this is so, then the distinction between sensation and perception does not eliminate the presence of elements of reflective consciousness from perceptual experience and so does not eliminate from such experience the possibility of the unique sort of error which flows from reflective consciousness.

While I think this is substantially correct, I would, for the moment, like to bypass this problem and look in more detail at the sensation/perception distinction. If, within the spirit of the distinction, we claim that perception, shorn of all additions, reduces to sensations of color, size and shape, what are thought to be the ordinary objects of perception, that is, trees, rocks and dogs, turn out to be constructions out of the primitive sensations. But if this is so, since all of our everyday perceptions involve constructs flowing from reflective consciousness, they are all potentially erroneous. This, then, puts us back with the problem of the contribution to perception of reflective consciousness. To overcome it, we would have to focus not on the objects of everyday perception, but on sensations of color, etc. If we did so focus, there would only be direct "unmediated" sensations and the source of error stemming from reflective consciousness would be eliminated.

There is, however, a price to pay for such a shift. For in talking only about sensations, one ceases to make perceputal judgments—unless one is talking about perceiving sensations, and then we have introspective judgments — and is involved exclusively with perceptual experience or the having of sensations. But this, in turn, focuses the problem of error, not on perceptual judgment, but on perceptual experience. With this focus, we become involved not with whether or not our perceptual judgments can be immune from error, but rather with whether or not our perceptual experiences can be immune from error.

This, or something like it, is the standard move in such situations. For when people typically talk about perceptual infallibility or immunity to error, they do not do so in terms of perceptual judgment or the nature of the object of perception, they do so rather in terms of perceptual experience, conceived of as sensation or appearance or "seemings." This, of course, is an appropriate move, for there is, for good reason, a near universal agreement that infallibility cannot attach to perceptual judgments. However, rather than seeing this as a reason for questioning the notion of content infallibility, many people seek to attach that infallibility to the sensation or seemings. Let us look at this latter point more carefully.

Virtually everyone agrees that "this is a tree with green leaves" or "I see a tree with green leaves" are not infallible; but many suggest "there seems to be a tree with green leaves" or "I seem to see a tree with green leaves" are infallible. The move is from a claim about how the world is to one about how the world appears; and it is suggested that while the former can be mistaken, the latter cannot.

The first thing to notice is that an equivalent move cannot be made for pre-reflective creatures. Such creatures can make perceptual errors in the form of misidentifications. But it does not follow that one can say that they seem to perceive the misidentified items. From *their* perspective, this does not make sense, for they have no reflective standpoint from which a seeming/not seeming, appearance/reality distinction can be made. The *kind* of infallibility which allegedly adheres to seemings is contingent on the development of reflective consciousness and so is not applicable to pre-reflective beings.

Yet, it is possible to see the claim of infallibility of seemings as an attempt to capture the element of infallibility found in the perceptions of pre-reflective creatures. And there is indeed a significant similarity, for both sorts of creatures are, in the perceptual moment, fully absorbed in perceptual experience. They are having perceptual sensations, not reflecting or commenting on them. If we stay within this moment, there is the infallibility of experiencing, or *having an experience, whatever it is.*

But even within the experiential moment, there is significant difference between pre-reflective and reflective creatures. Since, as seems to be the case, particularizing elements are inherently part of sensations, both sorts of creatures have sensations *as of* this or that. The particularizing elements of pre-reflective creatures, however, are not tied to a larger reflective system consisting of concepts, perspectives and attitudes. Thus, their sensations, not in any way involving such elements, cannot display the kinds of errors which can be found in the sensations of reflective creatures which do reflect, even if indirectly, the presence of such elements.

Thus, again, we are led to the claim that the perceptions and sensations of reflective creatures are susceptible to a unique form of error. In its turn, this conclusion might lead us to conclude further that no sort of infallibility is applicable to the perceptual experience of such creatures. This, however, does not seem quite right; for there appears to be a real — though limited — infallibility involved in the having of sensations (and, beyond that, immersion in experience). This can be seen in the following.

Seemings or appearances or sensations can, I think, be thought about independently of their various contents. This, of course, does not imply that there are contentless seemings, etc.; but it does suggest that seemings can take different contents and that we can talk about what it is that takes different contents. Thus, "seeming to see a tree with green leaves" and "seeming to see a tall man" are not identical experiences, for they have different contents and so involve different sensations. But from the standpoint of seeming itself or having a sensation, the different contents are irrelevant. My suggestion is that the much sought after infallibility of perceptual experience is to be found attached to the sheer seeming, not the object of the seeming. The element of infallibility, that is, attaches to the seemingness of the experience itself, to the having of experience, or immersion in experience, and not to the content of the experience, for with respect to content, there is always a possibility of error.

This suggests that no matter what the content of the experience, there is a certain general kind of infallibility that attaches to the experience itself. Infallibility holds for the *that* of experience, *that* one is having an experience, not the *what* of experience. This is, I think, the element of infallibility which remains to reflective creatures once it is realized that all particularizations of sensation (and, beyond this, mental states) contain the possibility of error.

Now, if there is a possibility of error for reflective creatures within the perceptual moment itself, *a fortiori*, there is a possibility of error within all reflection and commentary on the perceptual moment. Thus, the *claim* that I seem to see a tree with green leaves may be mistaken, for I may not be in the mental state of seeming. (I may, for example, simply be seeing.) The concept of seeming is attached to a larger constructed, conceptual system, and if, as seems certain, the larger system can in various ways be incoherent, inadequate, distorted and the like, then so also may one's application of the concept of seeming and, beyond that, the very concept of seeming itself, along with its various contrasts.

It might be objected that it is far-fetched to suggest there is a possibility of error with respect to claims concerning states of seeming. I don't think this is so, for it might well be that our habit of talking about seeming to see rather than seeing is itself an error. But even if, in the case of seeming, talk about error is far-fetched, it is certainly not far-fetched with respect to other mental states, *e.g.*, belief, desire and especially particular emotions. If this is so, one cannot claim immunity from error for claims concerning states of seeming on the basis of a general claim to immunity from error for mental states. A claim to infallibility for seeming states would have to be based on narrower premises, perhaps even on an argument showing that, as a special class, claims concerning states of seeming are infallible.

The point which I think needs to be made here is similar to the one made concerning the having of sensations. Just as infallibility attaches not to the content of sensation, but to the having of sensation, the immersion in experience, the apparent infallibility of seeming statements attaches not to the claim that I am in the particular state of seeming, but to my being in some mental state or other, whatever it is. Thus, while I may be mistaken that I am having this mental state of seeming, being mistaken is itself a mental state, an absorption in experience, and as an absorption, immune from error at that basic and general level.

Reflective creatures can create more and more levels of reflection and commentary on experience. In its turn, this capacity creates more and more possibilities of error. But such creatures *cannot step out of being in the moment* and this absorption in experience, whatever its character, is again the element of infallibility.

There is thus a two-tiered possibility of error which is unique to reflective creatures. Both of these—the experiential and the reflective—flow from the larger constructed conceptual system, which it is the lot of such creatures to create. Obviously with regard to reflection, and perhaps not so obviously with regard to perception in its various forms, conceptual elements permeate the activities and make errors of content possible. Whatever becomes content becomes susceptible to error; what remains immune to error is immersion in experience.

Finally, just as outer perception is not immune to error, neither is "inner perception." "I have a green sensation" is not infallible, for I may misidentify the sensation as being one of green, perhaps due to an inadequate concept of green. If I then retreat to "I seem to have a green sensation," I have, as with perceptions of the world, regained infallibility, but again at the expense of content.

IV

There is, however, a powerful and important objection to the conclusions of the last section. This objection, which in large measure I agree with, will, when generalized, take us deeper into the problems generated by the claims that error is inherent in reflective consciousness and that reflective creatures must devise ways of coping with existence. It will then be seen that the objection, when elaborated and examined, is not incompatible with previously made claims, but rather provides the framework for a fuller consideration of these claims and their implications.

In line with the radical objection discussed above, it may be claimed that all sensations involve concepts in at least the minimal sense of classification. Thus, a sensation of red would involve the concept red, the latter element creating the sensation as a sensation of red rather than as another sort of sensation. In this way, the concept would be part of the sensation, indeed would *constitute* the sensation as the particular sensation it is. If this is correct, then so long as 'red' was employed in its standard use, it is hard to see how an identification error could be made. Since there is no raw, undifferentiated sensation which we come to call 'red,' there is nothing to misidentify. On this view, red sensation emerges as a totality and so sensations of red could not be misidentified, for there would be no sensations of red independently of their identification as red sensations.

As a corollary to the above, the use of 'red' could not come from one's own case, from applying 'red' to a previously identified, though as yet unnamed, private sensation. Red sensation, rather, would come into existence when a certain bit of language was acquired. And this acquisition would involve partaking in public experiences, including relating to other people and absorbing public teaching.

But these remarks seem to suggest that something I have asserted over and over needs to be looked at from a new perspective. This is my claim that concepts and conceptual systems can in various ways and to various degrees be incoherent, contradictory, inadequate and distorted. If sensations are constituted in their very existence by concepts and there are no sensations independently of such constructions, then there is nothing for concepts or language to distort. In order for A to distort B, B must exist separately from A. But if there is no B separate from A, if all that exists is AB conjointly, then A cannot distort B.

Now, as I have indicated, I, too, accept the view that there are no non-constituted, undifferentiated sensations which require labels or names. Yet, I also wish to claim that concepts and conceptual systems can be inadequate, distorting, etc. How can I maintain both views?

This is no slight matter. Indeed, it might be said that, when generalized, this problem reveals the basic plight of the reflective creature. Most generally, what is involved is how reflective consciousness finds its way, creates its place, within the larger world process. If, in creating a standpoint for action, reflective consciousness creates the human world, and in so doing constitutes or constructs this world as being of this sort and that sort, how can we say one constructed standpoint is better than another? In the absence of givens and values which are prior to construction, how can reflective consciousness make sensible, non-arbitrary choices?

This problem needs to be faced on both an abstract and a concrete level. Abstractedly, what needs to be shown is that while constructs are inherent to reflective consciousness, neither these nor the choices, ways of life, and ideas of fulfillment which are intimately connected to them, need be arbitrary. That is, the idea of non-arbitrary constructs, choices, ways of life, and ideas of fulfillment must be shown to be intelligible. Concretely, what needs to be provided are the details of these non-arbitrary constructs, choices, ways of life, and ideas of fulfillment. The latter problem I will postpone for our detailed discussions of personal integration; the former problem I will attempt to address now.

As suggested previously, in order to survive, certain creatures have to develop a reflective standpoint. Having such a standpoint enables the making of choices and so at least some degree of self-direction. But in order to make choices, the world in various of its aspects has to be represented within consciousness. Thus, a system of representations, including concepts, perspectives, attitudes, and the like, is developed and it is in terms of these that choices are made and purposeful action ensues.

But while choice is a significant phenomenon for reflective consciousness, it itself has a variety of limitations and so cannot serve unanalyzed and unexplored, as the key to human survival and fulfillment. First, not all behavior, and probably not all action, is a matter of choice, for there are a variety of forces in operation which are either not known to, or, when known, not controllable by, reflective creatures. Further, and more significantly in this context, not every choice is appropriate to the structure within which reflective consciousness emerges and chooses, namely, the physical world and the biological organism which is making the choices. From the fact that reflective consciousness constitutes or constructs the human world, it neither follows that it also constitutes or constructs the larger physical world, including its own physical nature, nor that its construction of the human world adequately accounts for the nature of the larger process within which the construction takes place. If this is so, it is, in a general fashion, relatively easy to see how inadequate concepts and conceptual systems can develop. As a result of faulty constructs, what is taken as real, important and valuable may lead to the adoption of ideals and the setting of goals which, when pursued and realized, make of the organism a less creative and fulfilled creature than it could be.

These remarks, however, create a deeper problem, for once we start talking about "creative and fulfilled creatures," we have at least implied a set of values. But if, as has been previously suggested, value only comes into the world with the creation of the reflective standpoint, what is the source of such values? My remarks seem to suggest that there is some standpoint, not itself a reflective standpoint, from which not only the elements of reflective standpoints but the reflective standpoints themselves can be evaluated. But I have also suggested that for reflective creatures there are no standpoints other than reflective standpoints. Again, how can both of these views be consistently maintained?

Here, once again, we seem to come face to face with the peculiar and disconcerting plight of the reflective creature. Within a situation of neither value nor disvalue, the reflective creature must create a standpoint which generates action. Action, however, involves choice, which, in turn, involves values and so the reflective creature must create values. But these values are created within the very standpoint they direct. They are generated from within the standpoint, do not have an existence independent of the standpoint, and so cannot be used to justify the standpoint. Yet, the values develop along with the standpoint, help to produce movement within the standpoint and so, along with other elements of the standpoint, serve to modify and expand it. The standpoint, then, is the source of the values and is itself directed by these self-same values.

But if this is so, how can the created values and the standpoint of which they are an inherent part be evaluated? Certainly, not by the standpoint itself, for it is, in part, constituted by the values it generates and so it, as much as the values, stands in need of evaluation. If this is so, it eliminates the possibility of self-justification, both for the values and the standpoint, for these interconnected constructs are generated within a developmental flux or process and must be understood and, if possible, justified within that flux. Self-justification seems to imply the possibility of severing such constructs from their developmental contexts, an exercise which, I think, distorts both the nature of the constructs and the process within which the constructs emerge.

Justification, then, seems to be available only from a larger, more inclusive standpoint. From this larger perspective, one would be able to evaluate the ideals, goals and values, as well as the claims about the world, of the more limited standpoint. But the larger perspective is also a standpoint, containing values created by reflective consciousness in the same manner values are created within the less inclusive standpoint. If this is so, the larger perspective stands in need of evaluation as much as does the more limited standpoint. And if we then move to a still more inclusive evaluative standpoint, the very same problems emerge anew; and *ad infinitum*. Thus, there is no non-constructed standpoint which can stand outside of constructed standpoints and evaluate them; and since, in addition, there is no constructed standpoint which can certify itself as final and authoritative, we are once again back with our problem of how it is possible to say that some standpoint or some set of values is better than others.

In response, my suggestion is that reflective consciousness cannot, literally cannot, step out of the process of which it is a part. It can, of course, attempt to do so — as the claim to self-justification apparently does — but the attempt will simply be one more way of being within the process, though a way less successful than would develop if reflective consciousness openly acknowledged and embraced its participation in the process. In addition, reflective consciousness cannot, again literally cannot, cease constructing ways of coping with the larger life process of which it is a part. Again, it can seek to cease such constructions, but such an attempt would just be another way of trying to cope. And, as with the attempt to step out of the process, the attempt not to create ways of coping would be less successful than those attempts which acknowledged and embraced the need to cope, and created reflective standpoints in maximum awareness of this need.

The general point is that *any* standpoint which attempts to extract itself from the process of which it is a part will produce distortions, misunderstandings, and so on, these reflecting the ways in which and the degree to which the extraction is attempted. Now this, of course, does not answer any questions concerning the details of particular, non-extracted standpoints. It does, however, remove from consideration as adequate those standpoints which either treat reflective consciousness as in fact not embedded within the larger world process or have, as a consequence of their explicit or implicit adoption, the concrete, personal experience of being disconnected or not embedded. In addition, it points us toward the need to create reflective standpoints which reveal and create the needed connections. I say "create" as well as "reveal," for given the need of reflective consciousness to devise ways of coping with its situation, it must from its own resources, come up with or create these ways. It thus must face and attempt to resolve, both conceptually and experientially, the question of what is and what is not creative connection to the process. Most generally, the dynamic nature of the process as well as the situation of reflective consciousness within the process is revealed; what must be created is the manner in which reflective consciousness can align itself with the process and its own peculiar nature.

But now, one final time, what about the status of these last remarks? Do they, too, express just one additional standpoint among others? If they do, it is doubtful I can draw from them the conclusions I am attempting — and, as we proceed, will attempt — to draw. If however, this is not just another standpoint, but somehow reveals the necessary structure of all reflective standpoints, what can justify or, if justification is the wrong notion here, account for this phenomenon?

The assertion, "no standpoint can escape being a standpoint within the life process" does indeed express a standpoint within the life process. But while the assertion expresses a standpoint, the standpoint expressed is not a typical one. Typical standpoints express the existence of some content or other; they do not point back to or express the conditions of their existence. The standpoint we are now considering does include itself within its assertion, and in so doing reveals something absolutely basic and necessary about the construction and nature of reflective standpoints. Reflective consciousness is such that it has the capacity to look endlessly at its constructions, thereby creating ever new standpoints. But in looking at its constructions, it is not simultaneously looking at the looking. The *always* present level of not looking establishes the presence of a further standpoint, which reflective consciousness may wish to make explicit, explore and seek to justify. Any standpoint, then, no matter how fundamental, implies a further standpoint, the one generated by reflecting on the original standpoint. This *is* how reflective consciousness works; and, try as we might, we cannot escape it.

But does this in any way detract from the claim that some reflective standpoints are better than others? Again, my answer is no, unless we think that validity is a function of a standpoint which is *not* subject to the constitutive and reflective movement of reflective consciousness. As should be clear, however, I take the idea of such a standpoint as itself a construction of reflective consciousness; and, as should also be clear, I think this idea is ultimately incoherent and so the standpoint it expresses not as good as other standpoints.

While standpoints which are thought of as independent of reflective consciousness are incoherent, they are not without influence on how reflective creatures deal with their life situation. However, if the above is correct, no matter how such standpoints are thought of, they are nonetheless a way reflective consciousness is operating within the process. But when this is not seen, the actual operation of reflective consciousness — including both the creation of the idea of a standpoint independent of reflective consciousness and the particular standpoint itself — is concealed from the individual. As a result, one does not need to face directly the question of the degree of responsibility one can take for the creation of the standpoints in terms of which one lives. Consequently, one's way of life is limited, involving distortions and misunderstandings and one does not fare as well as one otherwise might.

V

This long excursion into the possibility of justifying reflective standpoints grew out of the discussion of perceptual judgment and experience and, especially, perceptual infallibility and error. The problems connected to these latter topics are versions of similar problems that attach, in general, to reflective consciousness and, in particular, to its various modes of operation. As we proceed through analyses of these other modes, many of the suggestions put forth in the preceding discussion will again prove relevant.

What has emerged is that reflective consciousness, with its array of intricately interwoven concepts, perspectives, attitudes, and other attributes, creates the possibility of a unique sort of non-reflective, spontaneous perceptual error of the world. This is so even if it is the case that basic perceptual experiences, such as seeing red, emerge as wholes and are endorsed through public systems of communication; for these systems of communication are themselves outcomes of reflective consciousness and are thus susceptible to all the distortions attendant on reflective consciousness. In light of this, errors of this sort are not limited to non-reflective, spontaneous perceptual experience, but spill over to the totality of non-reflective experience. But the story does not end even here, for reflective consciousness also creates the possibility of a many leveled, deeper, but parallel, class of errors. These are the errors which can flow from the concepts, etc. which are employed in reflection on spontaneous experience and, one level deeper, those which can flow from reflection on the reflection on spontaneous experience.

If this is correct, reflective consciousness has within it the seeds for significant alienation, fragmentation and distortion. And such possibilities easily, all too easily, turn into actualities. It is in light of this that the need to arrive at a coherent notion/experience of integration is as pressing as it is.

Before leaving this topic, I wish briefly to point out that the primary conclusion reached above — *viz.*, that reflective consciousness cannot step out of the process of which it is a part and so is always, within this process, manifesting a particular standpoint which is not capturable in its moment of operation by itself — is of a piece with and is mutually supportive of two previously reached conclusions. The first of these is that there is no self, and especially no Cartesian Ego, which is simultaneously both the source and object of attention. This is at least similar to, and perhaps identical with, the present point that there is no absolute standpoint of evaluation and so no self-certifying source of evaluation which can be employed in the evaluation of other reflective standpoints. In both cases, the self and the absolute standpoint, the reason for non-existence is the same: they both presuppose another self or standpoint by which or within which the self or absolute standpoint is known. This implies that what was thought to be "the self" of "the absolute standpoint" is not that at all, but is one more temporary, partial construction or vantage point, more or less adequate than others. In other words, the inability of self to capture or know or introspect itself implies there is no final, observing self; and the inability of any standpoint to justify itself implies there is no final absolute standpoint.

The second point of coherence involves the previous claim that perceptual infallibility is limited to immersion in experience, some experience or other and does not involve any *specific* content. This is, I think, supported by the claim that reflective consciousness cannot escape the process of which it is a part and out of which it arises. If reflective consciousness is inherently and inescapably part of this process, infallibility is simply non-reflective immersion in experience: the inability to escape the process is tantamount to immersion within the process.

Consciousness, Pain and Error

Chapter Five

I

Much of the last chapter was, in general, concerned with the manner in which the products of reflective consciousness come to permeate the various experiences of reflective creatures and, more specifically, with how those products come to permeate perceptual experience. The conclusion was that given the emergence of an intricately interwoven set of concepts, perspectives and attitudes, the experiences of reflective creatures are all susceptible to a unique form of error and so do not display content infallibility.

This conclusion, however, may have been a bit premature, for there is an additional phenomenon, namely, organic sensation which, it is often argued, is not susceptible to error of any sort. Indeed, it might be argued that due to its nature, it is organic sensation, and not perceptual sensation or any other kind of mental state, which ought to be treated as the test case for claims to content infallibility.

While at various times in the past it has been claimed that either all or most mental states are transparent to consciousness and so could, through simple attention, be known infallibly, this is rarely, if ever, claimed now. Today, infallibility is typically claimed only for those mental states which have a phenomenology or qualitative content. Since most states of consciousness are now thought not to have a phenomenology, most states of consciousness are not claimed to be infallibly known.

But both perceptual experience (sensation) and organic sensation do have a phenomenology or qualitative content and so they become the prime candidates for infallibility. However, while perceptual experience does have a phenomenology, it can be claimed that this phenomenology has elements which preclude it from displaying content infallibility. Perceptual experience is almost certainly intentional, that is, it takes an object or is about something beyond itself. But the presence of an object or of something beyond itself, what I have been calling a content, provides an essential element of differentiation. And, in reflective creatures, this element of differentiation is provided for by the conceptual system which is the very source of the possibility of error which is unique to such creatures.

Another way of putting this matter is to point out that the phenomenology of perceptual experience involves the look of something or other. For a look to be the look of this rather than the look of that requires a mode of differentiation which is internal to the look. With reflective creatures, this differentiation seems to involve a mentalistic aspect of the look, a category or concept; and this again flows from the larger constructed conceptual system of such creatures.

These are some of the considerations which led to the conclusion that there is no content infallibility attached to perceptual experience. Indeed, it also led to the claim that the failure of content infallibility for perceptual experience implies that the only sort of infallibility which can be claimed for reflective creatures is that they are experiencing something or other. Anything more specific than this immediately becomes susceptible to error due to the presence of elements of the constructed conceptual system.

This point also affects claims to infallibility for states of seeming, for these, too, involve differentiation, not only for what one seems to see, but for the state of seeming itself. If we retreat from a characterization of the state as this or that, and simply attempt to treat it *qua* experienced as infallible, we again have only the contentless infallibility of experiencing something or other.

But it is precisely a generalization of this conclusion to the whole of consciousness which, on the basis of the example of organic sensation, can be resisted as at least premature and perhaps even as mistaken. It might, that is, be suggested that organic sensations are significantly different from perceptual sensations and that these differences provide for at least some bit of content infallibility.

Before we proceed with this matter, a brief word must be added on how organic sensations are treated in contemporary philosophy of mind. Obviously enough, organic sensations are the bodily sensations of the organism. As such, they range from the extremes of pleasure to the extremes of pain. Within this range, there is an enormous diversity of phenomena. Yet, virtually all contemporary discussions of this matter focus on some instance or other of a distinct, vivid sensation of pain. Perhaps the reason for this is to find some one clear type of example which can settle, once and for all, the question of the infallibility of organic sensations. Although I think such a focus is misleading, I will also initially adopt it. However, as we proceed, we shall find reason to expand this focus.

The first thing to notice about pain states is that they are almost certainly not intentional. That is, pain does not point beyond itself to something that it is of. In a perhaps not misleading way of speaking, pain is its own object. Being non-intentional, pain does not include an element of differentiation which intentional states do include, and thereby does not contain at least one element which is a source of possible error.

Pain states, however, do of course involve an element of differentiation; for if one is in pain, one is in that state and not another state and this is a differentiation. It can, however, be argued that such a differentiation is non-conceptual. Although we can, perhaps during the fact, and certainly after the fact, characterize the state conceptually as a pain state, the immediate onset of the state is not so characterized at all. Rather, at the onset of the state, it is differentiated, *i.e.*, experienced *as* pain, simply by its non-conceptual felt character, its phenomenology or qualitative content. Unlike perceptual sensations whose phenomenologies involve the look of the sensation and so, for reflective creatures, a conceptual element, pains, and more generally organic sensations, have a phenomenology of feel, bodily feel. Such feels, it may be said, are immediate in such a fashion that they are completely unmediated by concept, category and the like. If this is so, it may then be argued there is a class of pain states which is not permeated by the elements which flow from reflective consciousness and so are immune to the type of errors these elements make possible. It may be that some pain sensations are so direct and immediate that they, as it were, bypass both reflective and non-reflective consciousness. In such cases, one is overwhelmed by pain in so basic a fashion that the elements flowing from reflective consciousness only attach to the experience during and after the experience of the sensation, but not at its onset.

Before looking at this matter in greater detail, it is important to see that even if this claim is correct, it only holds for a very limited class of pain states. Within the class of pain states, we make a variety of distinctions concerning the kind and degree of pain that is present. In addition, we distinguish pain states, especially at their edges, from a variety of other states of consciousness. In doing so we are, of course, employing a range of elements derived from reflective consciousness. As a result, all such distinctions, and their concomitant claims, are susceptible to error. So whatever is said about the infallibility of a limited, though significant, class of pain states, it does not follow either that whenever we are in fact in pain and know it, that we do so infallibly or that we always infallibly know that we are in pain or that we are not in pain.

If these latter points are correct, one outcome is that it is possible for one to be in pain, and not know it or not be in pain, but think one is. But if this is so, pain cannot simply be the felt nature of pain, nor non-pain the felt nature of non-pain. Or, perhaps better, pain cannot simply be the acknowledgement—or even the sincere acknowledgement—of pain, and non-pain the denial—even the sincere denial—of pain.

My suggestion is that it is not only possible, but quite common, for one to be in certain sorts of pain and not to acknowledge these states as pain states even, or primarily, to oneself. What makes this possible is the expansion and development of reflective consciousness. As it expands, it enlarges the range, *i.e.*, the variety and depth of pain states. But with reflective consciousness being a divided consciousness, such developments need not be noted or acknowledged. When they are individually not noted or acknowledged, one may be in pain but not know it. In light of this, it is a very interesting question whether unacknowledged pain states are—whatever the individual notes or acknowledges—felt as pains or as something else.

II

Let's look at these matters more closely. It has been insisted throughout these chapters that reflective creatures experience the world by means of constructed conceptual systems. Since these systems arise from the constructive activity of such creatures, they need not adequately account for the reality they reflect or represent. Thus, all such systems are at least theoretically susceptible to error. This, in turn, implies that the concepts and language employed to understand the world are also susceptible to error. It would seem to follow that no experience whatsoever is thoroughly immune to error.

If this is so, I must conclude, as I did in the case of perceptual sensation, that no instance of organic sensation is immune to error. For if the previous conclusions are correct, the conceptualization and language of pain can, in any number of ways, be defective. But there seems to be something not quite right about such a conclusion, for even if the conceptualization and language of pain are somehow incoherent, inadequate, or the like, there is still the *felt experience* of pain, what is experienced spontaneously without — and this appears to be possible — the mediation of concept and language. If it is therefore insisted that such experiences are infallible, this appears to be very similar to what was said about perceptual experience, namely, that what is infallible is immersion in experience, some experience or other. But while there is this similarity, there is also a significant difference, for the immersion in pain experience seems to be a *more particularized* experience than is the immersion in perceptual experience.

The sort of immersion in pain experience I am referring to precludes a characterization in terms of intensity, tone, depth, and the like, for these explicitly introduce conceptual elements and so the possibility of error. But in the absence of such characterizations, the sheer onset of vivid pain seems to involve a content, a specificity, that is not to be found in perceptual sensation. If this is so, a certain class of pain states may involve not only the infallibility that attaches to any immersion in experience, but also a degree of content infallibility.

I think there is something to be said for this position, for it is difficult to see how someone suddenly hit with, say, a sharp, stabbing pain would not know, and know absolutely and infallibly, that he was in pain. In order to properly delimit the class of cases for which such an analysis seems to hold, we stipulate that such cases occur against the immediate backdrop of a complete bodily calm and equilibrium. In this way, the contrast between the pain and what immediately precedes it is so dramatic that being in pain is not at all primarily a matter of knowing, rightly or wrongly, that one is in pain; rather it is a matter of being overwhelmed by pain. What possible source of error could there be here?

Let's take a look at an example. It will, I think, enable us both to solidify the position which seems to be emerging and to see its limitations and move beyond it. Imagine someone at the dentist having a tooth filled without the benefit of anesthesia. Now contrast this with an identical case, except for the fact that the patient did have an anesthetic administered. In both cases, the dentist starts to drill, but only in the former instance is pain felt. Isn't the latter instance a case of someone being hit with pain, yet not feeling pain? If it is, then it would seem to counter the claim that there are a certain class of cases, namely, those in which one is hit with sudden pain, in which pain states are infallibly known.

But, of course, the typical response to this analysis of drilling with anesthesia is that in such a case there is no pain, for there is no pain felt. Pain, it would be claimed, is simply felt pain. The notion of unfelt pain is absurd or incoherent. To travel this path, however, is to come perilously close to defining pain as "what is felt to be pain;" and if we do this, we rule out the possibility of unfelt pain or mistakes about the existence or non-existence of pain states before we've even begun to explore the phenomena. As a result, we wind up treating all pain states as infallibly known. What is said to be pain is pain, for if one feels something as pain, it is pain; and what is said not to be pain is not pain, for if one does not feel something as pain, it is not pain.

What I think misleads us here is a pre-occupation with one kind of pain state, the kind in which one is hit with vivid, overwhelming pain. From such cases, we seem to conclude both that all pain states are infallibly known and that the notion of unfelt pain is absurd. When hit with vivid, etc. pain, there seems neither to be a possibility of error nor any sense to say that such pain is unfelt. But in addition to such modes of pain, there are other modes of pain; and for these a different, expanded sort of analysis seems to be needed. The case of the applied anesthesia may serve in one way as a bridge between what we take as the typical case and these other cases, for with the presence of anesthesia a barrier is placed between the physiological imposition of pain and the feeling of it. Something like this occurs also, I think, with the other cases, except the barrier is not chemical and the question of whether or not the pain is felt is both more complicated and difficult.

But what are these other sorts of pain states or modes of pain I am alluding to? They are all states which have developed as a result of the emergence of reflective consciousness and include anguish, anxiety, a sense of loss, grief, the fear that is contingent on reflection, and so on. Typically, such states do not involve a localizable, distinct sensation as do the standard instances of pain discussed above. They do, however, involve somewhat diffuse and often vague feelings of negativity and so have a phenomenology or qualitative content. But these phenomenologies, because they emerge from elaborations and developments of reflective consciousness, not only can become obscured within the complexities of such emergent phenomenologies, they can also exist at the edge or limits of awareness and understanding and so not be adequately grasped. Unlike the pain which overwhelms one, this sort of pain does *not* bypass reflective and non-reflective consciousness. Rather, it is the outcome of the movement and development of reflective consciousness and so is constituted by the elements and constructs of such consciousness. Given this, such pain states can be obscured, misnamed and even ignored.

The pain that is contingent on reflective consciousness is, I think, tied to the sense of mineness which emerges from reflection. Once a creature becomes aware — reflectively aware — that it is leading a life, that it can identify this life as its own, a new form of vulnerability arises. The creature becomes explicitly aware that various harmful and destructive things can happen to *it*, that *its* life and well-being can be threatened in any number of ways. This realization diffuses itself through the consciousness of the reflective creature. As a result, the various ways in which the creature encounters and experiences life can become tinged with this new form of pain.

To ignore pain of this sort is to treat pain essentially on the model applicable to pre-reflective creatures. For such creatures, it appears adequate to treat pain exclusively as being overwhelmed by certain sorts of localizable, distinct sensations. They cannot reflect on their experience, contemplate their life situation and develop attitudes and perspectives in terms of which they see their life as ebbing and flowing, and at some point coming to an end. Their pain states are limited to the immediacy of experience in two senses: 1) they cannot take up a standpoint to the immediacy of experience and so cannot experience the pain that is connected to such standpoints; and 2) stemming from this inability, elements derived from such standpoints cannot be absorbed within the immediacy of experience. There are, then, for such creatures, no pain states which *could* be other than and at a different level from those pain states found in the immediacy of experience. Since such pains involve feeling pain as a localizable, stabbing, or aching sensation, it appears correct to identify, in total, the pain of pre-reflective creatures with just such phenomena.

As we've stressed, reflective creatures can also be hit with pain, overwhelmed by pain. When they are, the proper analysis of such pain is probably very similar to — perhaps even identical with — the analysis available for pre-reflective creatures. However, it does not follow from this either that all instances of the pain of reflective creatures can be treated on this model or that there is no other mode of pain which reflective creatures experience. To draw such implications is precisely to eliminate from inspection those sorts of pain which are unique to reflective creatures and, in a fashion, are a manifestation of the particular nature and situation of the reflective creature.

III

I am focusing on the mode of pain which is unique to reflective creatures because I think such pains are not only known fallibly, but, more, may not be known at all by the person who has them. But what can it mean to say one may not know one is experiencing pain of this sort? How can one *have* such pains and not know one has them? Isn't this some sort of contradiction or incoherency?

As long as we think of pain exclusively on the model of being hit with distinct, localizable sensations of a certain sort, we shall find the notion of unknown or unfelt pain very puzzling. And we shall find it still more puzzling if we see the typical situation of pain as one in which tranquility of being is interrupted by a vivid stab or ache. As suggested, from such a perspective the notion of unknown or unfelt pain does indeed seem absurd. But not all experiences of pain are of this sort. For example, people can lead lives in which they do not have readily available the clear contrast which makes many instances of pain so vivid and manifest. They may, that is, lead their lives within a background of a steady, underlying unease, anxiety, and the like, which is *not identified as such*. To the extent that there is an explicit acknowledgement of such states at all, they could be taken as the norm and assumed to be present, in this manner and to this degree, for all reflective creatures. If they are so thought of, there is no imaginative contrast available — one in which the unease, anxiety, etc. would not be present or at least not pervasively present — and such states would be regarded and named as instances of "feeling o.k." or even "feeling good."

In such situations, the degree of awareness and acknowledgement of the underlying feelings — and the forces connected to them — would almost certainly be determined by the interaction of those phenomena with environmental circumstances. That is, various shifts in the intensity of the underlying phenomena would determine what description the individual would provide to himself and others concerning how he felt at some moment. When, due to circumstances in the individual's life, the underlying feelings became more intense than usual and the unease, etc. began to seep through to reflective awareness, there would be some vague acknowledgement of pain; but when, again through the vicissitudes of circumstance, the underlying feelings diminished in intensity and receded still further into the background, the individual would describe himself as content or even happy.

Thus, one clear way one can be in pain and not know it is to misidentify the pain state as some other sort of state. In such a situation, however, is the individual actually in pain, even though he does not call it pain or acknowledge it as pain? Again, part of what confuses the issue here is the implicit assumption that in such cases we are talking about the kind of pain which is universal to virtually all creatures and so not dependent on the emergence of reflective consciousness. When pains are of this sort, there is no possibility of misidentification and so no possibility of actual but unacknowledged pain. The cases now under consideration, however, are not quite like this. These pains exist within the elaborated structure of reflective consciousness. But having been developed within the structure, they have a distinct nature relating to their particularity and mode of development within this structure. But if this is so, questions relating to the possibilities of unknown and unfelt pain must be answered within this perspective and not from another perspective — *i.e.*, pre-reflective consciousness within which such questions cannot even arise. To be sure, while the proper naming and acknowledgement of such states brings them more vividly to reflective awareness, their misdescription and non-acknowledgement does not cancel their existence. It just ensures that their nature and mode of operation will be hidden from the individual.

My suggestion is that unknown or unacknowledged pain states are indeed possible. Although the individual's comments on his pain states — and beyond this, all his mental states — must be given a special standing, they are by no means always correct or final. In seeking to make explicit the peculiar and unique authority which the individual *does* have with regard to his inner life, we sometimes fail to see the limitations which are inherent to this authority. This is a result, I think, of our implicit belief that we can extract and isolate the individual from the larger process of which he is a part. But to extract the individual from the process is also to extract him from those aspects of the process which are operating within him. To treat pain states — and other mental states — as existing only if felt and acknowledged is thus a manifestation of a deeper misconstrual of the individual existence of reflective creatures.

Let's elaborate these matters a bit more. The initial question is: can an individual be said to be in a state—X—which that individual sincerely calls by another name or description—Y—which is incompatible with X? One argument against such a possibility is that at least some significant behavior of the individual will almost certainly indicate that he is not in state

X, but will rather seem to indicate he is in state Y. If one is in pain, but does not acknowledge it, one will not, at least not obviously, behave in the ways typical of one who has acknowledged pain. For example, one will neither seek to extricate oneself from the immediate situation, nor seek to find out and explore why one feels as one does. Since one does not call one's experience painful, there is no immediate reason to do either of these things. [1]

These acknowledgements, however, seem to lead to peculiar conclusions. For if one is in pain, but displays no behavior which is indicative of being in pain, we seem to have to say that pain is a private phenomenon having no inherent connection to behavior. And not only would it be a private phenomenon, but one which, in such a case, is not even known to the person who has it. This, incredulously, would be to make of such instances of pain isolated, private but unacknowledged states. But this, of course, is not being suggested. What is being suggested is that if the individual does not acknowledge his pain, he will not behave in ways which are *immediately* characteristic of those who do acknowledge their pain. This does not imply, however, that he will not act in other ways which are characteristic of how those who are in pain do act (even though he who is denying he is in pain will almost certainly not grasp the significance of such action). Indeed, it will typically be because of such actions that one will be tempted to say that the individual, though denying he is in pain, is in fact in pain.

So we are asking a question about the felt nature of certain experiences independently of how they are described, named or thought of. My suggestion is that in the case of certain instances of certain sorts of pain, no matter how we describe, name or think of these, they are nonetheless pains. That is, they are painfully felt, even though they might not, within the capabilities of reflective consciousness, be felt *as* pains, that is, named as pain. [1]

IV

Now, however, I seem to have stepped into troubled waters. I have, on the one hand, been insisting throughout these chapters that there is no undifferentiated given to which we attach names. But, on the other hand, my latest remarks seem to suggest precisely what I have been denying, namely, that independently of any names or descriptions, there are such states as pain states. Can both of these views be consistently maintained or is there a blatant contradiction present?

This is a complex matter and to deal with it we again have to return to our distinction between pre-reflective and reflective creatures and see how that distinction impinges on the present difficulty. Pre-reflective creatures are immersed in experience and within such experiences feel pain. That is, they experience pain *as* pain and not as something else. But they are incapable of reflecting either on such states or on their life situation and so the range, variety and depth of their pain cannot expand. Given their ongoing immersion in experience and the non-expandability of their pain, they are not susceptible to errors of misnaming, misidentification and misdescription. For such creatures, the given is simply the immersion in pain experience and there is no question of the existence of a given independently of a name or description.

Now, although the case of pain and other mental states is extraordinarily more complex with reflective consciousness, I have suggested there is a type of pain experience had by reflective creatures which is perhaps identical to that had by pre-reflective creatures. These are the cases in which one is hit with or overwhelmed by pain. In such cases, it appears the pain is so direct (unmediated) and bodily that at its onset it simply bypasses both reflective and non-reflective consciousness. If this is so, there again is no distinction between the given and the naming of it; there is only the immersion in the overwhelming givenness of the pain. In such instances, it appears that there is no possible question to be asked concerning what is given as opposed to what is its name, description, etc.

If this is correct, then the only area in which questions can arise concerning a distinction between what is given and its name is that of reflective consciousness. Given the ability of reflective consciousness to attend both to its particular pain states and its life situation, the range, variety and depth of pain states and complexes can expand; and given this expansion and the continued ability to reflect, it becomes possible for the pain states to come apart from reflection. When this occurs, we can indeed ask: is there a given separate from the name or description we apply to it?

My response is yes, there is, within the reflective creature's expanded experience of pain, a given which can be separated from the naming of it. This given, however, is *not* an undifferentiated given. It is rather a given which exists *within* the constructed system of reflection. As such, it is a *differentiated* given, a given which has its existence and nature through the workings of reflective consciousness. It is *not* a given which pre-exists the system of reflective consciousness and can be identified independently of that system. In cases in which the name or description applied to the pain state is other than pain, what is given is the felt nature of pain within the system of reflective consciousness, and what is occurring is that the individual experiencing the pain is misnaming or misdescribing it.

But how is this possible, how can reflective consciousness not know what it is experiencing? As indicated previously, reflective consciousness is a divided consciousness. That is, it is a consciousness with one aspect or several aspects knowing other aspects of itself. Given such a division, it is possible for the aspect or aspects of consciousness which know not to know what it or they could know. When we couple this point with the claim that pain is not exhausted by the pain which overwhelms, we can easily see how one could be in pain and yet sincerely deny it. In addition, we can see that to admit the existence of unknown or unacknowledged pain is not also to admit the existence of an undifferentiated given.

Before moving on to a related and very interesting point, I would like to present, in support of the claim that misidentifications of pain are possible, an additional short argument which is, I think, implicit in our common sense view of these matters. People often come to realize that what, on past occasions, they had called "not pain" were in fact clear instances of pain. This seems to be a clear recognition that one can misname or misdescribe one's pain.

It is, however, possible to avoid this conclusion by saying that at the time of experience, in the past, the experience was indeed of non-pain, and that it is only now, in the present, that it feels as if there were pain in the past. In this way, it would be claimed that both experiences, *i.e.*, the non-pain in the past and the pain in the present, are accurately described. But even if one takes this line, there is still an error of description remaining, namely, the error of now calling pain what was in the past non-pain. However, those who insist that mistakes about pain are not possible would attribute this error not to a mistake about pain, but to the unreliability of memory. That is, it will be said that the present experience of pain is correct, but the assigning of the pain to the past event is mistaken due to a faulty recollection of the past event.

This response, however, will not quite do, for while it is, of course, possible to recollect past events in a faulty fashion, it is also possible to recollect—or, better, *re-experience*—past events in an accurate fashion. If one accurately re-experiences a past event and claims that such an event, previously claimed to have been without pain, did indeed involve pain, then if we continue to maintain that the act as originally experienced was without pain, we are placing the error in the present experience of pain. Thus, once we recognize that what was once thought not to be pain can later be claimed to be pain, we are recognizing that pain can be misnamed, misdescribed, and so forth.

V

Although much of the present chapter is preoccupied with establishing that there are modes of pain which, in a significant sense, can be unknown, unacknowledged, and, in a specific manner, unfelt, pain is typically defined and known through its phenomenology. I say "typically" rather than "always" because this phenomenology can, in various ways, be eliminated or obscured. Through the introduction of a chemical, for example, pain may be completely eliminated, while through often unconscious psychological maneuvering pain may be misnamed and so become obscured and hidden. The existence and use of such methods, however, does not negate the essential phenomenological nature of pain. Recognizing that the feeling of pain can be blocked by chemical or physiological factors is simply recognizing that pain as phenomenologically experienced has a physiological component and to affect this component in a certain way is to alter what is phenomenologically available. Similarly, recognizing that certain kinds of pain can be unknown, etc., is not to deny the phenomenological nature of pain; it is just to recognize that this phenomenology can be misnamed and so obscured. In these latter cases, pain retains its phenomenology, but the phenomenology is misconstrued.

These remarks raise some interesting problems. Pain is clearly a behavior producing phenomenon; and presumably it produces behavior in terms of its phenomenology, its felt nature. But if there are unknown, unacknowledged and, in the sense we've explained, unfelt pains, it seems such pains cannot perform their behavioral function. In the absence of the properly identified and acknowledged negativity of pain, certain sorts of behavior will not be forthcoming.

While this is a significant problem, it can, I think, be handled within the structure of the views already presented. On these views, it is true that when pain is not properly recognized as pain, certain sorts of behavior, e.g. immediate avoidance of the pain inducing situation, an attempt to understand the situation, etc., will not occur. However, it does not follow from this that no behavior at all will be produced by those inadequately recognized pains. Behavior will indeed develop; but it will be behavior which must be seen in the light of pain which is being experienced under descriptions other than pain. In such cases, the unacknowledged and misdescribed phenomenology of pain takes over and produces its outcomes independently of what is consciously acknowledged. Thus, while pain is productive of behavior in terms of its phenomenology, the individual who is behaving may not acknowledge the pain nor have any understanding of how his behavior is being produced by the pain. On this view, in order to function as pain, pain must be painfully felt, though it need not be acknowledged as pain or recognized as functioning at all.

If correct, these remarks eliminate the possibility of pain not being pain, *i.e.*, of pain being experienced, independently of what it is called, as other than what pain, properly acknowledged, is experienced as. This conclusion, however, seems to engender a conflict with one of the currently most popular views of the mind, namely, functionalism. Functionalism is the attempt to tie — indeed, to identify — all mental states with functional states of the organism. Functional states are said to be those states which are the outcome of certain causes and which in turn are productive of other outcomes. Within such a view, however, the exact ontological nature of such states is typically left open. But not only is the ontological nature left open, capable of being filled in by different physical natures in versions of physicalism and even by different non-physical natures in versions of non-physicalism, so also is the phenomenology left open. And the matter must be left open, for if different creatures — never mind machines — have suitably different physical natures, then identical functional states, *i.e.*, states produced by the same type of causes and productive of the same type of effects, may, due to the radically different physical natures, be experienced in radically different fashions — and so pain may not be pain, that is, painfully felt.

Another way of looking at this is that according to functionalism, there are contingent identity statements linking the experience of pain — and all other mental states — with specific functional states of the organism. However, since these identity statements are held to be contingent, it is at least conceivable that experiences of pain could be identified with *different* functional states. In light of this, what is now pain might not have been pain, and what is not now pain might have been pain. [2]

The Functionalist is not, of course, simply claiming that the experience we now call pain might be called by some other name. That, of course, is true, but, in this context, uninteresting and irrelevant. Rather, the suggestion seems to be that the experience, the actual felt experience, of pain could be different. Since, on this view, mental states are functional states which stand in certain causal relationships to input and output, a different functional state could be prompted by what now causes the functional state which is pain and this different functional state could produce the behavior which is now caused by the functional state which is now pain. And given the alteration of the functional state, presumably the felt nature of pain could also be altered.

But is this in fact possible? Could some state which is not immediately experienced as hurtful, or damaging or unpleasant, or is not immediately linked to other elements of experience that do feel this way, function as pain now does? I don't think so.

Of course, what we take to be painful, that is, what makes us feel pain, can vary to some significant degree, especially when we move away from the standard stabbings, drillings, etc., to take account of pains of loss, anxiety and the like. In addition, we can imagine a species which seeks to avoid sensations of pleasure and cultivates sensations of pain. In such cases, however, there would need to be associations to the opposite sensation which would enable the postulated sensations to function as they are said to. That is, pleasure would be avoided because of an immediate and direct association to something negative and painful; and pain would be sought because of an immediate and direct association to something positive and pleasurable. In the absence of such associations, these states simply could not play the role they are being asked to play in the imagined examples. The adversiveness of feeling which produces adverse behavior would not be present and so what is said to be pain could not be pain for it is not serving the function of pain. If this is so, then for a state of the organism to be and to function as what is now pain, there must be a distinctly negative and hurtful feel to the state.

This, however, is not to claim that there are necessary connections between pain and its causes, for there may be cases in which there are pain-inducing causes and yet nothing is painfully felt. Nor is it to claim that there are necessary connections between pain and the behavior it produces, for there may be cases of pain which produce no characteristic behavior or even any behavior at all. But it does not follow from this that there is an entirely contingent or accidental relation between pain states and their causes and outcomes. For pain to be pain, it must feel like pain,[3] i.e., have a negative and hurtful phenomenology; its connection to input and output must be considerably tighter than sheer contingency.

Whatever is to play the role of what is now pain must, if it is to play that role, have a negative feel. If it does not, it cannot play the functional role it has been assigned. Functionalists have a tendency to miss this point because often their attention, interest and theoretical commitments are focused on the functional, that is, the physical side of the alleged identity, and not on the phenomenological side.

VI

There is another interesting phenomenon concerning the awareness of pain which merits brief attention. This involves what appears to be an asymmetry beween sincere assertions of the first person pain avowals "I am in pain" and "I am not in pain." Both of these are allotted somewhat privileged status, for they reflect the unique access each of us has to our mental states. While I have questioned and found wanting almost all of the standard claims to infallibility for experiences of pain, I do not wish to question the general reliability of sincere expressions of these avowals. However, granting general reliability is not equivalent to granting universal reliability.

Although I think it is possible for both sorts of avowal to be mistaken, claims that one is not in pain are much more likely to be mistaken than are claims that one is in pain. People are very rarely in error when they sincerely say "I am in pain," for typically they have no stake in believing they are in pain when they are not. As a result, most such assertions can be taken at face value.

There are, however, exceptions to this. For example, someone needing constant attention may come to believe (without being quite aware it is believed) that being in pain gains attention. In consequence, a variety of physical and/or psychological states may be taken as pains and the individual sincerely think of himself as in pain, though he is not in pain.

But this is a too simple rendition of the situation. The person who is often treating non-pain states as pain will, over time, come to be pained. The operating attitudes and reactions are themselves kinds of pains and constant repetition of such phenomena will produce a dour, complaining person. In addition, such a person is almost certainly in pain at a deeper level, the level which is producing the surface complaints. There is then perhaps a sense in which this sort of person is indeed always in pain when he asserts he is in pain. However, what he focuses on as pain is not the significant pain in the situation. It may in fact be argued that his focus on surface pain is precisely a way of avoiding focusing on and acknowledging the deeper, more significant pain. If he were asked whether there is pain at this deeper level, he would almost certainly respond in the negative. And here is where the asymmetry between mistakes concerning "I am in pain" and "I am not in pain" becomes apparent.

The reasons for the disinclination to acknowledge pain are many and complex and I wish only to offer a few suggestions. First, and most obviously, pain doesn't feel good and so most of us are adverse to feeling it, especially when it is possible not to. Secondly, and related to this, we often have a sense we are not supposed to be in pain. Although this is certainly in part cultural, we feel that pain is a sign of weakness and that if we are in pain, we will be unacceptable to others. Finally, and beyond all cultures, pain is one way, a very stark way, of opening ourselves to certain realities of the human situation: aloneness, sickness, aging and death. Facing these realities takes us to the core of the incomprehensibility and perhaps absurdity of the human situation. Although I think facing and dealing with these realities is a necessary condition for the attainment of maturity and anything resembling happiness and fulfillment, it is not an easy thing to do. It is not surprising, then, that so much of what is pain is not faced as such.

In light of these analyses of pain, I think we can say that if our treatment of mental states — pain included — is to reflect the actual nature and workings of those states, we must focus not just on the abstract ideas of those states, but also on their interconnected ongoing place in the movement and development of reflective consciousness.

Finally, before moving on, I wish to offer a few general remarks on the perspective so far reached. I have suggested that reflective consciousness is an outgrowth of pre-reflective consciousness and that the elements of reflective consciousness are compatible with an infallibility which is limited to general, contentless absorption in experience. This conclusion, however, was modified in light of the limited, but apparently real, content infallibility that is a property of a certain kind of pain.

While this latter conclusion may seem to create an inconsistency with the former conclusion, I don't think it does. Indeed, this is just the way things should be if the more general perspective is adequate. Since infallibility attaches to absorption in experience, making escape from experience impossible, it is not surprising that certain sorts of pain represent a limited content infallibility. These pains are first and foremost *bodily* in nature and since it is our bodily nature which grounds our existence within the process of which experience is a part, it will, of course, be vivid, bodily experience which yields a degree of content infallibility.

Desire

Chapter Six

I

The discussions of types of consciousness and the sorts of possible errors adhering to these types have focused on perceptual and organic sensation. Shorn of their reflective developments, these phenomena are, given a certain degree of animate development, probably universal. Although not all living organisms perceive and feel, those of any significant complexity do. In this respect, then, there is a uniformity between reflective and pre-reflective creatures.

Through their ability to reflect on perceptual and organic sensation, however, reflective creatures, among other things, expand the range of these sensations, as well as develop the capacity for judgement concerning these phenomena. While this move into reflection modifies non-reflective awareness, it does not cancel the primordial, spontaneous absorption in experience which is displayed in perceptual and organic sensation and which is common to pre-reflective and reflective creatures.

Throughout these pages, I have claimed that reflective consciousness is a divided or separated consciousness. But no consciousness can be an entirely divided consciousness. However pervasive and persistent reflection is, there is at some point — even if it is only the non-reflective nature of the reflective moment itself — a direct absorption in experience. This absorption is to be found both "externally," with the world, and "internally," with one's mental states. In the absence of such absorption or connection, consciousness is simply an unintelligible, ungrounded, floating will-of-the-wisp. Thus, however far reflective creatures remove themselves from first order non-reflective immersion in experience, there is always another level order of immersion which is inescapable.

However, for reflective creatures, the point of connection to what are not themselves constructions of reflection is most likely to be achieved in experiences of perceptual and, especially, organic sensation. Since these experiences are the most likely candidates for instances of non-divided consciousness, they are also the most likely candidates for states of consciousness displaying content infallibility.

As suggested, however, perceptual sensation and, in many cases, organic sensation are modified by the operation of reflective consciousness. When this occurs, the resulting mental states are no longer merely what arise in the interplay of instinct and environmental situation. These modified mental states rather involve constructions emanating from reflection and this disrupts the original unity of consciousness and object. The result of such disruption is division both within consciousness and between consciousness and the world.

But this is not all there is to the matter, for while the emergence of reflective elements does, I think, alter the whole range of perceptual sensation, it does not alter the whole range of organic sensation. This is because the former, but not the latter, involves — at least prior to the ability to construct imaginary objects — an object of attention which is other than the mental state itself. Obviously, in the absence of reflection, this object cannot be altered, modified or misconstrued by reflection. Once reflection does emerge, however, the object of the mental state is affected and this produces both a unique form of separation from the object and the possibility of a new and unique kind of error.

This situation does not exist for those organic sensations which are vividly and overwhelmingly felt. Since they do not involve an object outside of the sensation, there is no object to be altered, modified or misconstrued. Like all mental states, organic sensations involve a content, but unlike most other mental states this content is not an object which is other than the mental state itself. Through the operation of reflection, however, this situation can be modified. As the range of pain (and pleasure) is expanded, the content of such states need no longer be inherent to those states. That is, the content of such states can now be an object — i.e., another aspect of consciousness — which is other than the mental state itself. So here also we can have both the division of consciousness and the kind of error which is unique to reflective consciousness.

As it expands its range and depth of awareness of objects outside of itself, consciousness becomes divided from the world in a new and unique fashion; and this division increases into a further dimension as consciousness becomes able to take its own awareness and constructs as objects of attention. Indeed, the greater the range of awareness and the larger the number of types of mental states which emerge as the result of such an awareness and the constructions which accompany them, the greater the possibility of division, error and solidified separation or alienation.

In light of these remarks, it is appropriate to take a look at those mental states which have come to be called "propositional attitudes." These are mental states which involve a "that" clause, *e.g.*, "x believes that y is tall," "z hopes that r will arrive on time," etc. Because the propositional attitudes inherently involve an element beyond the form of the mental state, they all, depending on the degree to which consciousness can place constructions on this element, involve separation. Thus, a creature with virtually no ability to provide constructions on the object of the attitude is a creature which experiences virtually no separation from the object of the attitude. A creature, however, which has a great capacity for providing such constructions is a creature which, at least potentially, can experience a great deal of separation from the object of the attitude. Given this variation of operation relative to type of consciousness involved, those propositional attitudes which can be found on both sides of the divide between reflective and pre-reflective consciousness merit special attention. An examination of such attitudes, hopefully, will yield further insight into the operation of the two sorts of consciousness as well as the special problems of reflective consciousness.

Of the various propositional attitudes (or mental states which can be seen as propositional attitudes) which do overlap the two types of consciousness, desire is the one most appropriate to focus on initially. There are a number of reasons for this. First, desire is clearly a state which is common to pre-reflective and reflective creatures. This is not a matter of controversy in the way, for example, it is a matter of controversy whether or not beliefs are attributable to pre-reflective creatures. Second, desire clearly does involve an object, state or situation outside of itself. A creature desires that something be had or realized or attained or the like; and what is had, realized or attained is something other than the desire itself. Third, desire, initially at least, is bodily. It is part of the "equipment" of the creature who has it. Fourth, and related to the previous point, it appears that the desires of pre-reflective creatures have a phenomenology or qualitative content. Since such creatures cannot reflect and so cannot deceive themselves concerning what they do or don't desire, their desires are known from *within* experience in the impulse or urge toward the object of desire. Such impulses or urges do indeed appear to have a phenomenology. Fifth, there are a number of interesting, but puzzling and confusing, contrasts between perception and desire. To focus, for now, on one of these, both clearly are capacities which are had by pre-reflective creatures. In addition, both seem to involve a phenomenology at this level: perception, the phenomenology of some look or other; desire, the phenomenology of some impulse or other. Yet when we talk of these phenomena in the context of reflective consciousness, perception often, but desire never, is said to involve the possibility of infallibility. Of course, I think neither type of mental state involves content infallibility. At this point, however, I'm questioning one dimension of the different treatment these two sorts of state receive. Perhaps it is thought either that desires do not involve impulses or urges or the like; or that while such impulses, etc. exist, they are not transparent or simply available to consciousness. If they are thought not to be available to consciousness, they will be thought of as contrasting with perceptions which always and necessarily involve some look or other — the look obviously being available to consciousness.

II

Given these preliminary remarks, let's look at desire in greater detail, touching both on the above and other issues as we proceed.

Like perceptual and organic sensation, desire is given with the organism. In their most fundamental operation, these phenomena are not created or even developed by the organism which displays them. However rudimentary, the existence and operation of such capacities is a pre-condition of the creature's survival. In the absence of desire, there is no impetus to action and so no possibility of obtaining what is needed for survival. As creatures evolve and physiology and consciousness develop, these capacities take on new dimensions and capabilities. But in all of this, the energy which is basic to all living, conscious beings — and probably also to all entities and events — maintains its presence, though its particular manifestations or expressions change. Primordial energized instinct or appetite proceeds into desire and, along the way of development, into modification of desire and the creation of still new desires.

But if desire is not only central to survival but also expands with the enlargement of consciousness and so plays a central role in the constructions of reflective consciousness, it again becomes crucial to gain a sense of the kinds of error which desire, at various levels, is susceptible to. The conclusions here will be consistent with what was previously said concerning perceptual error: pre-reflective creatures, because they cannot reflect on their desires, cannot misunderstand or modify either the mental state itself or its object, and so cannot make errors based on this capacity. As a result, they cannot desire something which is detrimental to their well-being. Or rather they cannot modify their given desires in light of a constructed view of what could or ought to be in such a manner that the modified desires, if fulfilled, would be detrimental to their well-being.

They can, of course, desire an object x, perceived as y, which is detrimental. That is, they can go for the bait and get caught in the trap. But this is an error of perception, not of desire. Pre-reflective creatures are immersed in experience. Their desires are one aspect of this immersion and so there is no standpoint, other than misidentification through physical and/or physiological factors within the desiring situation, from which errors of desire could be made.

The situation is similar to that of perception. In both cases, errors flowing from reflection are not possible, for such creatures do not reflect on their perceptions or desires. They therefore cannot import into perception or desire the elements produced by reflection, thereby altering their instinctual relationship to what they see or desire. As a result, pre-reflective creatures cannot be mistaken about the state of desiring itself; they cannot confuse desire with some other state. Similarly, they cannot desire something as severed from their energized instinct or appetite. They cannot, that is, construct layers of desire, such that the last desire, presumably productive of a new type or level of fulfillment, is in reality an instance of severance from original, productive energized instinct or appetite.

While spontaneous, non-reflective desire is, of course, also possible for reflective creatures, this is not the only, or perhaps even the distinctive, form which desire takes for such creatures. With reflective creatures, desire characteristically is tied to other elements of reflective consciousness, especially beliefs and goals or purposes. As such, desires deeply reflect the conceptual system, *i.e.*, the concepts, attitudes, perspectives, and the like, which reflective consciousness generates. Since these latter elements can be inadequate and distorted, so can the desires which are a part of the system. That is, due to the expansion and re-routing of energized instinct and appetite, the desires which become a part of the system can become separated from and even contrary to the organism's original survival focused desires. Although reflective creatures must modify existing desires and create new sorts of desires, these modifications and creations need not be adequate to the nature of the life situation reflective creatures face.

The desires of reflective creatures, then, are susceptible to a number of kinds of error. Within this class of errors, there are those which relate to the state of desiring itself and those which relate to the object of desire. If we start with the latter category, we will find, often interconnected with each other, errors of misidentifying (or misnaming), misunderstanding, misevaluating and probably more.

To begin with a somewhat trivial example, error can occur when one desires something because one has a faulty recollection of it or confuses it with something else. For example, one may desire to read a certain book because one "remembers," mistakenly, that it is the book one's friend has recommended. In such a case, one is misidentifying and so misevaluating the object of desire.

Strictly speaking, of course, this is an error of memory, not desire. As such, it may be compared to the kind of error of desire made by pre-reflective creatures. Previously, it was claimed that errors of desire stemming from misidentification were not really errors of desire, but were errors of perception. On this basis, it was then claimed that pre-reflective creatures do not and cannot make errors of desire other than those based on perceptual mistakes flowing either from physical factors in the environment or physiological factors within the organism or both. But if we take this line with pre-reflective creatures, don't we have to take a similar line with reflective creatures when their errors of desire are, strictly speaking, not errors of desire, but errors which stem from other of their capacities?

While there is an overlap between those errors of desire in reflective and pre-reflective creatures which flow from capacities other than desire itself, there is also a significant difference. This difference has to do with how the other capacity which is causing the error of desire is functioning. In reflective, but not in pre-reflective, creatures the relevant capacity is tied to the system of reflection in such a way that the type of error we are discussing is made possible. That is, the capacities within reflection have a range of application, an array of elements and a dimension of reflective self-awareness which allows for the book to be picked out, commented upon, evaluated and remembered. It is within this larger range of activities that memory can falter and the book be misidentified. This type of misidentification is not possible for pre-reflective creatures and so the misidentifications of reflective creatures are not simple misidentifications.

More complex and of more direct psychological significance are the following two examples. One can know what one is desiring, *i.e.*, not be mistaken about the immediate object of desire and so name it properly, but at the same time be desiring, from a larger perspective, what is not beneficial to oneself. Assuming that one does not wish to desire what is not beneficial, there is a clear sense in which one's original desire is in error. Since from the broader perspective, one wishes to desire what is beneficial, one's narrower desire is in error, for it leads, not to what is beneficial, but to what is detrimental. Concretely, one may desire to eat some particular sort of food, knowing it as that sort of food, but not knowing that the food is almost certainly not beneficial to one's health.

What was properly named, understood and evaluated at one level, can turn out to be misnamed, misunderstood and misevaluated from a broader perspective. Among other things, this perspective contains second order desires. And it is characteristic of reflective creatures to form such desires which, in turn, can be employed to evaluate and modify first order desires either directly by overt examination or indirectly, often by unconscious and covert means. This is another way of pointing out the manner in which reflection alters and expands the phenomenon of desire, making possible new kinds of misidentification, misunderstanding and misevaluation.

A variation of the above type of error occurs when the original desire turns out, upon examination, to be a substitute for a deeper, hidden desire, the latter not consciously acknowledged. Thus, to take an obvious example, one may desire a great deal of money without being aware that this desire is standing for a deeper desire for security or power or self worth. Here, one is correctly naming the immediate or first level object of desire, but misunderstanding it and so misevaluating it.

The difference between the two examples is that in the first, it is assumed there is a second order desire for what is beneficial and that on becoming aware of the nature of the object of the original desire, it becomes clear that this desire, if acted on, will not yield beneficial results. The error has to do, then, with a proper understanding of the nature of the object of the original desire in light of the broader desire for what is beneficial. In the second case, however, there is a non-acknowledged desire which is directly masked by the acknowledged desire. This error concerns a failure to acknowledge what is actually and more deeply desired.

The above are examples of error that involve the object of desire. But within reflective consciousness, it is also possible to be mistaken about the mental state of desiring itself. That is, it seems possible for one to be in a mental state other than desire, yet sincerely think that one is desiring; and, conversely it seems possible to desire, yet sincerely not know and deny that one is desiring. With respect to the former, it is, I think, possible to want or to crave, but to think one is desiring. Presumably, wanting is a less and craving a more intense form of desiring, and so given the validity of these gradations, it is possible either to want or to crave, but to think one is desiring. While in certain circumstances — especially those which involve craving — this can be a significant error, it leaves one wondering whether grosser forms of error are possible, ones in which one is in a state significantly different from desire, but sincerely thinks one is desiring.

If there are such cases, they will almost certainly not be cases in which all desire is absent from consciousness, but will rather be cases in which that aspect of consciousness within the situation which is said to involve desire does not. There are, for example, cases in which we induce or try to build up desire. We may be lukewarm or even quite indifferent to some situation, yet, for any number of reasons, manufacture desire. In response, it could be said that manufactured desire is still desire and so we have yet to give a case in which one is in a state other than desire, but thinks one is desiring. But I doubt this is an adequate response, for certainly the desire that is induced or manufactured is not an immediate, genuine desire, of the desirer. It does not reflect the nature of a direct interaction of the organism with the particular environmental situation. The desire rather is mediated by other factors within the person and his situation, say, frustration and boredom, and the desire to escape these, or a sense that one is supposed to desire something within the situation. Given these remarks, it is of course true that at the moment of manufacturing desire, the person does have other actual, but unacknowledged desires. Since, however, these are not acknowledged, they are not available to awareness. As a result, when the individual says he desires x, that is, the manufactured desire, he cannot be referring to the unacknowledged desires. In such cases, at one level the individual is in a state of boredom, frustration or indifference, but at another level desires not to be in those states and so attempts to alter the original state. My suggestion is that the alteration of the original state does not involve an instance of genuine desire, though the individual in question may call it that.

The converse case in which one desires, but sincerely denies it is, I think, much clearer. There is little doubt that this is a possible, and indeed even a common, situation. To take an interesting example, it is now almost common knowledge that people often harbor—along with other more positive impulses and desires — quite destructive impulses for intimate and central persons in their lives, yet consistently and persistently fail to acknowledge to themselves and to others the presence of such impulses and desires.

Denial of desire is, of course, a phenomenon unique to reflective consciousness; beings whose consciousness is always pre-reflectively immersed in experience cannot gain the standpoint or perspective from which desire, or other mental states, could be denied. This, then, is a phenomenon closely tied to fragmentation and alienation and the consequent need for integration. As such, we will have to return to it later; but for now, I wish briefly to mention a few of the many reasons why denial of desire is so common.

Perhaps the most common reason has to do with a belief or feeling on the part of the desirer that the object of desire is evil or that desiring such an object reveals a distasteful feature of the desirer's personality. Rather than acknowledge and confront this aspect of one's personality, one finds it easier to deny one is desiring any such thing. In another instance, the object of desire may be, or simply perceived to be, unattainable, and so as a way of avoiding frustration, the desire is denied. Finally, and perhaps more subtly, desire may be denied because it puts one in a position in which action becomes appropriate, namely, the action needed to fulfill the desire. But the prospect of action may involve a degree of anxiety which can only be alleviated by the outright denial of desire.

The above examples all involve errors which flow from the reflective capacity. But although desire does get caught up in the conceptual system of reflective consciousness, there is still non-reflective, spontaneous desire. Like pre-reflective creatures, reflective creatures can be immersed, and absorbed in experience. As a result it might be thought that just as pre-reflective creatures, given their absorption in experience, are immune to errors of desire, so are reflective creatures, so long as they, too, are absorbed in experience. This, however, is not correct; for the concepts, attitudes and perspectives which reflective consciousness generates come to permeate non-reflective desire. Non-reflective desire, though unmediated in comparison to reflective desire, is mediated in comparison to pre-reflective desire. These reflective additions, which modify and expand instinctual appetite or desire, create a permanent possibility of error. The errors made possible include those concerning the state of desire, the object of desire, the worth of the object of desire and even the worth of certain states of desire themselves. The only domain of non-error or infallibility is that some experience or other — perhaps not even desire — is occurring. This is consistent with previous claims concerning perceptual experience and many, though not all, kinds of pain.

III

The realization that reflective consciousness both modifies and expands pre-reflective instinctual energy raises, in an acute form, a large set of problems, perhaps the chief of which is the problem of rationality. These problems are unique to creatures who develop and create a standpoint which is to some significant degree both self-aware and self-directing, and which is directly tied to action. In their most general form, these problems can be seen as congealing into the problem of rationality, with notions such as appropriateness and worthiness subsumed within the larger problem.

But the notion of rationality is itself far from clear or uncontroversial. On one interpretation, it is conceived in a somewhat narrow and essentially intellectual fashion as involving the acceptance of a correct set of beliefs. Although people do not any longer talk much about faculties, rationality in this sense is virtually always tied to the ability to think or to reason. On this view, we come to have a correct set of beliefs through the proper application of reason to the various life situations we encounter. Even though there are obviously a number of questions to ask concerning this model — those involving, for example, clarification of its key terms, its use, range of application and possible successes — it clearly isolates a central dimension of rationality. Any notion of rationality must involve the notion of correct beliefs arrived at through correct thinking or reasoning.

This model, however, can be overly narrow in its apprehension of how reason works. It can see reason as separated from, and indeed as often needing to act against, other aspects or capacities of the organism. When this is the predominant image, reason becomes fragmented from the rest of the organism and we have trouble thinking of a rational organism. Instead, we are forced to think of an essentially irrational organism which has rationality imposed on it by one of its faculties.

In contrast to this notion, there is also a broader, and I think more powerful notion of rationality. This notion includes the idea of true beliefs arrived at through thinking or reasoning, but places this activity within a larger view of the activities of consciousness and the organism as a whole. The larger perspective provides the framework within which rationality, narrowly conceived, gets its explanation and justification. Rationality in the broader sense is a matter of how the organism as a whole, i.e., intellectually, emotionally and spiritually, responds to the environment of which it is necessarily a part. On this view, the thinking process, in various degrees of individual self-awareness, would be tied to and flow from the wider range of capacities of the organism as these relate to its environmental situation. Reason would not simply be a faculty over and against the organism's other capacities, perhaps covertly controlled by those capacities, but would rather be integrated with those capacities. Achieving rationality as so conceived is, of course, no small matter. Minimally, it involves establishing a productive integration, not only of the creature's various capacities, but also of the various items that fall within the particular capacities, *e.g.*, the various emotions.

Rationality, so conceived, is an outcome of and responds to the separation which creates the human world. But this separation need not issue in rationality; it can just as easily — probably more easily — issue in irrationality. Separation is the datum; but how the organism responds to separation determines its rationality and irrationality. The matter is complicated by the realization that separation is a condition for the emergence of the reflective or human world. Separation, then, must be acknowledged and embraced *and*, when possible and favorable to the organism, transcended toward unity. And, of course, it is the very task of the reflective creature to determine when and how to produce this new form of unity. From this perspective, rationality is the ongoing construction of an integrated, unified standpoint.

This calls for some comment and clarification. Rationality as described above is an ideal, almost certainly not achievable at every moment over the whole range of one's activities, yet certainly achievable at various moments of activity. Given that such moments can increase in number and in depth, rationality becomes a matter of degree, something to be attained. But talk about degrees of attainment can be very misleading. It may suggest there is some static, pre-existing datum — rationality — which due to any number of factors cannot be fully attained. The problem, however, is both more radical and more fundamental, for the standpoint of rationality is itself one aspect of the larger reflective standpoint created by reflective creatures. As such, rationality does not stand outside of the standpoint and so cannot be reached when the elements within the standpoint are operating properly. There is nothing to reach in this way, for rationality is itself an inherent part of the ongoing, changing standpoint. It, too, is changing and it is doing so in relation to other developments within the process of which it is a part. Rationality, like consciousness and as an aspect of consciousness, is thoroughly and endlessly dynamic.

This conclusion is of a piece with a number of previously reached conclusions. The denial of a fixed criterion of rationality is consistent with the denial of both a Cartesian Ego and an absolute standpoint from which particular standpoints can be evaluated. Indeed, these conclusions are all connected to the larger point that consciousness is developmental and creative of its particular and peculiar standpoint. But if consciousness is creative of its standpoint, it follows that integration is also something created. And this, in turn, suggests that integration—and its concomitant phenomenon, rationality—cannot be understood as a function of one favored part of the organism, namely, reason, but rather must be understood as an aspect of the organism as a whole.

When reason is treated as the exclusive "organ" of rationality, we create precisely the sort of deep and extended separation which reason is ostensibly employed to prevent. When this occurs, rationality becomes an agent not of integration and unity, but of increased separation or alienation. As a result, not only is there a solidified separation of self from the world—for we are now relating to the world essentially through reason as so conceived and not with the totality of our being—but, more ominously, division within consciousness becomes near complete and virtually tangible.

In all of its forms, consciousness is emergent; that is, it develops out of the larger evolutionary process. But if this is so, rationality is a more particularized development of the larger process *through* the development of consciousness. These points provide us with a new perspective from which to view and extend a previously made point, namely, that the notion of a disembodied consciousness or a disembodied rationality is, in some significant sense, incoherent.

It is, however, not clear what the incoherence is, for such notions neither express logical contradictions nor display what is unimaginable. We can, for example, provide consciousness or rationality with some sort of wispy form and imagine it floating about in some equally wispy place. But though such pictures can be formed, I do not think they establish the coherence or intelligibility of what they picture. Indeed, such pictures are possible only because consciousness can reflect on and take itself as a separate existent. The ability to so picture itself is thus not an indication of the intelligibility of what is pictured, but is rather an indication of the degree of separation or alienation which consciousness is capable of.

Still, however, it is not clear how this claim can be established, for it is saying that what is imagined as possible, namely, a disembodied consciousness or rationality, is itself an incoherent expression of what has incoherently been taken as a possibility and is, in its present operation, mistakenly being lived or experienced as actual. That is, the notion of a disembodied consciousness or rationality is itself an expression of consciousness as alienated. But it is not clear how this can be explained or demonstrated to a consciousness which is functioning within the confines of such alienation.

In any case, my suggestion is that the notions of a disembodied consciousness and rationality are the expression of a false consciousness, that they are illusions, for consciousness, at its deepest level, cannot lose the tie to the process from which it emerged. To be sure, it can obscure, lose sight of, not know of, and twist the connection; but none of this is to cancel or obliterate the connection. Consciousness always and necessarily remains embedded within the process. If this is so, claims to disembodied consciousness and rationality are incoherent and not just matters of empirical non-occurrence.

Consciousness and rationality must be understood in their direct absorption in the world. As such, they need to be temporally and spatially grounded. Any instance of consciousness or rationality is an instance of such at a particular place at a particular time. When rationality is conceived exclusively along the lines of reason, armed with its unique resources, grasping various truths, it cannot satisfy these requirements. For such a notion abstracts from the situation in which reason is operating. But this is not to say that such abstractions are always either impossible or unfruitful. These abstractions have themselves been creations, at various times, of reflective consciousness and are, in addition, *one aspect* of how reflective consciousness relates to its situation *in the present*. Reason attempting to determine what is true is one dimension, interconnected with others, of how the reflective creature encounters its situation in a *rational* manner. Properly understood, rationality is an embodied expression of consciousness which relates to, or is involved in, the world in a productive, non-destructive fashion.

IV

The introduction of the problem of rationality in the context of a discussion of desire is somewhat, though not entirely, arbitrary. The arbitrariness stems from the fact that, given the general position being developed, rationality could have been introduced into the discussions of perceptual and organic sensation without too much of a strain. Since the fruits of reflection are not wholly absent from almost all of the relevant phenomena, the standpoint of rationality is at least a possibility. More specifically, the elements which, typically, are spontaneously produced by the activity of reflection are absorbed within non-reflective consciousness. These elements can then be made objects of explicit reflective awareness, evaluated and either maintained, cultivated, modified or rejected. As long as elements of experience are not entirely instinctual, and can both be made objects of awareness and in some fashion actively influenced by the organism, the assignment of rationality and irrationality is, to at least some degree, appropriate. From this perspective, almost every kind of mental state of reflective creatures is susceptible to treatment in terms of rationality—a phenomenon which is in striking contrast to that which holds for pre-reflective creatures.

Traditionally, however, perceptual and organic sensation have not been a focus for questions of rationality. They have been thought to be spontaneous, non-rational phenomena, quite beyond the control of either the will or reason. Perceptual judgments, of course, have been treated from the standpoint of rationality, but this is due to the fact that they are typically treated as explicit or implicit beliefs, and belief is taken as the paradigmatically rational or irrational mental state. The psychological pain I have suggested is an expansion of organic pain is rarely, if ever, treated in this context. As a result, it is not clear whether or not it is thought to be susceptible to rational considerations. My position on this matter, which I will return to later, is that while the organic pain that is overwhelmingly and vividly felt is not susceptible to considerations of rationality, the psychological pain which is an extension of organic pain is.

Desire, too, is often taken as something given and spontaneous and so not susceptible to rational assessment. My sense, however, is that the strategic connection of desire to action within the system of reflective consciousness makes desire susceptible to rational considerations. In addition, while being a propositional attitude, desire is not a belief, though if we are considering anything beyond the most primordial urges or impulses, it almost certainly involves beliefs of some sort. Thus, desire can be something of a test case for the broader notion of rationality. If desire turns out to be susceptible to rational treatment beyond the beliefs it involves, then rationality is not limited to belief and it becomes possible to extend considerations of rationality to a larger range of mental phenomena, precisely what the broader notion of rationality requires.

Let us take a look at this problem, with special attention to the similarities and differences between belief and desire as they relate to action. Though both are typically tied to action, this is accomplished in different ways. To function effectively, belief must more or less *adequately* present or represent the world. If it does and, in conjunction with desire, produces action, then in the absence of obstacles, we will get what we in fact want. Belief, here, displays that the object, event or situation fits and satisfies the desire. If, however, belief does not adequately represent the world, but again in conjunction with desire, produces action, we will not get what we want; desire will not be satisfied. From this perspective, beliefs need to fit the world, to reflect or represent the world adequately; and it would be fool-hardy and irrational to adopt beliefs which do not fit the world. In general, beliefs function in such a fashion that they must fit the world, *not* the world fit them. This, of course, is being said from the standpoint of seeking sur-vival and fulfillment, and understanding belief as it functions within such a standpoint.

Desire, however, in at least one of its aspects is very different from this. For desire, so conceived, is not concerned with how the world is, but with what it should be. It does not seek to represent the world, but to have the world be a source of fulfillment for itself. Thus, desire is not the sort of phenomenon to conform to the world; rather it wishes to have the world con-form to it. However, if desire is taken *exclusively* in this fashion, with its objects thought to be any and all aspects of the world, it becomes inherently irrational, for the world is not in any wholesale fashion going to conform to individual desire. Indeed, when desire is seen in such a fashion, it is no longer desire in its primordial operation. For primordial desire, being in-stinctually determined, is very specific and limited in its focus. The desire which has indiscriminate and unlimited focus is in fact the desire which is the outcome of reflection. Unleashed from its exclusive tie to instinct, desire can increase its range of focus in a virtually unlimited fashion. If desire is not centered, *i.e.*, constructively disciplined, by reflective consciousness, it can indeed range over anything and everything, independently of the worth of what it is focusing on. This, however, is not a description of desire as it always functions, but of desire as it can function in the context of re-flective consciousness.

The upshot of the view that desire has unlimited focus is that desire is simply irrational. This is, I think, a distortion of another more sensible, but much more limited view, namely, that desire is neither rational nor irra-tional, but is non-rational or pre-rational. On this view, desire simply is, with the categories "rational" and "irrational" not applying.

This view does, I think, hold for the primordial urges and impulses of pre-reflective creatures. These phenomena pre-date the emergence of re-flective consciousness and so function in a situation that is non- or pre-ra-tional. However, once desire becomes a part of the system of reflection, with its need to direct action, and its categories of rational and irrational, desire is no longer simply a matter of primordial urges and impulses. The latter phenomena do, of course, remain, but the energy which informs them expands into both new types of desire and complicated interconnections with other elements of the reflective system.

Desire, that is, undergoes ranges of alteration as it is "taken over" by reflective consciousness. As a result, non-reflective, spontaneous desire comes to include elements absorbed from reflection and so is modified beyond simple instinctual energy. In this way, desire expands and finds a place within the multi-leveled, highly complex and developed conceptual system which produces a significant degree of self-aware, self-directed action. In order, therefore, for desire, in its various expressions, to direct itself onto what is — or is most likely — productive of survival and fulfillment, it must be looked at, explored, evaluated and developed. It must, that is, be seen as a functioning part of the system of reflection and be evaluated by the devices, *i.e.*, the notions of rationality and irrationality, which are generated precisely for such a general purpose.

There is a clear sense, then, in which desire needs to fit itself to the world. This, of course, is not to say that desire must exclusively fit itself to the way the world is; often it is both possible and wise to desire beyond this framework. With the aid of the imagination, desire can stretch well beyond the narrow confines of the present and the presently existing. This must not be discouraged. But the outer limit of this is the attempt to reconstruct the world in terms of one's own particular, unexamined desires and their related fantasies. This is to impose oneself on the world in a destructive fashion, to fail to see the nature and limits of one's being in the world.

The ability, however, to attain the measure that is here appropriate is very difficult to come by, for in line with our previous remarks, there is no pre-existing, fixed world, the knowing of which reveals the needed nature and limits. The world, and so its nature and limits, is in constant dynamic development, as is the standpoint which reflective consciousness takes up within the world. But the recognition of the reality of development and creation does not negate the recognition of the reality of limits. Indeed, to create implies a recognition of the nature of the medium in which creation is taking place, the materials out of which the creation is emerging, and the form or limits placed on what is being created. In the present context, failure to grasp these elements is to see oneself as larger, more powerful, than the world. This failure, and the attitudes and actions which flow from it, creates an imbalance between oneself and the world, the outcome of which is disharmony and alienation. Although within such a state the individual can become quite sophisticated in his constructs, he is essentially relating to the world as an infant, wanting and demanding that the world be as he wishes it to be. In the context of the broader sense of rationality, this attitude, and the desires which are a central part of it, are indeed irrational.

V

I have claimed that it is appropriate to speak of the desires of reflective creatures as rational or irrational. If this is so, it seems to follow that, whatever their content, conflicts of desire fall within the rational/irrational distinction and would themselves be irrational. If a particular desire can be irrational, then within an inconsistent set of desires, at least one of these desires must be irrational and so the holding of such an inconsistent set would also be irrational.

The situation, however, is not quite that clear, for desires cannot simply be assimilated to beliefs. It is, of course, irrational to hold conflicting beliefs, since the world will not match these beliefs. But desire, in one of its aspects, does not function so as to match up with the world; rather it seeks to impose itself on the world. If we follow out this line of thought, we will most likely claim that having a conflict of desires is not a sign of irrationality.[1]

I've suggested that though desire is a phenomenon which places demands on the world, this is not a sufficient reason to claim that desires cannot be assessed in terms of rationality and irrationality. This suggestion stems, in part, from the claim that desire cannot fruitfully be understood as an isolated phenomenon functioning by means of its own discrete essence. Desire, rather, must be seen as part of a larger system of consciousness which is attempting to make a place for itself within the somewhat changing limits provided by physiology and the larger environment. From this perspective, conflicts of desire appear to be irrational, for so long as they persist, they at least tend to inhibit consistent, integrated action. But while this appears to be so, conflicts of desire can also be seen as providing a foci for the kind of self-understanding which is a condition for the overcoming of alienation or the attaining of integration. In this light, while conflicts of desire may in themselves be irrational, they can be seen as opportunities for the attainment of a deeper form of rationality.

Let's take a closer look at these matters. Conflicts of desire take at least two typical forms. There is the obvious case in which one both desires to have and desires not to have the same object; and there is also the case in which one desires both A and B, but the satisfaction of one desire makes impossible the satisfaction of the other.

What accounts for the existence of such conflicting desires? A prime explanatory candidate is that the inconsistent desires flow from different aspects of the personality (or consciousness). One aspect of the personality desires A while another either desires not having A or desires B, which is incompatible with A. Within this general situation, there is a large range of possible configurations and I think the question of irrationality can only be fruitfully addressed in terms of these varied details. If, to take one extreme example, the conflict occurs in an individual whose awareness of what is involved is limited to the experience of two or more strong, contradictory pulls, there is irrationality present. In such a case, the individual does not have a clear understanding of the situation and so is not able to choose what to do in an effective fashion. The conflict, and whatever behavior that results from the conflict situation, is produced by inner forces which the individual is not even aware of and still less understands.

If we consider an example at the other end of the spectrum, the conclusion will be somewhat different. Suppose one has the same sort of conflict present in the above example. Now, however, instead of being caught primarily in the whirlwind of strong, mysterious conflicting desires, the individual is reflectively aware of the conflict, has a significant sense of what aspects of his personality and which of his values are involved, and is able to act within this understanding. If this is so, I think it unlikely we would say the conflict is irrational. Indeed, in this case the conflict is being used as a means to increased self-understanding and personal growth.

Within the above extremes, there are countless gradations of interconnected awareness and blindness. As a rough rule of thumb, perhaps we can say: the greater the degree and depth of awareness, the less irrational the conflict; and the less the awareness, the more irrational the conflict.

This, however, still leaves open the question whether, independently of the actions they may or may not produce, conflicts of desire, because they are conflicts and involve inconsistent desires, are irrational. There is a sense in which this question is suspect, for it seems to require that we look at desire separately from the larger system of consciousness of which it is a part and against the background of which its nature and modes of operation can be comprehended. In certain circumstances, it is of course legitimate and helpful to treat desire and other mental phenomena as abstract, separate, discrete; but it is not legitimate to take the results of such treatment as providing insight into how these phenomena — desire included — are actually functioning as parts of the larger system.

Desire relates us to the world in a particular way; it does this in conjunction with a number of other phenomena; and in combination with these, it produces actions of various sorts. When these actions are not adequately understood and chosen and/or produce destructive consequences which could have been, but were not, foreseen, we say that irrationality is present.

If we now abstract from this larger situation and ask simply whether the having of conflicting desires is irrational, then from my perspective, there will be a temptation to answer both yes and no. Yes, for even though desires are not entirely meant to match the world, they must, in order not to be irrational, recognize the nature and limits of the world, and when there is a conflict of desire this recognition seemingly cannot exist. No, for although desire is being considered in abstraction from reflective consciousness, it is still an aspect of such consciousness and so displays and contributes to its expansion. Thus, a conflict of desires can be seen as an *experiment* of consciousness, as a way of moving into an area that was previously unexplored, thereby providing the materials for increased awareness and, perhaps, subsequent coherence.

Let us back up a bit and develop these points. It seems uncontroversial that desires can conflict and so be inconsistent. But it is not clear either that having inconsistent desires is always irrational, or that having consistent desires is always rational. With respect to inconsistent desires, my suggestion is that a large part of the determination of irrationality turns on the agent's degree of awareness and understanding of the conflict situation. Mere consistency of desire, however, is not equivalent to rationality, for one's desires may be unified, non-conflicting *and destructive*. And destructive desires, whether unified or not, display a deep irrationality, for in the absence of mitigating background circumstances, *i.e.*, circumstances which allow the destructive desires to restore a previously upset balance, they create a significant imbalance or disharmony between self and the world. If consistency is a condition of the rationality of desires, it is not the only one. An additional condition, that the unified desires are productive and creative, would have to be added. The notion of productive and creative desires — and, more generally, mental states — is, as suggested in a number of previous contexts, to be understood in terms of the establishment of internal and external harmonies.

The above remarks concerning consistency, inconsistency, rationality and irrationality are still lacking a larger, informative context. This can, I think, be provided by our distinction between pre-reflective and reflective creatures. For both sorts of creatures, desire is a crucial phenomenon in the unfolding of their existence. In some cases, indeed, desire functions in near identical fashion for the two sorts of creatures. In other cases, however, desire functions in a significantly different fashion. Failure to recognize the relevant differences can result in assigning to one sort of creature the modality of desire found in the other sort of creature. Thus, the ambivalence and uncertainty concerning the predication of rationality/irrationality to desire and to conflicts of desire is grounded in a genuine cross-creature overlap of operation.

There is a significant sense in which conflicts of desire are limited to reflective creatures. Pre-reflective creatures, not having the ability to reflect upon and modify existing desires or to create new ones, are not subject to the conflicts these abilities produce. To be sure, if an object is desired and also surrounded by palpable danger, a pre-reflective creature can both desire and not desire it. (Or, perhaps better, can both desire the object and desire to avoid the danger, which, under another description, is not to desire the object.) Additionally, such creatures can desire two objects, not both of which can be had. But conflicts of this sort flow from the circumstances of the situation, not from the creature's constructed relationship to the environmental situation. Since there is no constructed relationship within which desire is developed, modified, and the like, no question of the rationality or irrationality of desire or conflict of desire can even arise.

The modification and alteration of desire which is created by reflective consciousness and is unique to reflective creatures is precisely what creates the problem of rationality. And this, on the other side, creates the *possibility* of rationality and the *possibility* of irrationality. Insofar as desire is instinctual and pre-reflective, it simply is and cannot involve the *kinds* of inconsistencies which raise the question of rationality. If we employ this model when treating the desires of reflective creatures, it is quite unlikely we will treat conflicts of desires as irrational, for the category doesn't take hold. When, however, we stress the elements of desire which are unique to reflective creatures, we introduce the possibility of rationality/irrationality and shall probably be of two minds whether or not to call conflicts of desire irrational. If, within the expansion of reflective consciousness of which desire is a part, we see conflicts of desire as manifesting minimally understood splits within instinctual energy which lead to destructive and ultimately unfulfilling behavior, we shall probably regard those splits as irrational. If, however, we see such conflicts as opportunities for gaining insight into the development of instinctual energy and, in addition, as a way of channeling these developments in positive, productive ways, we shall probably regard the conflicts as, perhaps not themselves rational, but as an element or device in the creation of a larger system which can be rational.

VI

A final, additional question about desire I wish to discuss concerns whether or not desires can be said to have a phenomenology or subjective feel. This is obviously an important question from my perspective, since I have been suggesting that personal integration directly involves how we experience our various moments of existence and, in addition, that such integration is achieved, in part, by means of identifying and working through the elements found in pre-integrated or fragmented experience. If it turns out that desire (and other mental states) have no phenomenology, then it would seem to follow that desire (and other mental states) could not be identified through awareness of one's subjective states. In addition, it would also seem to follow that integration would not entirely, or perhaps even primarily, be an experiential state of the organism.

It is sometimes suggested that neither desire nor belief have a phenomenology, that there are occurrent desires and, especially, beliefs which simply have no subjective feel. I do not think this claim is entirely correct for either desire or belief; but whereas it seems to have a large degree of plausibility when applied to belief, it seems to have much less plausibility when applied to desire. Occurrent desires typically involve an urge, impulse or impetus towards an object, event or situation and these urgings involve an experienced subjectivity or feel. Indeed, it is most often this subjectivity which enables one to say both that one is desiring and what one is desiring.

To be sure, not all desires are strong, short term phenomena focused on a particular object, event or situation. Desires can be of varying degrees of strength and, while being fulfilled, may exist over an extended period of time. One class of desire is exemplified by a desire for this piece of cake now or putting on this pair of pants now. But another class of desires is exemplified by a desire to build a desk or write a book; and about such desires it is quite implausible to say they are being felt through the duration of building the desk or writing the book. At various times during such activities, the desires recede into the background of awareness and are not directly and immediately experienced.

However, since typically the energy or impulse of desires of the latter sort is immediately connected to the particular activities involved in carrying out the desire, the larger, central desire moves easily from the background to the foreground of awareness or consciousness. This suggests that such desires can be thought of as having a partially dispositional nature, for given certain circumstances, they will no longer be in the background, but in the foreground, of awareness. This dispositional element, however, does not rob such desires of their status as occurrent desires. It is within their status as occurrent that the dispositional element is to be found, allowing the desire to move from dim to clear awareness.

If such desires maintain their status as occurrent, they also maintain their phenomenology, albeit dimly and in a diffused fashion. As suggested above, the energy and so the subjective feel of the desire gets placed onto other aspects of the activity, onto the larger mental/physical network of which the desire is a central part. Because all mental states occur within a network of other mental states, the feel of a mental state — in this case, the larger desire — does not have to remain permanently and exclusively attached to that particular mental state. Rather, it can get attached to other aspects of the network, providing them with an original or an additional phenomenology or subjective feel. Indeed, how the energy of the desire connects to those other mental states and the various activities involved in fulfilling the desire determines the degree of success of the activity. If the energy of the desire is obscured and distorted in its diffusion to the larger mental/physical economy of the person, the activity will falter and perhaps even the original desire will become obscure and unclear. However, if the energy of the desire connects coherently and clearly to the other elements of the activity, then, in the absence of uncontrollable factors, the activity will be carried out successfully. And in such a case, the larger desire, not having been obscured or distorted, will, given certain circumstances, move easily into the foreground of awareness.

There is an additional class of desires whose members are occurrent, have a phenomenology—though typically of a background nature—and are dispositional within their status as occurrent. These are the general but persistent desires which many people have for world peace, personal health, the well-being of one's family, etc. Although these are standing, persistent desires, one is often not directly aware of them.

I do not think such desires can be given a full dispositional analysis. It is not that under certain circumstances I will have such desires and that in the absence of the circumstances I do not have the desires. Rather, I think I always have such desires, but that only under certain circumstances do I directly experience them. What, in part, distinguishes desires of this sort from those like the desire to build a desk is that they are often not tied immediately to the activities of the day. Such desires are much more general than the desire to build a desk and so it is easier to fail to see their connection to one's everyday activities. They are, of course, also much deeper desires, connected to other fundamental aspects of the mental network. As such, it is easy to get confused about them, and to obscure their nature, as well as their modes of expression in everyday existence. Thus, for such desires, the movement from background to foreground of awareness is not accomplished as easily as it is with the desire to build a desk.

Such remoteness from awareness may tempt us to claim that in the absence of direct awareness such desires do not persist, are therefore not occurrent and so do not have a phenomenology. This would, I think, be a mistake. Such desires do not go out of existence; rather their energy or impetus gets diffused, sometimes quite thinly, over a wide range of not obviously unified aspects of the mental network. While this gives the impression that such desires have no phenomenology, this impression is mistaken, for if we find that no degree of the energy of such desires is to be found in the larger mental/physical economy of the person, we conclude that the person simply does not have such desires. So the presence of confusion and obscurity at this level, along with the absence of a clear and distinct phenomenology, does not preclude the presence of the desire along with a diffuse and unclear phenomenology.

There is an additional consideration here. When people do begin to work through the obscurity of such desires, they often are able to tie them directly to their everyday activities, just as the desire to build a desk is typically tied to the everyday activity of building the desk. When this occurs, the movement from background to foreground of awareness is accomplished as easily in the one case as in the other and there is as little reason to deny an occurrent status and phenomenology to the more general, persistent desires as there is to deny them to the less general, more specific desires.

In contrast to the above sorts of occurrent desires, there are also clear cases of fully dispositional desires, desires which when not actually experienced are not in any sense occurrent. The desire to eat or sleep would be examples of this sort of desire. At certain times, the desire to eat is occurrent; but when it is not occurrent, it does not slip into the background of consciousness and continue as a low level occurrent desire. This, however, does not imply that there are not degrees of hunger. Surely there are and, in some cases, an occurrent desire to eat could wind up in the background of awareness, given an individual's involvement with other, more pressing activities. However, I do not think the desire to eat persists over time as do the desires for world peace, good health and the like. Once hunger is satisfied, the desire passes out of existence, not to arise again until certain circumstances are realized. This is what gives hunger its non-occurrent, dispositional form and distinguishes it from the former sorts of desire. In its merely dispositional form, though certainly not in its occurrent form, the desire to eat does not have a phenomenology. It is because of this kind of desire — and the following two less significant classes of desire — that I agree with those who claim that not all desire has a phenomenology.

Of the two additional classes of desire, the first consists of those desires of which it can be said that I have them, though they have never been occurrent. An example of such a desire might be that I not be hit by a green bullet shot from a red rifle. Until this moment, I have never experienced or formulated such a desire, yet there is an extended sense of "have" in which I have always had the desire. Second, there is the class of possible desires. These are not desires which I have though they were never articulated, but desires for which the circumstances of their being had have never existed. An example would be the desire for a specific object which has yet to be invented.

While such desires have no phenomenology in their purely dispositional form, they do acquire a phenomenology when they become occurrent. In fact, it is probably the case that their becoming occurrent and their acquiring a phenomenology are two sides of the same coin.

Although the existence of these classes of desire complicates the relationship between desire and its phenomenology, it does not detract from the claim that desires typically do have a phenomenology. The fact that desires — and other mental states — can be prompted regularly by certain circumstances, or said to be "held" given more general interests, or can come to exist when situations change and develop, does not imply that in their occurrent status they do not have a phenomenology. It only suggests that because creatures have a repertoire of actions and reactions to the various situations they encounter, it is the case both that mental states not yet existing could come to exist and that those mental states which one can be said to have are at the moment quiescent.

Perhaps the mental state which will most severely test this general perspective is belief; and to that we now turn.

Belief

Chapter Seven

I

The essential focus of these writings has been reflective consciousness in its ability to attain reflective awareness of its own states. As suggested, such awareness involves a division or separation within consciousness itself, and provides the materials for a unique and apparently pervasive form of error. In becoming aware of aspects of itself in this fashion, consciousness loses the immediacy of direct, absorbed, pre-reflective experience.

To be sure, immediate, non-reflective experience still occurs, for the reflective awareness of some particular mental state, as that act of awareness, need not itself be reflected upon; and, in addition, particular mental states are often themselves initially non-reflective. Thus, the advent of explicit reflective awareness does not destroy all absorption in experience. Indeed, as previously suggested, every mental state at bottom involves a direct absorption in experience. However, while reflective consciousness does not obliterate such absorption, it does alter both the original, undivided wholeness of consciousness and the nature of direct, absorption in experience. The former is altered, for consciousness now has reflective awareness of itself; and the latter is altered, for now absorption in experience contains elements derived from the conceptual systems generated by reflection. Any attempt, then, to reunify consciousness—and, of course, its relations to what is other than consciousness—must recognize the radical problem created by reflective consciousness.

As suggested in the last chapter, the forms of consciousness which most readily and clearly display the unique changes brought on by reflective consciousness are the propositional attitudes—as they are employed by reflective creatures. This last proviso is necessary, for there is a clear, relatively non-controversial sense in which not only reflective, but also pre-reflective, creatures display propositional attitudes, or at least the intentionality that is the hallmark of propositional attitudes. Pre-reflective creatures have beliefs and desires, and at least the rudiments of some of the emotions had by reflective creatures. These phenomena, like their counterparts had by reflective creatures, have an object or directionality, are about something or other, and are instrumental in the production of behavior. But along with these similarities, there are also significant differences. The propositional attitudes of pre-reflective creatures somehow emerge exclusively within the immediacy of or absorption in experience. They contain no elements derived from the activity of reflection, nor can they be made the objects of reflective consciousness. This dual absence of reflection assures that the propositional attitudes of pre-reflective creatures will not involve the kind of separation we have been discussing. As found in pre-reflective creatures, the propositional attitudes display a nature which is conducive to activity within the environment and which is commensurate with *their* consciousness and the physiology which constrains it.

Environmental conditions, however, produce pressures which in a very complicated, obscure fashion lead to the alteration of pre-reflective consciousness and the emergence of reflective consciousness. A creature which cannot depend on its instinctual, spontaneous reactions to the environment for survival must, if it is to survive and physiology permits, develop a locus of explicitly self-aware directedness. Input both from the environment and the creature's own being must be reflectively monitored and, in light of this awareness, information, belief, attitudes and perspective developed which produce behavior conducive to survival and perhaps flourishing.

Such activity involves the ability to reflect on the states one pre-reflectively experiences. But it also involves the inclusion within non-reflective experience of those modifications of consciousness developed by reflection. The former is necessary, for in the absence of reflective awareness of at least aspects of direct experience, redirection of energy and so modification of behavior is not possible. The latter is necessary, for if non-reflective experience is not itself modified enabling the modified behavior to proceed relatively spontaneously, the locus of directedness, *i.e.*, reflective consciousness, will be overloaded beyond its capacities.

Once again, then, reflection is a two-edged sword. On the one hand, it provides the condition for a new sort of behavior and indeed for the emergence of an essentially new sort of being and life. On the other hand, it does this, and must do this, by creating a distinctively new form of separation.

This latter point and its importance can be seen if we take a more detailed look at something said in Chapter 2. Particular pre- or non-reflective mental states come to be in the immediacy of experience. When we reflect on these states, we are no longer in the immediacy of experience of the mental states we are reflecting upon. To be sure, the mental state of reflection is itself an instance of the immediacy of experience; but it is not the same immediacy of experience as the state reflected upon. A state of reflection can itself be made the object of another state of reflection; but again, the latter state, in its immediacy, is not identical to the immediacy of the state of reflection it is taking as its object.

In this way, all mental states, at bottom, involve a dimension of immediacy, *i.e.*, are immersions in experience. But althouth this is the case, the immediacy of reflective states is not identical to the immediacy of the state being reflected upon. As such, the state of reflection can only seek to capture or comprehend the state being reflected upon in terms other than the immediacy of the state being reflected upon. If the state of reflection could grasp the state being reflected upon in the latter's immediacy, there would no longer be two states; rather there would be but one state.

One might, however, object to these remarks and claim there might be two instances of the same state, *i.e.*, that the reflective state and the state reflected upon might be identical, though non-numerically identical. But this will not do; for if the state of reflection becomes identical to the state being reflected upon, it is no longer a state of reflection. Rather than taking the state being reflected upon as an object of reflection, it would itself become identical, perhaps even numerically identical, to the state being reflected upon. It would no longer be a reflective state; rather it would be a state of non-reflective immediacy.

In this way, reflective mental states are necessarily separate from the states they take as their objects. But not only is the one separate from the other; they are also significantly, and perhaps radically, different forms of activity. As such, reflection must employ its methods and tools to grasp what is essentially different from it; and this it can do only to a limited extent. Being able to describe or talk about an experience is a very different sort of thing from having that experience.

There is another, related way of making the above point. Immediate, non-reflective experience has a distinctive feel or subjectivity or phenomenology depending on the particularities of the experience. In contrast to this is the feel, etc. of reflection. Both in general and in particular, the latter is not identical to the former, again displaying the separation of reflection from immediacy or non-reflection.

This matter, however, is not quite so straightforward. While I do think the above remarks are essentially correct, I also think they apply only to reflection understood in a certain fashion. In Chapter 3, I distinguished between "introspection as observation" and "introspection as revelation" and suiggested that the latter, but not the former, typically provides significant knowledge of experience. The basis of this claim was that while introspection as observation is an activity essentially external to experience, one which is conducted from the outside of the state being reflected upon, introspection as revelation flows out of the particular experience itself. Although it is not easy adequately to characterize what happens in the latter case, a version of reflective awareness seems to occur when the immediate experience somehow switches (or is switched) into a new and perhaps implicitly conceptualized awareness of the experience as an instance of this particular type of experience. This state seems to be intermediate between full absorption within experience and the separated awareness which takes the experience as an object to be understood and commented upon.

Reflective creatures seem to be capable of at least three stages of awareness of experience. First, there is the direct, non-reflective awareness of an activity or mental state, let's say dancing or being jealous. At this stage, one is simply dancing or being jealous. Second, there seems to be a perhaps somewhat fleeting, elusive state which is an awareness that one is immersed in is dancing or jealousy. In this stage, the awareness *flows out of* the experience, and if it is possible to express the awareness, it will be done in a way that avoids the sorts of errors which flow from talking about an experience that one is not *now* experiencing. (Although, of course all such talk will be susceptible to the sorts of errors which are made possible by the conceptual systems generated by reflective consciousness.) The third state, introspection as observation, is what stage two often quickly and imperceptibly slides into, namely, being absorbed in reflecting upon the original activity or mental state while no longer being directly immersed in the activity or mental state. It is reflection as so conceived that is susceptible to the objections raised above.

The significance of these remarks is that there appears to be a mode of reflective consciousness which is not, *as reflection*, separate and debilitatingly different from absorbed experience. As a result, it appears that reflective consciousness can have a direct, though of course fallible, connection to and knowledge of its first order, non-reflective activities and mental states. This will be a very crucial matter when we get to our detailed discussions of fragmentation, alienation and integration.

II

As developed in their reflective form, propositional attitudes are both distinctively human and involve separation from the original immediacy of experience. As such, besides enabling the creation of a new form of life, they are also a condition for the emergence of extreme forms of separation and so inner fragmentation and both inner and outer alienation. Any attempt, therefore, to deal with the latter phenomena must take a detailed look at how reflection functions in the form of the propositional attitudes. The need for this is still clearer when we realize the pervasiveness of the propositional attitudes. For once the standpoint of reflection emerges, virtually any aspect of the world, any aspect of consciousness and anything imaginable can be taken as an object of reflection.

This development creates an enormously complex situation, one which includes not only the range of objects of reflection and so the range of propositional attitudes, but also the complexity of the propositional attitudes themselves. Emotions, for example, almost certainly are complex propositional attitudes, consisting at least of interconnected beliefs, wants (or desires) and evaluations. Given this, an attempt at this point to explore the propositional attitudes in detail would be premature. What, however, is not premature is an examination of belief; for, among other things, belief seems to be a building block for other, more complex propositional attitudes.

But there is another reason to look at belief at this stage. Obviously, all of the mental states we've discussed so far — perceptual sensation, organic sensation and desire — are shared by pre-reflective creatures. In addition, each of these types of mental states becomes altered with the emergence of reflective consciousness. While the overlap of belief is not as clear as it is with the other mental states mentioned, there is an aspect of the mental functioning of pre-reflective creatures which is similar to the functioning of belief in reflective creatures. Although pre-reflective creatures probably do not actually have beliefs — they certainly can't articulate them — they are capable of distinguishing aspects of their environment and this is sufficient to allow one to say they have a mental state (or states) something like belief. In addition, belief shares the second characteristic of the mental states we've mentioned, namely, a significant alteration with the emergence of reflective consciousness. Indeed belief, or what was similar to belief, probably undergoes the greatest change of any pre-existing mental state once reflective consciousness emerges.

In the ways mentioned, then, belief seems both similar to and different from the mental states shared by pre-reflective and reflective creatures. Perhaps these differences will enable us to see why belief appears to be special and perhaps even transitional.

What seems unique about belief is that while all pre-existing mental states take on a new dimension with the emergence of reflection, belief in large part appears to be the vehicle for such changes. A non-instinctual, non-spontaneous creature needs to direct itself to what is valuable and avoid what is not valuable (and especially what is dangerous) in the environment. In order to do this, it must construct beliefs about what is and what is not valuable, as well as beliefs about ways to attempt and ways not to attempt to obtain what is valuable. The existence of such beliefs provides a larger network within which pre-existing perceptions, organic sensations and desires become embedded, often redirected and even internally modified. Having such a type and range of belief takes the creature out of the realm of those creatures which are primarily instinctual in their relationship to the environment. This development not only alters the nature of the mental states already existing pre-reflectively, it also, perhaps even more significantly, provides the groundwork for the development of the more complex mental states — i.e., the emotions — which are the outcome of a self-aware, self-directed and expanded relationship to the environment.

In short, the having of reflective beliefs, that is, the creation in part from one's own resources of a set of beliefs, places the creature in a new relationship to the world. The hub of this relationship — the center from which all the other mental states of the creature seem to be effected — is the set of beliefs one has. If these beliefs are coherent and adequate to the developing process within which they are created, the creature achieves a new form of unity; but if the beliefs are incoherent and inadequate to the process, the result is disunity and alienation.

In and of itself, belief is a state of unity. There is the state of belief which relates itself to its object in the manner characteristic of belief, and there is the content of the belief which varies with the particularity of the belief. All beliefs have these two features and as such are a unity. But belief is only potentially a unity with respect to what the content of the belief represents. If what is represented is represented coherently and adequately, a unity of sorts is achieved; but if it is represented incoherently and inadequately, disunity results. In the instance of incoherent and inadequate representation, belief becomes a phenomenon of distance. When we couple this point with the more fundamental point that in its dominant form of expression, reflective belief is not, except as the belief itself, a matter of direct experience, but is rather a comment on experience, we can see the thrust toward separation and disunity that is inherent to belief. Indeed, as reflective belief expands its capacities and domain, it can take as its content virtually anything that is imaginable or statable, including non-existent and contradictory objects, thereby creating various further ranges of distance from direct, absorbed experience.

Such expansions of belief are linked to the reflective creature's ability to be articulate concerning direct experience, to construct further beliefs about these articulations and to develop the wide ranging conceptual systems previously mentioned. In the absence of such capacities, belief is not a phenomenon of distance. Thus, the beliefs or, perhaps better, the categories or means of classification of pre-reflective creatures emerge spontaneously in the interaction of creature and environment and do not create a distance between experience and belief (or category). The beliefs are merely extractable from the experience; they are embedded within the experience and are not separate from the experience.

This, in turn, suggests a conclusion wholly consistent with previously developed conclusions in like circumstances. It is that the only sorts of error which the beliefs of pre-reflective creatures are susceptible to are those which flow from physical and/or physiological factors within the experiencing situation. Given environmental obstacles or physiological limitations or both, the object of perception or desire may be misidentified. Errors of belief which are contingent on the ability to reflect and to create conceptual systems do not arise for pre-reflective creatures, for they have no such ability.

In contrast to this is the range of error of belief reflective creatures are capable of. Indeed, I think it the case that probably all the beliefs of reflective creatures are susceptible to error.[1] Since the typical belief is a claim about something external to itself, the belief may not reflect the nature of what it is about. This is certainly the case with respect to beliefs that are articulated, either aloud or silently. The belief is constructed and so is portraying or reflecting some object, event or situation other than itself. But a possibility of error also holds for those beliefs which are not articulated, but are embedded, non-reflectively, in the immediacy of experience. Here the possibility of error emerges from the conceptual system of which such non-reflective beliefs are a part. The system, an outcome of reflection, incorporates the fruits of the latter activity, and insofar as the system is susceptible to error, so are the beliefs which are created within and are a part of the system.

If, then, reflective beliefs are both devices of distance and susceptible to error, they are crucial factors in the development of alienation. If we come to have false beliefs, we are in a state of separation from or disunity with the object of the content of the belief. And if these beliefs are false due to elements generated by reflective consciousness, we have a deep, systematic and pervasive form of separation.

If this is so, the question emerges as to whether or not reflective beliefs are necessarily productive of separation and alienation. If they are, creatures who must have reflective beliefs in order to operate effectively in the world have a built-in defect. And if this is so, the possibilities for fulfillment beyond survival, *i.e.*, the attainment of some form of unity or harmony within the larger process, are, at best, meager. Indeed, perhaps even this is too optimistic; for if there is such a built-in and ineradicable defect, survival itself is in question. (Witness the widespread and seemingly unending use of energy, skill and natural resources in the production of the means for total destruction.) From this perspective, it is important to see just how belief does (and can) function within reflective consciousness.

But perhaps we're going too fast here. For if false beliefs involve a separation or disharmony of the reflective center (or self) and the object of belief, true beliefs would seem to involve a harmony or unity of the reflective center and the object of belief. And there is nothing I have so far said concerning belief which implies that beliefs must be false. I have indeed claimed that beliefs are always fallible, but fallibility is not at all equivalent to falsity and still less is it equivalent to necessary falsity.

This, of course, is a reasonable point; and it suggests that in order to overcome or avoid alienation, reflective creatures must develop a certain sort of reflective center or self. From this reflective center or self would flow the various true or adequate beliefs which would, in part, establish the unique form of unity reflective creatures are capable of. From this standpoint, belief becomes a central phenomenon in the overcoming of alienation, of the development of integration, and this is as it should be given the centrality of belief to the very emergence of reflective consciousness. However, while this stress on correct belief is appropriate, it can also be misleading; for while belief is probably the central feature in the emergence of reflective consciousness, it is not necessarily the most powerful or dominant force within reflective consciousness. That is, although belief may appear to take over reflective consciousness and may be thought by many to do so, this is not the case. To be sure, belief does seep into the other elements of consciousness, modifying and altering them; but the route of influence also often goes in the other direction, with the other elements of consciousness determining belief, often without the individual being aware this is happening. That is, belief is often determined, not by evidential considerations, but by the unacknowledged strength of other elements within consciousness.

What complicates the matter enormously is that the other elements within reflective consciousness, being part of reflective consciousness, also involve beliefs, but beliefs which are often not acknowledged by the person holding them. The upshot of this situation is that given the centrality of belief in the development of reflective consciousness, much of the energy of the reflective creature becomes entangled with all sorts of beliefs, many of which the individual is not even aware of. If this situation is typically one of fragmentation and alienation, the overcoming of same would involve focusing on the beliefs which entangle the primordial energy. Freeing this energy from false or inaccurate beliefs and attaching it to true or accurate beliefs is one major dimension of creating both internal and external harmony or unity.

In light of these suggestions, it is crucial that reflective creatures have the capacity to become aware of a good deal of what at various levels they believe and why they believe it. With such awareness, they can constructively modify and develop their beliefs so these are unified not only with other of their beliefs and mental states, but also with what is other than their mental states, *i.e.*, the larger world process.

III

In order to develop the above remarks, it is necessary to make two sets of distinctions concerning the manner in which beliefs can be held. The first of these I will introduce now and the second later in the chapter. There is a distinction between, on the one hand, beliefs which are either sincerely stated, silently or aloud, or about which there is reflective awareness and, on the other hand, beliefs which are only implied given the particularities of the experiential situation. Beliefs of the first sort are clearly occurrent and it is their status as occurrent which enables us to say that the individual in question holds them.

It is less easy to provide a status for beliefs of the second sort, since if they are merely implied by the experience, they are not occurrent. The alternative that they are dispositional also seems not quite right, for the point is not that given certain circumstances such implied beliefs would become occurrent — this is true, but I think irrelevant — but rather that it is a mistake to think of the experience as inherently involving beliefs of any sort. However, if we take this line, it becomes unclear whether we can say such implied beliefs are held by the experiencing individual. In some sense, they are held, for as an example will presently show, not only are they immediately extractable from the experience, but they will also be stated — and so become occurrent — if and when the agent is asked the right sort of question. But in another sense, they are not held, for neither being constituents of the experience nor occurrent, there is a distinct sense in which they are non-existent.

What is at stake here seems to be the following. I have suggested that belief is often a phenomenon of separation, that belief being about something other than itself can distort and misrepresent the nature of this something other. But I have also suggested that belief can provide one dimension of a new form of unity. Part, but not all, of this difference can, I think, be accounted for by how beliefs function when we are involved in experience. When we come to experience and view it through an articulated (or unarticulated) belief, we are separating ourselves from the experience, even if in some general fashion the belief is accurate. Saying, muttering and thinking the belief separates us, sometimes subtly, sometimes grossly, from the experience we're having. This matter, however, is complicated by the fact that probably all the experiences of reflective creatures involve conceptual phenomena and so imply beliefs. Such beliefs, however, need not be the filters through which experience is had; rather they can be what flow out of the experience, are extractable from the experience and will, on reflection, be stated, by the agent. Beliefs functioning in this fashion are not devices of separation. In these situations, the individual is immersed in experience and the belief, as a particular phenomenon, is only something which can be said to exist through the mediation of the experience. These beliefs do not precede, but succeed, or at most parallel, the experience.

The sense in which such beliefs can be said to be held should be sharply distinguished from the sense in which other beliefs neither articulated nor about which there is reflective awareness can be said to be held. There are, I think, beliefs which fit the latter description, but which yet precede and structure certain experiences. Although such beliefs are not articulated, they are nonetheless held in a strong sense. What I have in mind are those beliefs which we can perhaps call unconscious. Such beliefs are not only extractable from the experiences of which they are a part; they are also constitutive of these experiences.

Some examples should provide clarification for the entire discussion. Suppose one is walking down the street and sees a red car. Assuming one is non-reflectively absorbed in the experience, clearly there is no actually stated belief that this is a red car. No doubt the concepts "red" and "car" provide some of the conditions for seeing the red car, but there is not in addition to these concepts a belief that this is a red car. Such a belief is only implied by and extractable from the experience; it is not a part of the experience. If this is so, the concepts "red" and "car" are constituents of the experience; but the belief that this is a red car is not another constituent of the experience.

Let's now contrast this with a similar situation in which one walks down the street, sees the red car and is frightened by it. In contrast to merely seeing the car, this example involves the emotion of fear. But for fear to be present, the agent must, at some level or other, in some way or other, believe there is danger in the situation. In the absence of this belief, however we come to specify it, the individual simply is not afraid. In this way, the belief which is producing the fear precedes the experience and is constitutive of the experience in its aspect as frightening.

However, the claim that the fear producing belief (or beliefs) precedes and structures the experience might raise the following objection. It might be said that the individual did not have any such belief in mind on walking down the street and that simply looking in front of him as he walked produced the fear just as, in the previous example, looking about produced his seeing the red car. In the one case as in the other, the experience flows out of what is encountered, not out of previously existing beliefs. Now, to be sure, the occasion of seeing the red car produced both the experience of seeing the red car and the experience of fear. However, whereas seeing the red car does not imply a pre-existing, constitutive belief that there is a red car, being afraid of the red car does involve a pre-existing constitutive belief concerning red cars and danger. Since in normal circumstances parked red cars are not dangerous, this is not the sort of case in which one confronts an objectively dangerous situation and as a result of the objective danger becomes frightened. This is rather a case in which the element of danger is provided by the specific beliefs which the individual brings with him to the situation.

I have, of course, chosen an example in which the distinction between what is and what is not objectively dangerous is virtually non-contestable. But this is not always — or perhaps even often — the case. When it is not the case, it is a difficult matter to determine to what degree the fear is a product of pre-existing constitutive beliefs the individual brings to the situation and to what degree it is a product of the objective nature of the situation. In many instances, it is probably a product of both. But certainly, part of the task of the reflective creature is both to become aware of the pre-existing, often irrational beliefs, with which he confronts experience and to gain (or, perhaps better, to create) as clear a sense as possible of what is in fact objectively dangerous. This latter task, in its turn, involves becoming aware of the very basic beliefs which are often constitutive of how one views oneself and one's relationship to the larger process.

If we return to the specific case of fear of the red car, it seems we can say that although the specific beliefs which link red cars to danger are not directly known by the individual, they are nonetheless held by the individual in a strong sense. That is, although unacknowledged, they are occurrent within the individual's experience of fear of the red car. Such beliefs, of course, also have a dispositional form, for they become operational or occurrent only in certain circumstances, say, when the redness of the car appears in a certain shape and is seen in a certain light.

We seem to have reached the following position. Beliefs which are constitutive of experience are occurrent, even when they are unconscious or simply not available to awareness. Beliefs, however, which are not constitutive of experience are occurrent only if they are sincerely stated, silently or aloud, or become objects of awareness. All of these types of beliefs, besides having an occurrent form also have a dispositional form, for given certain circumstances they become operational, or are stated or become objects of awareness. But there is another type of belief, namely, those which are implied by experiential situations, which while they can become occurrent and can be seen as dispositional are perhaps best regarded as neither occurrent nor dispositional.

The latter suggestion, previously made, needs a bit more discussion. In order to provide it, let's return to the simple case of seeing the red car. If we treat the belief that is extractable from this experience as either occurrent or dispositional, seeing the car becomes a cognitive act in, I think, a quite misleading fashion. To be sure, seeing the red car is a cognitive act in the sense that one is seeing what one sees *as* a red car rather than as something else; and such a discriminatory activity is indeed cognitive in nature. However, I would like to suggest that the dimension of cognition involved here is significantly limited. It is the sense in which any entity, animate or inanimate, which can display differential reactions to the environment can be said to be performing cognitive acts. But it is very misleading to equate the beliefs of reflective creatures and their mode of functioning within reflective consciousness, with the mere capacity for having such differentiating reactions. As a phenomenon of reflective consciousness, belief occupies a unique, creative role which is unclear and problematic; and it is in this form, as a development/creation of reflective consciousness, that we need to explore belief so as to gain a sense of how it does and can function. Our main concern with belief ought not be its capacity to differentiate, for all sorts of things can be built to do that.

If we fail to recognize these different dimensions of cognition, we may wind up treating all the experiences of reflective creatures as involving beliefs in the unique form in which beliefs *can* be employed by reflective creatures. As a result, we are likely to treat all the experiences of reflective creatures as involving the element of distance or separation which many such experiences do. This, however, would rule out an apparent possibility, for although *non-reflective* experience is permeated by the elements derived from reflection, including beliefs, it yet appears possible that in at least some instances such experience can be direct and unmediated. Of course, because such experience is permeated by the fruits of reflection, it cannot be unmediated[2] in the manner in which the experience of pre-reflective creatures is unmediated; but this does not rule out the possibility that such experience need not be *additionally* mediated by belief.

Again, what is at stake here is the possibility of overcoming solidified separation or alienation and achieving harmony or unity. If reflective belief is both inherently a device of distance and inherent to all experience, the possibility of achieving non-distanced absorption in experience is probably non-existent. I will return to these problems as we proceed.

IV

Much of what was said in the preceding section is connected to problems concerning the legitimacy of assigning to beliefs a phenomenology or qualitative feel. There are two clusters of problems here. The first arises in the following fashion. Beliefs which are held in the weak sense seem not to have a phenomenology for they are either dispositional or merely extractable from experience. Some philosophers,[3] however, claim that such beliefs are somehow parts or constituents of experience. But if they are and do not have a phenomenology, they cannot be involved in the awareness of how an experience *actually feels*. That is, the feel of the experience will have to occur independently of the beliefs embedded in the experience, for these beliefs are said not to have any feel at all. If this is so, such beliefs cannot be involved in the process of working through and altering the felt nature of experience. If, then, one thinks, as I do, that integration emerges only from such working through, one must argue that beliefs which are held only in the weak sense are neither constituents nor parts of experience. In the last section, I argued for just this point.

The second problem concerns whether beliefs *ever* have a phenomenology. If, as many do, we say that beliefs never have a phenomenology, then what is true of beliefs which are held merely in a weak sense becomes true of all beliefs. As a result, the exploration of belief in its experiential aspect would never be a dimension of the process of becoming aware of and working through the felt nature of experience. But this seems to be a highly unlikely situation, for belief appears to be the central phenomenon in terms of which consciousness develops and expands. If it in fact does play such a role, the various forces and energies of consciousness become entwined with belief in complex ways and at a variety of levels. From this perspective, beliefs absorb and disperse energy within the system, for it is largely in this manner that the development and expansion of consciousness takes place. But if energy is in this fashion tied to belief, it would seem that at least some beliefs have a phenomenology.

Let's take a step back and look at various kinds of belief to see whether or not they do have a phenomenology. First of all, it seems beyond dispute that not all beliefs do. Dispositional beliefs, not involving a modification of consciousness which is the belief, do not have a phenomenology. Since they are not occurrent, there is not anything which could involve a phenomenology. The class of such beliefs is vast. Besides those beliefs which I once adhered to and/or articulated, but am not now adhering to and/or articulating, there is the virtually limitless set of beliefs which in a weak sense of "hold" I hold, but which I have never even articulated. For example, now that I think of it, I believe that Socrates had a left foot, that no strawberry weighs over 50 lbs., etc. Like the beliefs which are extractable from certain definitely circumscribed experiential situations such as seeing the red car, these beliefs also seem to be extractable from our various experiential situations. The difference is that while beliefs of the former sort are directly and obviously extractable, beliefs of this latter sort are more indirectly and less obviously extractable. Such beliefs seem to be almost endlessly extractable from almost any experience. In any case, neither of these sorts of extractable beliefs appear to have a phenomenology.[4]

I have been suggesting that in order for a belief to have a phenomenology, it must be occurrent. While I think this is true, it does not follow that all occurrent beliefs have a phenomenology. How then do we distinguish those occurrent beliefs which do have a phenomenology from those which do not? I think we can gain initial entry into this matter if we see what happens when the belief "this is a red car" is no longer simply extractable from the experience of seeing a red car, but becomes a full-fledged occurrent belief.

If the experiential situation within which one sees the red car is in any number of ways either questioned or challenged, one may take a harder look and affirm, with conviction, one's original perception, but now in the form of a belief. When this occurs, it appears the belief involves a phenomenology, for there is a feeling of conviction that accompanies the belief. But of course, this will be objected to on the ground that belief is one thing, the conviction another, and that the phenomenology attaches to the latter, not the former.

This is obviously an important and interesting objection, which, among other things, provides the occasion for introducing a variation of the second distinction alluded to in Section III, concerning the various ways in which beliefs can be held. Occurrent beliefs can be seen as essentially logical phenomena, implied or entailed by certain situations, facts and other beliefs, having an existence independent of the way they are actually held. But they can also be seen, not just as logical phenomena, but as modifications of consciousness, often internally connected to other elements of consciousness which do have a phenomenology. If we treat belief in the first fashion, we separate the logical entity, belief, from its place within the consciousness of the individual, and shall on that basis deny it a phenomenology. If, however, we treat occurrent belief as a modification of consciousness, variously interconnected with other elements of consciousness, we shall, at least sometimes, see such beliefs as having a phenomenology.

These considerations introduce a major problem, for it must be said that belief is internally and essentially connected to action; and it is not at all clear how beliefs conceived exclusively as logical phenomena, lacking a phenomenology, can be connected to action. It would seem that for belief to connect to action, it must involve the various forces and energies of the organism and so have a phenomenology.

I think that what misleads us here is a certain model we derive from focusing on conscious occurrent beliefs. Such beliefs, because they are conscious, can be treated as logical phenomena. Being known, it is possible to abstract them from their manner of being held and to treat them from that perspective. This, however, is not possible for unconscious occurrent beliefs. Not being known, they cannot be treated as logical phenomena, for the abstraction which would make them logical phenomena cannot be performed. Yet, such beliefs, as argued previously, do have an effect on experience and behavior and so this effect must be due to the actual manner in which the belief is being held and this would involve a phenomenology.

I am here invoking a distinction between first and third person perspectives. It is, of course, possible from a third person perspective to continue to employ, with regard to unconscious occurrent beliefs, the distinction between the manner in which a belief is held and the belief as a logical entity — assuming the third person knows of the first person's unconscious belief. But this distinction cannot be maintained from the first person perspective, for the belief is not conscious to the first person. Since the first person perspective is the locus of action, and beliefs are tied to action, the beliefs must be functioning in terms of how they are being held. And this is true even though unconscious beliefs at their moment of functioning are not available to consciousness *as that* particular belief.

The upshot of this is that our perspective on occurrent belief — conscious and unconscious—should reflect what follows from an understanding of how, in general, unconscious occurrent beliefs are tied to behavior. While a focus on belief as a logical entity is often helpful and appropriate, it need not and should not lead us away from seeing the necessity of treating belief as a modification of consciousness often involving a variety of forces and so having a phenomenology.

Above and previously, I suggested a number of things about unconscious beliefs: that they have a phenomenology; are often productive of behavior; and are productive even when their phenomenology is not consciously attached to them. This calls for some brief comment. What I think happens with unconscious beliefs is that their phenomenology—that is, the complex of feeling which originally and properly belongs to the belief — somehow becomes attached to some other belief and/or complex of mental states of which the individual is conscious. Indeed, what appears to make a belief or other mental state unconscious is that its phenomenology becomes separated from it and instead becomes attached to something else. The outcome of such misplaced attachment is that the phenomenology gets focused onto something which is in one sense easier for the agent to handle — for it is not the actual situation out of which the phenomenology flows.

I think we can sketch how this works if we return to the case of a person's fear of the red car. Seeing the red car brings forth a fundamental and powerful fear in the observer. The fear, however, is not attached to the beliefs which are connected to the fundamental fear; rather the fear gets attached to the belief that this is a red car. This enables the individual to avoid having to confront the fundamental, truly powerful fear and allows him instead to focus on something which he can see, and others can tell him, is silly and irrational and so not to be taken seriously. Although any short way of stating this needs considerable investigation and explanation, the unconsciousness of the deeper beliefs are the outcome of a basic fear "preventing itself" from becoming conscious to the agent, or of the agent's "refusal" to become conscious of the basic fear, or even perhaps in some obscure way, both.

If these remarks are on the right track, they have a significant impact on the possibility of overcoming fragmentation and alienation, and achieving integration. Awareness of misplaced phenomenologies yields the possibility of awareness of the origin of such phenomenologies; and awareness of the latter yields the possibility of the creation of new, more adequate perspectives on one's situation within the world.

V

Although many of these matters have been alluded to or discussed above, at this point it may be helpful to concentrate on how belief affects non-reflective awareness and how the question of the presence or absence of a phenomenology for belief, in turn, affects our ability to understand and modify such awareness. As indicated, the ability to reflect produces intricate and extended conceptual systems, perhaps the key elements of which are reflective beliefs. Along with other aspects of reflective consciousness, these beliefs create an explicit sense of self and so a new way of experiencing both one's existence and the world within which one's existence unfolds. In addition, the elements of reflective consciousness seep into pre-reflective experience, altering it and necessitating that it be reconceptualized as non-reflective experience.

The transition from pre to non-reflective immersion in experience is also a transition from non-mediated to mediated immersion; and mediated immersion is susceptible to forms of error non-mediated immersion is not susceptible to. As a result of this range of alterations, all the experiences of reflective creatures involve at least some degree of distance, the distance which stems from the failure of a certain sort of immersion in experience — the sort which does not involve items derived from reflection.

But while distance is ineliminable, the degree to which it occurs is determined both by the nature of the mental state expanded or created by reflective consciousness and by how this state is functioning within reflective consciousness. Of these mental states, the one which seems, at least potentially, the most distancing both as a type and in its functioning is belief. Even here, however, the problem can be mitigated, for if the beliefs which are constituents of the awareness are "true," "adequate," "appropriate," or the like, non-reflective awareness will be less distanced (and distorted) than if it involves beliefs which are "false," "inadequate," "inappropriate," or the like. Indeed, types of non-reflective awareness, such as spontaneous emotions, which include beliefs as constituents are, when the beliefs are true and the other elements which constitute the emotion are commensurate with the situation, instances of the new and unique form of harmony reflective creatures are capable of creating. This, it might be added, appears to be the limit of direct immersion in experience for creatures who are no longer pre-reflectively immersed in experience.

When beliefs seep into non-reflective experience, they become integral to such experiences and so become a dimension of the felt nature of the experience. As a result, either they themselves have a phenomenology or, as modifications of consciousness, become entwined with other elements of consciousness which do have a phenomenology. In this manner, beliefs become a pathway to other elements of the experience—and they also to belief—and so to a deeper grasp of the experience. Of course, in order to maintain such views, we must treat beliefs, not just as logical phenomena, but as modifications of consciousness. As a way of supporting such treatment, I will now introduce the second distinction concerning the ways in which beliefs may be held. This distinction was alluded to in Section III, above, and a variation of it was discussed in the previous section.

This distinction does not apply either to beliefs which are mere implications of experiential situations or to beliefs which are constitutive of experience but have not been articulated. It is, rather, a distinction within the class of explicitly articulated reflective beliefs.

For want of a better term, we can say that one way such beliefs can be held is intellectual. A belief is assented to because the weight of reasons, abstractly and impersonally considered, presses in that direction. But there is an additional way in which such beliefs can be held, although it is not easy to provide a clear and concise characterization of this way. In such cases, one assents to the belief, not only through the activity of reason, but also through the active involvement of one's broader emotional being. The belief, as it were, links up with various elements of one's being, becoming a part of and expressing one's "whole being." Perhaps a general way of characterizing this distinction is to call the former "belief as abstract or impersonal"; and the latter "belief as lived."

Before providing an example to clarify this distinction, and especially the notion of "belief as lived," it must be pointed out that not all occurrent, articulated beliefs are covered by the distinction. For example, it would be a mistake to treat the presently articulated belief that Albany is the capital of New York as a belief that is lived; for such a belief involves virtually no aspect of my emotional being—though, of course, there are circumstances in which it could. If an articulated belief does not connect with elements of my emotional being, it is then simply impersonally or intellectually held and so does not have a phenomenology. Or, perhaps better, it has no significant phenomenology, for while it may involve assent—as opposed, say, to entertainment—the feel of the assent is tied only minimally, if at all, to my emotional being. Here, then, is a case—and there are many, many more—in which an occurrent, articulated belief has no significant phenomenology.

There are, however, many other beliefs for which the distinction between being held intellectually and being held with one's whole being is crucial. Take, for example, the question of personal immortality. In such a case, one could examine the various arguments for and against personal immortality and come to the conclusion that the arguments against immortality outweigh those for immortality (or vice versa). On the basis of such reasoning and weighing, one could come to believe that there is or there is not personal immortality. While such a belief is actually held or adhered to, the holding occurs only in an intellectual, impersonal, perhaps even uninterested, fashion. The person remains untouched by the process which leads to the belief and by the belief itself.

In contrast to this is the belief of a person who has not only weighed the various arguments and considerations relating to the logic of belief in personal immortality, but who also has explored the matter as it relates, multi-dimensionally, to his sense of his own concrete, personal existence. These explorations would, of course, include bringing to consciousness a whole range of emotional states and desires and the beliefs which are connected to them. In their turn, these would reveal both facts about one's situation as a human being and how one understands and reacts to or feels about this situation. In the midst of this ongoing process and in reaching a provisional conclusion, the beliefs which are involved are rich and resonating; they vibrate through one's being and their phenomenology is vivid and distinctive. The only way this phenomenology can be missed is if we separate the beliefs from the fuller range of mental and organic states with which they are inherently connected and treat them in an abstract, disconnected fashion.

Belief is a multi-faceted phenomenon as it functions within the consciousness of the reflective creature. In many cases, belief has no significant or any phenomenology at all, while in others, it seems clearly to have a distinctive and significant phenomenology. Given the range and complexity of reflective consciousness, it seems a mistake to treat belief as having one unique and exhaustive mode of operation.

Before ending this chapter, I wish to return briefly to the point that belief is in various ways and to various degrees a phenomenon of distance. Since I have been arguing that belief is perhaps the central mental phenomenon in the development of reflective consciousness and this development creates the possibility of fragmentation and alienation, it is appropriate to close with some explicit remarks on these matters.

When occurrent beliefs are either constitutive of experience, and/or the vehicles — explicit or implicit — by means of which an experience is had, it is relatively clear how belief can be a device of distance. In such cases, the individual is not directly immersed in experience, but is rather having the experience through the window of the belief; the belief places a structure on the experience, removing the individual from direct immersion in the experience. Although typically the individual is not aware of this, the belief becomes the state of consciousness one is immersed in,[5] as opposed to the experience which the belief is structuring. One mistakes a state of mind in which one believes something about an experience or through which one is having an experience, for the direct having of the experience. As a result, it is possible to live many of one's experiences within one's head or by means of beliefs rather than with the absorbed totality of one's being.[6]

To be sure, one can step back and focus — now with one's whole being — on such beliefs and their interconnections with other elements of consciousness. Doing so puts one in touch with how one sees and experiences particular situations on a deeper level. As such awareness expands, one can slowly develop and refashion how one sees and experiences various situations, enabling a fuller and more coherent relationship with various aspects of existence.

There is a sense, then, in which beliefs serve as a flap within consciousness. When they mediate experience in ways that are unknown and distorting, they create disconnection, fragmentation and alienation; but when they are coherently interconnected with the rest of consciousness and the totality is in a viable and productive relationship with the world, they help create a new and unique sense of unity and harmony.

For the latter to occur, however, beliefs must first be identified and then purged and/or modified. For this to happen, beliefs cannot be treated simply as logical or intellectual items, impersonally held. Rather, they must be seen and experienced as interconnected parts of a vast psychic apparatus. Seen in this fashion, beliefs almost certainly have a phenomenology of their own and, without doubt, have a phenomenology in their interconnection with other aspects of the psychic apparatus. It is by means of this phenomenology that one can come to identify beliefs and so come to find out what one *really* believes, not just what is "rational" to believe or what one says one believes. Becoming aware of what one really believes provides one with the opportunity of working, not only with those items, but also with the deeper and more hidden aspects of the psyche with which they are connected. This ongoing, developing awareness and the modifications in attitude, belief and value which it makes possible is one of the keys to integrating and harmonizing both one's consciousness and one's relationship to not-self. As such awareness and the resulting modifications continue to deepen and entrench themselves, they, in turn, become absorbed within non-reflective experience, enabling such experience to be spontaneous, fluid and productive. To the extent this is possible for reflective creatures, one is now illuminatingly absorbed within the range of one's activities.

Fragmentation, Alienation and Self

Chapter Eight

I

In the preceding pages and chapters, in a variety of ways and contexts, I have discussed the claim that consciousness in its movement to humanity via the phenomenon of separation can become fragmented and alienated. These latter notions, however, are obscure in a number of ways and it is time now to attempt to provide some clarification. Dealing with these notions will also lead more deeply into the question of the structure of self and so the interconnected problems of self integration and integration with not-self.

In their primary sense, "fragmentation" and "alienation" are properties which attach to consciousness only in its reflective phase. They refer to phenomena which have as their condition the very existence of consciousness as reflective. In the absence of reflective consciousness, fragmentation and alienation, in their primary sense, cannot exist. As argued previously, pre-reflective creatures are immersed in experience. Being so immersed, there is no standpoint within their consciousness which could provide the source or foundation for the separation which can yield fragmentation and alienation. Seen from this perspective, pre-reflective consciousness is a harmony or whole, but, being pre-reflective, it is a very limited harmony or whole.

Reflective consciousness involves not only the ability of consciousness to become aware of itself as a reflective consciousness, but also the ability to become aware of various of its aspects. But being so aware, it is also capable of not being aware. That is, having attained the capacity to reflect upon, know, be aware of, aspects of itself, it is also capable of not knowing, not being aware of such aspects — either aspects it was once aware of or aspects it is now, in the present, not aware of. When reflective consciousness is in a state in which aspects of itself are hidden from itself and these aspects are effective in the production of belief, desire, emotion, mood, attitude and action, we have fragmentation. Unawareness can exist over a wide range of mental states, and it usually does so not in terms of total oblivion of the states in question, but in degrees of unawareness.[1] In its various manifestations, unawareness is tied directly to fragmentation. As such, it raises a series of difficult and intriguing questions concerning its own structure and the structure of reflective consciousness.

Reflective consciousness involves the possibility of an internal rupture within itself, whereby different aspects of consciousness can be severed from each other and can work against, or contrary to, each other. This is a situation of non-harmony or non-wholeness. Parts of what could be a whole are not integrated, but exist as discrete units operating, at least as far as reflective awareness is concerned, independently of each other. Again, it is in this sense that reflective consciousness can be fragmented.

But separation within consciousness, i.e., the at first non-articulated awareness that these are my states of consciousness, that it is I who is experiencing such and such, simultaneously brings with it the (non-articulated) awareness that there is also not-self or the world. Knowing there is a world other than the self provides the possibility for separation from the world or alienation. The creature is now no longer-pre-reflectively immersed in the world, innocent of the awareness that the world is being experienced by an "I" which is not, at this emerging level, any longer identical with the world. Rather, the creature slowly becomes reflectively aware that (its) consciousness is the standpoint by means of which the world is experienced. Thus, the emergence of the possibility of alienation.

In all of this, of course, there is the phenomena of degrees of reflective awareness, degrees of insight into the situation, degrees of fragmentation and alienation, etc. Tracing the history of such developments poses a monumental task; but whatever the difficulties and obscurities involved in providing such a history, the core point, I think, remains. This is that the move from pre-reflective to reflective consciousness creates a situation in which the new form of consciousness involves a separation or rupture within what was a harmony or wholeness and so there emerges the possibility of a two-fold extended rupture occurring both within the "organ" of awareness, i.e., consciousness, and between consciousness and that of which it is conscious, namely, the world.

II

The phenomenon of reflective consciousness, with its concomitant possibilities, fragmentation and alienation, raises in an acute form the problem of self. Reflective consciousness involves the felt, though not always articulated, awareness that these are *my* feelings, this is *my* life, I am this creature. To employ the expression previously used, a sense of "mineness" develops which transcends the brute, pre-reflective awareness that accompanies organic sensation. What is this sense of mineness? How is it related to self? What is the structure of self? And, finally, what is it to be (to have) an integrated self?

What bedevils many discussions of self is the explicit or implicit claim that it is a substance or entity of some sort, one which in some way or other exists and can be grasped outside of the historical and developmental flow of consciousness. When self is seen in this way, the question of origin, which is most obscure from any perspective, becomes still more obscure. For self, thus understood, is not seen as internally and necessarily connected to the world of which it is a part and out of which it emerges at a certain stage of development. Rather, it is seen as an entity in its own right, one which can have a separate existence and whose relation to the world in which it finds itself is contingent and adventitious.

As a corollary to the above, self so understood is typically seen and experienced in contrast to and separate from body. And this, in turn, leads to an immense cluster of problems concerning respective ontologies and the nature of interaction — for, after all, self as substance does appear to be "within" the body.

The approach I am suggesting is radically different. It sees self as emerging out of the developmental and historical flow of consciousness within the wider developmental flow of the universe and its energies. From this perspective, although individual selves within the process can experience and think of themselves (the self) as outside the historical flow of consciousness, this must be a false or distorted experience or thought. For, on my view, self is inherently part of the process of development and to be adequately grasped must be seen and experienced in this fashion.

Exactly how one would establish this claim is not clear, but if self is not an emergent aspect of the process, inherently tied to the process, where could it come from, how could it arise? Perhaps there are two questions here, one dealing with origin of self, the other with the status of self independent of origin. I suppose one could argue that self is historical in origin, yet separate in its nature and operation. But it is hard to see what the possibility is here, for the only form of separation which appears to be intelligible in this context is self thinking of and/or experiencing itself and its operations as separate. Surely, however, such a thought or experience does not establish the actual separate nature and operation of self. Indeed, as I have suggested, it appears to be a form of distorted understanding of self which is unique to reflective consciousness.

My claim, of course, is that self is both historically emergent and inherently tied to the process from which it emerges, and that any view of self which in any way separates it from this process, while possible as a psychological or conceptual thought, is mistaken and/or distorted. Although consciousness can come to reflect on itself, thereby creating a sense of mineness or self, and in that way achieve separation or transcendence, this is not a separation from, or transcendence of, the process, but is rather a development *within* the process. As argued previously, however many levels of reflective awareness reflective consciousness achieves, the awareness remains and must remain within the developmental flow of consciousness — indeed it is simply another development or wrinkle or extension of consciousness.

But if we see self as emerging within the developmental flow of consciousness, and if the condition of emergence of self is the ability of consciousness to become aware of itself, we must then see self as some aspect (or aspects) of consciousness itself. Self would somehow become identified with that part of consciousness which is reflectively aware and so operating in some form of executive capacity, that is, interpreting situations and making decisions. It appears that the sense that one is indeed a particular person living this life arises from the fact that consciousness can take a self-aware look at itself and its situation. In light of this, it is highly likely that self itself is identified with this capacity.

Of course, the aspect of consciousness which is self would consist of a cluster of mental items and configurations, a coalition or coalescence, as it were, of those aspects of consciousness which become predominant in the personality and do indeed provide interpretations and instigate courses of action. Seen in this manner, self is at least a somewhat flexible, moving and changing dimension of consciousness; for the coalition of mental items, operating as the self, will, depending on the awareness and maturity of the agent, vary through contraction and expansion.

This perspective enables us both to recognize the reality of a sense of self, a sense of mineness, and to avoid the perils of self as substance. Earlier, I claimed that the creation of a standpoint, a self, is needed not only for the emergence, but for the survival, of humanity. As the instinctual adaptability of the creature diminishes, a "device" of some sort must emerge as the at least partial "director" of behavior. The reflective capacity, identified as self, seems to fit this need. But recognizing the emergence of such a standpoint is not equivalent to seeing it as a substance or entity; it is simply to recognize that at a certain point of development, consciousness can reflect on itself and so, at a variety of levels, become aware that it is involved in living a life as a particular creature.

The point now reached seems to entail that self is not entirely constant nor entirely indivisible. If self is a coalition of mental items and configurations which take up an executive function within consciousness, the coalition need not be constant; it can shift in relationship both to the circumstances of function, *i.e.*, the situation in the world, and the degree of awareness and maturity of the individual in question. The degree of shift here cannot, of course, be limitless, for if it were, we would no longer have a functioning person. So there must be some reasonable degree of constancy present. What this degree is and how to evaluate various coalitions are, of course, questions that shall have to be returned to.

But, it might be said, this discussion of self is confusing metaphysical with psychological considerations. Self, as philosophers ought to be concerned with it, is a structural notion, one which transcends and is unaffected by considerations relating to particular, individual psychological situations or configurations. Although there is some force to this objection, I think it reflects back on the metaphysics of self that is presupposed by the objection rather than the claims about self against which it is directed. As I suggested in Chapter 2, it is a very short step from looking for the abstract structure of self to thinking of self as a substance or entity. So the rejection of doctrines of self as substance can be seen as the rejection of a certain sort of metaphysics of self. In its place, one gets a focus on self as psychological structure. Or, rather, within the present perspective, the metaphysics of self is located at the simultaneous emergence of separation and reflective consciousness. This latter becomes the formal, *i.e.*, metaphysical, dimension of self, while the content or psychological dimension of self consists of two levels, a descriptive-cum-evaluative version of an ideal integrated self, complete with the psychological details of such integration, and the non-ideal, particular psychological configuration of any particular self. This account, while focusing on psychological structure and so the concrete experience of being a self, also allows for abstract and metaphysical treatment of self, but with such treatment tied to the origin and nature of the lived self.

But considerations relating to constancy and indivisibility, especially when emanating from a non-substance account of self, raise questions concerning parts and wholes. Indeed, more fundamentally and primordially, the same problem arises from the emergence of reflective consciousness and the possibility of fragmentation, alienation and reintegration. While the problem of parts and wholes has a general form, dependent on the emergence of reflective consciousness, this problem takes on a particular and unique form when it is applied directly to reflective consciousness or self.

The awareness of the part/whole distinction is conditional on the emergence of reflective consciousness; and this, of course, also applies to the awareness that this distinction can apply to self. There is, indeed, a sense in which the distinction between parts and wholes holds of the world independently of reflective consciousness and so reflective awareness. It is, I think, safe to say this so long as we can say that some at least of our descriptions of the world are in fact based on the world and do in fact hold of the world. And even though I have previously suggested that there are built-in possibilities of error in all and any conceptual schemes and that there is no raw, undifferentiated given, it does not follow that our conceptual schemes need be thoroughly distorted impositions on the world. That we need to create the distinction between parts and wholes does not mean that the world does not consist of parts and wholes.

Yet, having said this, there is another sense in which consciousness, the world, and consciousness-in-the-world are neither parts nor wholes, nor not-parts nor not-wholes. For in the absence of reflective consciousness and so reflective awareness, things simply are as they are. From this perspective, however, we can also see that there is an additional sense in which consciousness, the world and consciousness-in-the-world *are wholes* because no rupture has yet occurred within consciousness to generate the reality of part/whole either within consciousness or between consciousness and the world.

So the general distinction between part/whole has as its condition the existence of reflective consciousness; and this distinction applied to self, *i.e.*, as fragmentation, alienation and re-integration, is itself an outcome of the rupture in consciousness which creates or is reflective consciousness. It is because of this rupture within consciousness that reflective consciousness becomes aware of (or, perhaps better, is) the problem of fragmentation/integration. So understood, the distinction (and problem) is not simply given by the world; it rather arises at a certain stage of the development of consciousness. As such, the problem of part/whole, as applied to self, is *internal* to reflective consciousness and so must be solved within the internal dynamics of reflective consciousness or self.

If this is so, and self is seen as that part of consciousness which is reflective, constancy of self emerges as reflective consciousness establishes a new form of unity or wholeness or integration both within itself and within the world. And this perspective parallels the earlier contention concerning self and psychological structure; namely, that constancy of self involves an ideal version of integration which is approximated to by particular psychological structures.

III

The above considerations propel us into one of the most perplexing and difficult problems in this area, namely, the problem of accounting for the identity of self over time. But perhaps "identity" is too strong a notion here. For if self is a coalition of mental phenomena and if this coalition is to any significant degree fluid and not constant, it would appear there could be continuity of self over time, but, strictly speaking, not identity. There would, that is, be identity or sameness with difference, not identity or sameness without difference. Strictly speaking, it would appear that identity of self could flow only from a substance view of self, one which saw the substance as continuing identical with itself over time.[2] Since I have denied a substance view of self in favor of a coalition view, I cannot call on the continuation of the substance to provide identity, or even continuity, over time.

There is, however, undeniably a feeling or sense of continuity and identity of self which, in all but the most extreme circumstances, we do experience. We think and feel we are now the same person who went to bed last night, attended college some years ago, grew up in the neighborhood we did, and so on. We are the same person, but yet as I have suggested, there is no self substance which accounts for this sameness, which remains constant over time. Thus, the experience of sameness must be accounted for in some other way. And the structural aspect of such accounting lies, I think, in the continuity of elements of the coalition which is self. This view would not involve an identity of elements of this coalition over time — though this could not be ruled out in all cases — but rather an overlap of such elements, with some of the elements (and their focus) more crucial to continuity than others.

This suggests both a general point and a somewhat more specific point. The general point is that if a reflective creature is to function in the world as a person, i.e., as a creature who is not essentially instinctual and so has to make choices, there must be some significant degree of continuity of self.

The elements which make up the coalition which is self cannot simply vary from moment to moment, for if they did, and there was little, or no, overlap through time of elements which constitute self, interpretation and understanding of the world, and action within it, would be whimsical, inconsistent and irrational. If this is correct, any view of self which sees it as a ramshackle of thoroughly discrete, disconnected items is defective, for it rules out the possibility of even reasonably coherent and consistent understanding and action.

The more specific point concerns the focus of the overlapping mental items and structures which constitute self. If self is a coalition of mental elements which occupy an executive function within consciousness so that the organism can adequately grasp its reality and determine how to act, the relevant elements must, first and foremost, focus on those aspects of the environment and the organism itself which pertain to survival. Thus, deeply, the mental items and structures which will overlap distinct moments of self concern or have as their objects basic biological and psychological needs of the organism. With no really sharp demarcation line to be run between the biological and the psychological, these will include the obtaining of food, shelter and clothing, sexual activity, curiosity, play and so on.

That is, self being a dimension of consciousness which arises given the plight of the creature, the fundamental and immediate objects of the coalition which is self will be those phenomena which pertain directly to that plight, namely, those phenomena which involve survival. Having to negotiate in the world in order to survive, self needs to be constituted by objects, as well as attitudes towards objects, which pertain to survival. In this fashion, self is grounded in, arises from, the *lived* reality of the organism. It is from this perspective that we need to look at the claim that at least in part, self is constituted by the objects of its mental states, not just the abstract mental states themselves. Desires, abstractly understood, may, for example, be elements of all selves, but it is only particular desires which, along with other particular mental items and structures, constitute a particular self. One needs to focus on the objects of mental states in order to gain an understanding of the constitution of self, for self is that aspect of consciousness which, in direct interaction with the organism and the environment, determines action.

The specific point, then, is still at a significant level of generality, for it is not only possible, but also quite likely, that the specific ways in which different selves relate to the elements which are relevant to survival will be different. Not only environments, but understandings of environments, vary both within cultures and cross-culturally. Consequently, the particular details of selves will also differ. But this is no puzzle; it is simply a consequence of the view that self is constituted by the details of its grasp of, or involvement with, its environmental situation. What remains constant here is the focus on those elements of the environmental situation — however understood by the particular self — which directly and immediately relate to survival.

What I am suggesting seems to be the following. Self is a coalition of mental items and structures which take up an exeuctive function within consciousness. This function needs to be established or be in place if the organism is to survive. As a result, self, at a very fundamental level, consists of mental elements which focus on those aspects of the environment and itself which are directly related to survival. And this focus and the continued need to operate in the world in an effective fashion involves the continuity over time of the relevant elements.

But not only is there a significant degree of generality in the point that the focus of self's mental states is on items directly relating to survival, there is also generality in the notion of continuity which both this focus and the plight of the creature produce. Continuity of self is a dimension of experience which must exist if an essentially, non-instinctual creature is to operate effectively in the world. But continuity so understood is very general and abstract, and becomes less so only when it is explicated in terms of those elements of experience which are essential to survival. However, if the items of the environment and one's organism which relate to survival can be understood and related to in a variety of ways, then the continuity which flows out of such attention and understanding can also have variable content.

In a word, self, both as constituted by objects which pertain to survival and by the continuity over time of such objects and the mental attitudes toward them, is permeated by change. Not only do environmental situations change, necessitating a re-orientation to the environment, but self's understanding and evaluation of its situation also changes, producing at least somewhat new options and orientations. Self, as it were, is a part of the environment, interpreting it, contributing to it and so changing it.

The perspectival and relativistic tone of these remarks must not, however, be taken to imply that any relationship of self to the world, any involvement of the creature with its world, is as effective (or as good) as any other. While there is latitude in a creature's sense of what specifically is needed for survival, and an even greater latitude in ways of relating to what is seen as needed, these are not unlimited latitudes. Certainly, any non-instinctual creature will need to develop the executive function which is self in relationship to its environmental situation. But this does not entail an equality of effectiveness of such selves; it rather suggests that some selves are more effective than are others, for it is not an arbitrary matter how self grasps, and so acts within, its environment. Failure to appreciate what is needed for survival—and this is an objective matter, although one which can be understood in more than one way—leads to a failure to survive; and beyond survival, failure to grasp what is needed for flourishing—though again selves can flourish in a variety of ways—leads to a failure to flourish.

Thus, the change which permeates self, if self is to survive, is limited by the objective demands of the organism and the environment, even when these phenomena are themselves changing. But this leads to an understanding of a further limitation on self's change, for such change is always *within* a context of development. Changes of self are not and cannot be large or total changes which bear little or no contextual relationship to what preceded them. While in the long run, over an extended period of time, context can get stretched out and the connections between past and present partially obscured, this cannot occur in the short run. Self's development is historical and concrete and as such is grounded in the realities of its situation. As a result, any changes must flow out of that situation and self's understanding of that situation.

Although this is just a corollary of the continued claim that consciousness — and so self — is historical and developmental, it is no small matter and rules out any view which sees self as capable of undergoing immediate and radical change. In addition, this is another way of restating the general view, namely, that identity of self over time is a matter of psychological continuity. While this raises problems we will have to return to, the developments of self are not, at least in the short run, radical or total in nature; rather they occur within a concrete context and are limited by the context, even when the context involves items and structures which are not immediately available to conscious or reflective awareness.

But if continuity of those elements of reflective consciousness which occupy an executive function within reflective consciousness is the measure of sameness of self over time, we need to look at that aspect of consciousness — memory — which makes such continuity possible. It is not, however, memory simply as an aspect of consciousness which enables the relevant sort of continuity; it is rather memory as found within the context of reflective consciousness. That is, it is reflective consciousness itself which provides us with the sense, the awareness, that we are continuous. And that part of reflective consciousness which, in complex ways, provides at least a significant dimension of that awareness is memory. The ability to recall, in a variety of ways, past events, situations and the like almost certainly arises out of the ability of consciousness to become aware of itself. Becoming so aware, consciousness develops a standpoint as well as a sense of itself, and so also a sense of itself over time, what "it" did or did not do, experience or not experience. From this perspective, memory is an extension within the structure of reflective consciousness of the pre-reflective operation of memory within pre-reflective consciousness. The emergence of a standpoint, that is, extends and modifies the operation of those aspects of the physiological organism which enable consistency of behavior at a pre-reflective level.

Having been extended and modified through the development of reflective consciousness, memory can no longer be pre-reflective. However, as opposed to reflective, it can be non-reflective. When memory is non-reflective, it operates in such a fashion that without explicit, reflective awareness of past events, situations and the like, it permeates and provides the structure within which present awareness and activity take place. Memory here is the non-reflective context within which continuity and understanding manifest themselves and — assuming reasonably accurate and adequate memories — coherent, survival producing behavior occurs.

But memory can also be directly reflective, with past activities and phenomena apparently becoming the direct objects of awareness. Although there are significant differences between these two manifestations of memory within reflective consciousness, in the present context the differences are secondary and the similarity, namely, that in either or both of these manifestations memory provides a continuity of past and present, is primary.

IV

The use of memory as the provider of continuity of self over time confronts us with a major problem, one which relates not only to the notion/experience of continuity of self over time, but also to the unity of self at any particular time. If, as I have insisted, self is not a substance, but a coalition of elements of consciousness, what is it which ties these elements into self at any particular time as well as over time? What is it which makes these elements into something other than discrete, disconnected items of consciousness at some particular moment of time and over an extended period of time?

Before attempting to answer these difficult questions directly, two pre-liminary observations are in order. The first is that although these questions do indeed need to be faced and responded to in some effective fashion, they are nonetheless at least somewhat suspect. This is because there is an im-plication to the questions that it is at least possible to ignore or obliterate the developmental and contextual nature of being a self. To be sure, self can be seen, thought of, in this fashion. As indicated in past chapters, self and its elements can be seen as separate, discrete, discontinuous; but this, as I have suggested, is a symptom of the fragmented and alienated state into which self can propel itself. So while our questions need a reasonable re-sponse given that they inevitably flow out of the development of reflective consciousness — indeed, they pose a challenge to the creative development of reflective consciousness — they must be treated with caution, for they also express an at least potentially alienating movement of consciousness.

The second observation which needs to be made is that one traditional way of answering these questions seems not to work at all. This would be to say that self is a substance and that, as a result, the unity of self at any moment and over many moments is accounted for by the unity, present and persisting, of the substance which is self. This, however, will not do, for it is simply to posit a very mysterious, unexplained entity just where expla-nation is needed. What is this self? Where does it come from? How are its properties related to it? What accounts for the unity of the substance? Pos-iting a self substance at this juncture serves not only to avoid the crucial, perplexing problems; it also apparently serves to turn the problem of sepa-ration, which is the origin of the problems of unity and continuity, into alienation, for, from this perspective, self appears to be a virtual entity unto itself.

There is, however, one crucial insight which the postulating of a self substance does involve. This is the recognition of unity and continuity and the need to account for them. How, then, if we reject a substance view of self, and adopt a coalition view of self, can unity of self at a particular time and continuity of self over time be accounted for?

In line with the general position developed in these chapters, namely, that self is an aspect of consciousness which emerges at a certain stage of the development of consciousness, and so is grounded in the reality of the *lived* experience of the organism, the source of unity and continuity must, it appears, be found *internal* to that development. From this perspective, whatever establishes unity and continuity must be something internal, some developmental aspect of consciousness itself. And this aspect of consciousness is, I think, the sense of mineness previously alluded to. However exactly it occurs, reflective consciousness is able to reflect on itself and its experiences and develop a new level awareness that this consciousness and these experiences are *mine*. It is, I think, this sense of mineness which is the foundation of both the unity and the continuity of self in the context of the sense of self had by reflective creatures.

The sense of mineness is, of course, subjective. In some not quite clear sense of "feeling," it is a feeling. In any case, it is a wrinkle, a development of consciousness and has a phenomenology. The sense of mineness can be reflective or it can be non-reflective. When the latter, it typically permeates and structures our activities at a quite fundamental level.

But since what we are aware of, what we have a sense of mineness about, both reflectively and non-reflectively, at any particular moment is quite limited, our sense of self at any particular moment is radically incomplete. Add to this the claim that no subjective state and so no sense of mineness is self-authenticating and we need to recognize that claims to unity and continuity, even when internally generated, are not infallible. Even though the source of both unity and continuity is internal (and internally felt) neither is the feeling of mineness equivalent to the establishment of unity or continuity nor is the absence of such a feeling equivalent to the absence of unity or continuity. The feeling of mineness may be inappropriate to the reality or the way the reality is being perceived; the absence of the feeling of mineness may also be inappropriate to the reality, due, say, to defensiveness.

Thus, the fact that we have a sense of unity of self at any particular moment and a sense of continuity of self over time does not entail that we have a full or complete, as opposed to a limited or incomplete, sense of self. But this should be expected, unless, that is, we think of self as fixed, as a complete, non-developing entity of some sort. The limited and incomplete sense of self is both an outcome of the changing and developing nature of self and is itself, in part, reinforcement for the notion of a changing, developing self.

But given such reservations concerning the operation of the sense of mineness, how does it establish—even in part—unity of self at a particular time and continuity of self over time? First, given our claims about the development of consciousness, it is the source or foundation for both unity and continuity within reflective consciousness. And second, it is the sense of mineness which *prima facie* at least establishes unity and continuity. For now focusing only on the sense of unity, such is provided by the sense of mineness which attaches to the experiences, the elements of the experiences, of the moment. Whatever in the moment has attached to it the subjective feeling of mineness constitutes the unity of self at that moment. But as we've indicated there are complications. There is not only the fact that mineness can be either reflective or non-reflective — a point I will return to later — but that not everything operating within the present moment of consciousness has the sense of mineness attached to it. In light of the latter point, the sense of mineness cannot be the sole criterion of unity of self, for if elements of self can be operating at any particular moment and yet not have the sense of mineness attached to them, the sense of mineness is an incomplete criterion.

There is thus a need for something (or somethings) additional if a more adequate and complete account of unity of self is to be provided. Unity of self would involve those elements of consciousness which have the property of mineness in a certain fashion as well as those elements of consciousness which do not have such a property but which nonetheless are at the moment part of the coalition which is self. The difficult point, of course, concerns the manner of identifying the latter elements.

Once the necessity of the latter addition is accepted, it is necessary to supply a non-subjective, non-internal criterion as a partial criterion of unity of self. This criterion, not involving the internal, subjective sense of mineness, can be classified perhaps as objective and certainly as external. But while this development removes the full elucidation of the notion/experience of unity of self from the internal domain of felt consciousness, it does not eliminate this domain from being the origin and essential focus of the notion/experience. The experience and awareness of the fact that self is unified remains necessarily wedded to the internal, dynamic development of (reflective) consciousness. It is in the context of the development of consciousness itself that the very experience of unity of self as we are now discussing it develops. But it is also in this context of development that consciousness ruptures or separates, thereby distancing itself from itself and creating a situation within which it is not transparent to itself. Given this, unity of self, in its reflective form, cannot simply be accounted for by what is internal to consciousness. Whatever theoretical troubles are presented by the need for a non-internal criterion of unity, such a need is no longer surprising once it is seen how both unity and the loss of what constitutes this new unity flow from the same development.

What, then, needs to be added to the sense of mineness properly functioning in order to account for unity of self? I think two things are needed here. One involves an account of what leads us to say of elements of consciousness to which the agent does not attach the property of mineness that nonetheless such elements are part of the functioning unity of that self. The second involves a claim about how any agent correctly attaches the sense of mineness to elements of consciousness. This latter claim would, I think, have to be elucidated through the notion of "ideal circumstances," that is, circumstances which involve the absence of those aspects of consciousness, such as defensiveness, which either prevent agents from acknowledging elements of the coalition as theirs or lead them to identify as elements of the coalition what is not part of the coalition. This latter point expands the problem, for, as previously mentioned, it indicates that the presence of the sense of mineness does not guarantee that the object of the sense is, as conceived, part of present unity. Thus, from this perspective, what is needed is an account of the integrated person on the ground that it is only the integrated person whose consciousness can approximate to the ideal and so is able to evaluate the objective claims concerning the functioning of consciousness. This state which, I think, involves a recognition that self as separate is an illusion will be discussed in more detail as we proceed. For now, I would like to comment on the first point.

It is clear that while we do give special standing to an individual's account of himself, we do not — and quite rightly do not — give such an account unquestionable and final standing. In addition to the individual's account, we have a more "objective" view, both theoretically and informally based, of what accounts for an individual's behavior. This includes a sense of which elements of consciousness are contributing to that behavior and so are part of the coalition which is self at that particular moment. This view is built up in very complex ways from a combination of awareness of oneself and observation of others. And while such a view, in general and in particular, is fallible, such fallibility does not entail that the view cannot account more adequately for behavior and what contributes to it than does the agent's rendition of what is going on and why.

In order to substantiate an instance of the objective view when it conflicts with the agent's rendition, the details of the view would have to be carefully spelled out and evaluated. But how would the evaluation take place if not in the context of the ability to assess from the internal perspective the claims made from the external perspective? Thus, as I suggested in Chapter 2, we are again back to the inevitability of the internal standpoint evaluating — and also producing — the external standpoint. And such an evaluation of what is functioning in behavior, of those elements of consciousness which are part of the functioning and so unified self at that moment, demand an integrated consciousness, one which is aware of those elements of consciousness which are operating even if unacknowledged, and not operating even if said to be operating.

The external perspective is created by the emergence of (reflective) unity; but it in turn necessarily leads back to, involves, the internal domain which is its source. The external perspective on unity is both created and evaluated by the internal; and it is only this internal perspective developing in a certain way which can provide appropriate evaluations and expansions both of itself and the external perspective. And none of this denies the fallibility of the internal perspective, however integrated it is.

But these remarks seem to return us, at a different level, to the original problem, for the suggestion seems to be that the subjective or internal feeling of mineness is — and must be — the last word on unity of self, while simultaneously acknowledging the fallibility and so the limitations of this sense. This, however, may be the best that can be done given the structure of reflective consciousness. We may, that is, need to rest content with the realization that, most fundamentally, unity of self is a subjective phenomenon, but that such unity cannot be established by the mere subjectivity of its nature. The subjectivity which is the source of reflective consciousness' awareness of unity of self at a particular time is not, by itself, capable of establishing with certainty such unity at any particular moment. The content of the subjectivity of unity, I am suggesting, is not simply given, but is developmental itself and so can be more or less adequate to the possibilities of unity within the structure of reflective consciousness and its involvement in the world. Thus, the productive enlargement of the subjectivity which constitutes unity is equivalent to the attainment of integration. But again, integration is itself a developmental subjective or internal state and as such is neither final nor infallible. It is, I think, within such a recognition that we need to deal with the problem of unity of self at any particular time.

V

As indicated above, there is, besides the fallibility and limitations of the sense of mineness, also the difference between reflective and non-reflective mineness. Although the reflective sense of mineness is not without its mysteries, it seems to be the more straightforward of the two experiences. This sense of mineness arises when I self-consciously or self-reflectively note some aspect of consciousness to be mine. I reflect on it, own it, in direct awareness feel it as part of my consciousness, my being.

The non-reflective sense of mineness is somewhat more difficult to explain. It involves a background, non-reflective, sense or feeling of mineness, one which permeates present awareness and activity. It is what enables one to relate to the present in a relatively coherent, ordered fashion. In a way, the non-reflective sense of mineness provides the grounding for one's participation in the world; in the absence of such grounding, coherence and order would dissolve into a whirlwind of discrete, disconnected units, a madhouse of bouncing, twirling shapes, colors and sounds.

On the feeling or phenomenological level, the non-reflective sense of mineness is that vague and taken for granted sense that I am having these experiences; or better, so as not to separate "I" from the experiences, I am these experiences, my life is now being constituted by these experiences. In part, what makes adequate characterization so difficult here is that once characterization begins, it involves reflection on the experience of non-reflective mineness, *not* non-reflective mineness itself. As such, it involves reflective explanation of the phenomenon, and such explanation invariably involves statements concerning the "I" or "self" which *has* experiences or subjective states which have the property of mineness. But this is precisely what non-reflective mineness is not. The latter involves absorption in experience, with this absorption including a sense of mineness which is not reflective and so does not involve any separation of "I" or "self" from experience. Reflective creatures have the experience of non-reflective absorption and the non-reflective sense of mineness this includes, while pre-reflective creatures do not because the former but not the latter have had absorbed into their consciousness the explicit or reflective sense of self which flows from the rupture in consciousness which is unique to reflective creatures.

I have, in a preliminary fashion, attempted to account for unity of self at any particular time by means of actual and ideal instances of the reflective and non-reflective sense of mineness. But how, using such experiences, can I account for continuity of self over time? In this case, the immediacy — actual or ideal — of the sense of mineness carries much less weight than it does concerning unity of self at the moment, for the sense of mineness refers to events and situations in the past, and the mere fact that there is a present sense of mineness attached to what is allegedly a past event does not confirm that event as continuous with the present self — unless, that is, memory can be trusted. But, as is commonly granted, memory is extremely deceptive. So how, if at all, can this difficulty be overcome? In line with what has been said previously, it is not so much a matter of overcoming the problems of memory but of working with and within them. In general, the phenomena which need to be accounted for emerge from the development of consciousness and an expanding subjectivity. So in order to properly grasp and develop such phenomena, we must work within that subjectivity. Self, unity and continuity are aspects or developments of reflective consciousness. As such, they are essentially, if not exclusively, constituted by subjectivity. If we apply this to continuity of self over time, the memories which subjectively supply the threads of continuity will involve feelings or subjective impressions both as to the object of the memory as a whole, *i.e.*, the event or situation which is being remembered, and the concrete details of the event or situation. That such recollections can be faulty in so many ways reveals the relative weakness of memory when it comes to particular phenomena and their details. But such weakness is not necessarily tantamount to weakness at the more general level of continuity of self. Even if the details of my past are vague and uncertain, the underlying sense of continuity cannot be denied. What is again helpful is the distinction between the reflective and the non-reflective sense of mineness. When reflecting on past experiences, seeking to recall them in the present, memories and the feelings associated with them can be seriously deceptive. But the non-reflective sense of mineness, while also capable of distortion, provides a more general sense of continuity, linking past and present.

The discussion concerning identity of self over time led to the related problem of unity of self at any particular time. Both phenomena have, in part, been accounted for by the subjective experience of mineness which, in its special features, is unique to reflective consciousness. But the use of mineness with respect to identity of self over time poses special difficulties since it depends on the use of memory, and that aspect of reflective consciousness is especially prone to error and distortion. Not only is memory subject to the standard limitations and distortions of constructed conceptual systems, as are all aspects of consciousness, there is, in addition, the dimming of memory over time and the more insidious demands placed on memory by present preoccupations. Memory, then, is no infallible guide to any particular event or situation in the past, including, of course, those which are felt to be continuous with self.

Nonetheless, fallible though it be, memory in both its reflective and non-reflective forms is a key aspect of that continuity which provides us with a sense of sameness of self over time. As suggested above, this is especially true of non-reflective memory which provides a context within which coherent and productive behavior can occur, that is, behavior which recognizes the physiological and psychological needs of the organism within a reasonably clear grasp of the situation in the world. While a pared down version of this description applies also to pre-reflective creatures, this does not vitiate the differences between pre-reflective and reflective creatures with respect to the operation of memory. To be sure, pre-reflective creatures typically do act "appropriately" within their environmental or survival situation; but such behavior is essentially instinctual and does not involve the kind of choices that require a reflective self, employing a developed memory. This difference registers a difference in kind and can be appreciated if we recall that reflective consciousness expands in terms of the conceptual systems it generates as a means of grasping its experiential situation, thereby enabling survival behavior. These systems come to permeate all of consciousness, including of course memory, and so the non-reflective memory that provides the context within which understanding, interpretation and action take place is of an order of complexity that is unique to reflective creatures.

At a very general level, then, memory provides the psychological continuity which is the sense of continuity of self over time. As memory gets more detailed, it becomes more questionable with respect to those details, but still does not lose its deeper and more constitutive function as provider of continuity. The latter is lost only with amnesia, and even then it is the details, the feeling, of being this person which is lost and not the non-reflective structure within which the person continues to live. If this structure were lost, the person would no longer be capable of functioning and in such a situation there would apparently be a total lack of anything resembling a coherent consciousness.

VI

The final remarks of the last section suggest something most interesting concerning the phenomenon of continuity of self over time. If amnesia can wipe out the sense of continuity and amnesia is the outcome of physiological factors, it might be suggested that the criterion of psychological continuity, even expanded beyond occurrent feelings of mineness, is not adequate to account for self over time. It might be suggested that besides the criterion of psychological continuity, a criterion of bodily continuity is also needed. Or, at least, that the recognition that amnesia — understood as physiologically caused — can erase the sense of continuity of self over time requires that we look at the relation between psychology and physiology as we explore further the notion/experience of continuity of self over time. If psychological continuity, however expanded and modified, is necessarily tied to physiological factors, then in some form or other the latter may well need to be included in any adequate account of continuity of self over time.[3]

In general, then, the problem of amnesia brings to the surface the fact that physiological factors can affect and interrupt the sense of psychological continuity. And, in its turn, this fact raises the far reaching problem of the embodiment of psychological continuity and indeed of all mental phenomena. Given that in previous chapters I have rejected as not expressing a possible reality any view of self as disembodied, it follows that I also reject as not expressing a possible reality any view of psychological continuity as disembodied. But even within this rejection, there are options available. For example, it is possible while holding the view that psychological continuity must be embodied also to hold that such embodiment can change, that psychological continuity can be transferred from one body to another. I wish to reject this view and hold not only that psychological continuity is necessarily embodied, but that it is necessarily embodied, in a sense to be explained shortly, by *this* body. Indeed, that this body is an aspect of psychological continuity and that psychological continuity is an aspect of the continuity of this body. In line with these remarks, I also wish to suggest that talk about embodiment, even necessary embodiment, is itself misleading, for it suggests that there are two things — psychological continuity and body — and they are necessarily together. I wish to suggest that there is only *one* thing, namely, embodied psychological continuity, but that because of the rupture in reflective consciousness, we are able to talk about psychological continuity in separation from its bodily existence. As a result, we often wind up losing all sense of the underlying, inherent unity.

In short, I am suggesting that psychological continuity is embodied in both a general and a specific sense. Generally, the suggestion is that psychological continuity cannot exist disembodied; and, specifically, the suggestion is that embodiment is particularized to this body. To deny either or both of these claims is to wind up with some sort of separate self or consciousness or subjectivity. To think of a disembodied psychological continuity, and so a self, which could inhabit this or that body is not only to treat self as some sort of ongoing substance, it is also to explicate the notion/experience of continuity of self in non-bodily terms, thereby sundering the unity of the person. That is, to place the burden of continuity of self over time entirely on psychological continuity is to treat the elements which make up such continuity as separate and disembodied. While such a thought is no doubt possible, it does not, beyond the world of thought, express a possible reality. In fact, I suggest it is an outcome of the rupture within reflective consciousness, a rupture which conceals the deeper unity of consciousness/body and self/world and which needs to be overcome at the level of rupture if fragmentation and alienation are to be avoided.

Self is an embodied reality; embodiment and specific embodiment are not accidental, contingent features of being a self; rather they are necessary features of being a self. As I will argue presently, eliminating body is also to eliminate the psychology of the creature and so the possibility of there being continuity of self over time in the manner that is relevant to this discussion. If this is correct, it is necessary to add to the previous conditions for continuity of self over time some sort of bodily criterion if we are to have anything resembling an adequate account of personal identity over time.

What appears to make these matters even more difficult and obscure than they otherwise would be are the underlying assumptions that often nourish them. It appears that the idea of separateness, of the disembodied existence of the psychology of the creature, entails both a general and a specific dualism. The general dualism involves the relationship of body and mind (and so the psychology of the creature), while the specific dualism involves the relationship of any particular psychology to the particular body of which it is an aspect. In both cases, the general and the specific, the relationships are seen as essentially contingent, or perhaps better, external, rather than necessary or, perhaps better, internal. To think of self, or what constitutes it, as an existent unto itself, placeable in any number of bodies, is to obliterate the underlying, deep unity of the person as an embodied self. That I am — I hesitate to say "have" — this body does not, of course, imply that parts of this body cannot change, but it does imply that this body is as inherently an aspect of my existence as is what is more commonly — and I think mistakenly — referred to as self.

Thus, to the question, "which body must be continuous if there is to be continuity of self over time?" the answer is: this body. To think any other body would do is to produce either of two types of dualism: the traditional non-materialistic dualism; or a somewhat new, apparently materialistic dualism. If, in accord with non-materialistic dualism, self is thought of as separate from body, as identical with a self substance, then body B might obtain the self of body A (say, in the form of the memories of A) and the question would arise as to whether body B in its new state (*i.e.*, with the memories of A) was B or A. While such a thought experiment can be stated — apparently coherently — I suggest that it involves a number of absurdities and so does not represent a possible reality. The absurdity which is relevant at this juncture is the implication that self has an existence either as disembodied or as only contingently related to its body, or both. As I have suggested, and will elaborate presently, the human person is an embodied creature with body/mind[4] separable only in (distorted) thought. Body/mind is an aspect of a unity, the unity that is self; the continuity, and so identity, of self over time is the continuity of body/mind over time.

But there are subtler versions of the above problem, for we now seem to have the capacity—and certainly have the imaginative capacity—to perform brain transplants. If we assume that the brain is a necessary condition for mentality and consciousness and so a necessary condition for the sense of self, then if the brain of A is transferred to B, and the brain of B to A, what should we say about the identities of the resulting creatures? Should we say that B, now having the brain of A, is no longer B, but is A; and that A, now having the brain of B, is no longer A, but is B? If we are tempted to say that having a new brain involves having a new identity, I think we are confusing a part of the body with self or with being a self. We might say that this is the materialistic form of dualism alluded to above, for apparently it is separating out, dualistically, one part of the body from the rest of the body and designating the separated part as self. In this fashion, we get a "brain (self)/rest of body" dualism.

To be sure, without a brain there is no self; indeed there is no life. But it doesn't follow from this that I am identical with my brain, that the brain is self. Individual A now having the brain of B is not therefore B. What (or who) this creature is is unclear, but I am suggesting it is not B, for a self— and so a person—is not just an externally amalgamated mixture of bodily parts (with one or more of those parts being the seat of mentality and consciousness). Self, rather, is an inherently interconnected or metaphysically unified "brain (and so mind)/body." Even if we grant that the brain is the seat of mentality and consciousness—which it surely is—this part of the body cannot simply be moved into another body, and, as a result, have the self which the brain allegedly is. The reason for this is that the rest of the body, how it is felt, how it is related to, how it has developed and is developing is *internally* connected to a particular brain, the brain which historically has developed along with and in interconnection with the rest of the body. If the brain is moved into another body, these historically developed, internal interconnections no longer exist and thus the unity and so the continuity and identity of the creature is sundered.

These remarks suggest that the continuity of the brain is fundamental to the continuity of self in a way that perhaps no other part of the body is.

But what follows from this is not that the brain is the self and so can be trans-ferred along with self (or identity) to another body, but that the brain is not to be understood in separation from the rest of the body. The particular brain is what it is and the other parts of the body are what they are, in large part, because of the organic involvement of each with the other. We fail to see this because again we focus on the separation which beguiles us, not on the more fundamental unity of the human creature. Consequently, this unity is lost to awareness and in its place appear fragmented and alienated forms of consciousness.

The point that self involves embodiment, indeed that such embodi-ment is and must be uniquely particularized, can shed light on similar, though somewhat alternatively focused, problems. Given our ability to re-flectively know we are selves, that we live a life, we can, in accord with the sense of separation this involves, ask a variety of questions concerning being this self. Once we grasp that being a self is to be a particularity in the world, we can ask: how is it that I am this self rather than some other self? and could I have been someone other than myself? A brief look at these dark, eerie puzzles will provide an additional vantage point from which to grasp the fundamental unity which is self and which allows for continuity over time in the midst of change.

Both of the above questions seem to imply that I is separable from self, that I becomes this self or could be another self. These thoughts, however, seem to be distortions, and again distortions which flow from our ability to reflect on experience and fashion an awareness of self. I and self are aspects of the same phenomenon, not detachable from each other in the way needed for the above two questions to have any bite. I simply represents the aware-ness that a life — the particular life which is being experienced as a partic-ular life — is being led. As such, it is an aspect of the complexity which is self within the structure of reflective consciousness. In other words, the ability to say I, to be aware one is an I, flows out of, and is an aspect of, reflective consciousness; it is a dimension of being a reflective self.

From this perspective, the question becomes, rhetorically: who else could I possibly be other than myself? To be sure, in the context of my ex-istence, I could have developed in ways other than I have. I could have, that is, gone to a different school, chosen a different profession, married a dif-ferent woman. These are all distinctly intelligible possibilities, but if any or all of them had been acted out, I would still be NR, not some other person. That my historical development could have been other than it has been is one thing; that I could have been other than who I am is an entirely different matter, one which I wish to suggest is quite unintelligible. The I (or self) I am develops historically as I live my life. There is no I separate from such living which could have found expression in another life. That I can say "I am NR" is a consequence of my ability to be aware that I am living a life and that this life is particularized as the life of NR, but it is in no legitimate way suggestive of the possibility that I could have been someone other than NR.

These remarks do, I think, provide reinforcement for the view of self as involving psychological and bodily continuity. In addition, it reinforces various previously stated objections to the notions of self or mentality or consciousness as separate existents. From this perspective, self is a unity, not the unity that attaches to a self substance, but the unity of a coalition of elements. These elements are in constant dynamic interaction with each other and the environment and so the content of the unity is developmental and not abiding. In large part, continuity is maintained by the complex, pervasive, but obviously fallible senses of reflective and non-reflective mineness. Self is a coalition of elements of consciousness which involves psychological/bodily continuity and which is quite specific in detail to the historical and contemporary situation of the reflective organism.

The unity of self, then, is a unity with difference, not a unity of identity. Self ebbs and flows, develops and changes. But if this is so, it is possible that such unity can come apart and there no longer be a functioning self. Thus, the continuity over time of those elements which constitute self must involve a certain degree of stable overlap and this overlap must be available to awareness, even if the awareness is primarily, though it cannot be exclusively, non-reflective awareness. Just what this degree is is probably not possible to state in any precise form. But in a more fruitful and preliminary fashion, it does force us to look more carefully at a central feature of the development of reflective consciousness, namely, the phenomenon of unawareness, the realization that for reflective creatures much of consciousness is not at any particular time available to itself. And this includes the realization that at least sometimes what in consciousness is available to itself is neither properly grasped nor described.

Although the idea of "unavailability," as it relates to aspects of consciousness, is ambiguous and needs sorting out, I wish first to say something additional about the notion/experience of unity which is fundamental to being a self. Within the structure of reflective consciousness, one is a self to the extent one's consciousness is integrated or unified. Though this is obviously a matter of degree, one can be a self only insofar as there is coherence of consciousness. But the coherence (or unity or integration) that is relevant here involves awareness of the relevant phenomena, even though the awareness is largely non-reflective, as opposed to reflective. Indeed, the awareness is and must be largely non-reflective, though capable of becoming reflective, for non-reflective awareness allows for spontaneous — rather than impulsive — activity within the objective environmental situation. The greater the productive coherence of non-reflective awareness, the more there is a unified self and the more effective behavior is. And, of course, the less the productive coherence of non-reflective awareness, the less there is a unified self and the less effective behavior is.

However, when unity of non-reflective awareness disintegrates, we get fragmentation, but only within the self of reflective consciousness. A unity remains, but it is now a causal unity which operates at the level of unawareness, producing the behavior that the aware self of reflective consciousness is no longer capable of producing. The breakdown of self is a splattering of the coalition and the concomitant awareness — non-reflective and reflective — that is self, of the center which reflective consciousness develops in its awareness that it is living a particular life; it is not a splattering of the elements of consciousness which are unavailable to the center, but which are obliterating the center and are producing behavior.

It is the expectation that there is such unity and coherence attaching to what is presently unavailable, but causally effective, that gives hope not only for the re-establishment, in degree, of a coherent, integrated self, but for the productive development and growth of those selves which are largely functional and partially integrated — a description which probably holds for all selves, other than those which are largely non-functional and significantly fragmented.

VII

It is now appropriate to discuss the crucial problem of unawareness, or the unavailability to reflective consciousness of aspects of itself. First, some general remarks. That there is such unawareness and unavailability seems to follow directly from the phenomenon of reflective consciousness, for the structure of such consciousness involves one aspect of consciousness reflecting upon itself. But if this is a proper model, it is not possible for reflective consciousness to be aware of all that is ocurring within itself at any moment. Being in structure selective, the gaze of reflection can fasten on to this or that, but not this and that and everything else.

In addition, reflective awareness is limited by the structure of the reflective moment itself, for there are the conditioning factors which are involved in such moments. These cannot be captured by the particular reflective act, for they are the items which constitute the reflective act itself. To seek to capture these is to step out of the particular reflective act into a meta-reflective act and when this is done the same problem of unawareness emerges with respect to the meta-reflective act.

Reflective consciousness involves unawareness in still another sense. For if consciousness is developmental and historical, present consciousness is permeated, in complex and subtle ways, by past consciousness. We do not come to present experience with a pristine consciousness; rather we experience the present through a consciousness which is structured by past experience. Though present consciousness can, to various degrees, become aware of such phenomena, present consciousness is by no means ever fully aware of such phenomena. Having staked out a center (*i.e.*, a self) within the flux of experience — including, of course, the flux of consciousness — reflective consciousness is limited to that center, though the edges of that limit are not clear. What, as always, exacerbates these matters is that reflective consciousness can, as pre-reflective consciousness cannot, conceive the idea of awareness and so the idea of full awareness.

It might, however, be objected that the above remarks apply only or primarily to reflective consciousness in its aspect as reflective, but do not apply to reflective consciousness in its other aspect, namely, as non-reflective. Non-reflective consciousness does not involve the gaze of reflection and so it might be claimed is capable of providing full or at least fuller awareness of consciousness than can be provided by reflection. This is, I think, an important point which leads through a series of difficult and obscure distinctions to the phenomenon of integration. Non-reflective awareness involves the dim but ever present structure within which present experience is had. As such, it involves both different degrees of awareness or availability (both to itself and to reflection) and different degrees of "correctness" or "appropriateness" in relation to the environmental situation, including both the world and the creature. Because it does not involve the gaze of reflection, non-reflective awareness omits one form of unawareness, that which flows from the selectiveness of reflection. But it doesn't thereby omit all forms of unawareness. There is, first of all, the implicit selectivity involved in relating to the present environmental situation. One is in this situation and one's attention, at various levels, is focused on this situation. This, of course, need not be distorting and is in fact an important aspect of relating successfully to the situation at hand. But even here there is the selectivity of focusing on this, and not that, aspect of the situation and how this is done almost certainly involves deeper aspects of consciousness than is usually — if ever — grasped.

But beyond this is the realization that the structure of non-reflective consciousness may, in so many diverse ways, not be appropriate to the environmental situation. One may, that is, structure a situation inappropriately or mistakenly and act on the basis of such misperceptions without realizing they are misperceptions. In such a case, the unawareness would be two-fold, involving both the perception of the situation and the factors which are producing the misperception. As suggested above and in previous chapters, such misperceptions may emanate exclusively from the inherent limitations of non-reflective (and reflective) consciousness; but they need not. They can also stem, more narrowly and obscurely, from consciousnesses' misunderstanding of itself and its situation or place in the world. This very general misunderstanding is, of course, expressed both in a variety of ways and in a variety of situations. In what follows, I will attempt to say something meaningful about the general misunderstanding and will deal with specific expressions of the misunderstanding as they are needed to throw light on the general problem.

Self and Integration

![black bar separator]

Chapter Nine

I

The position reached is roughly the following. Due to the operation of environmental and physiological forces, certain creatures can no longer survive depending entirely on instinct. As a result, though this does not necessarily imply a teleological view of the life process, such creatures need to develop a source of behavior which involves a new, and so not essentially instinctual, type of understanding. The source of behavior is the center or self which is an aspect of reflective consciousness and the understanding involves the reflective awareness which occurs when consciousness can both be aware of itself and its awareness of the world. With such multiple awareness, consciousness can, at least in part, direct behavior in a self-aware, intentional fashion.

As the reflective standpoint, *i.e.*, the center or self, develops, pre-reflective awareness becomes irreversibly altered through permeation by the fruits of reflection. For the reflective creature, pre-reflective awareness is obliterated and in its place there is non-reflective awareness. Thus, the center or self (reflective consciousness) includes non-reflective consciousness, an altered and developed form of pre-reflective consciousness.

Reflective consciousness and its by-product, self, emerge from the details of the historical development of certain creatures. As such, self is not an abstraction, but is rather a concrete aspect of the lived experience of these creatures; self, that is, is inherently interconnected with and tied to such development. But if self is tied to such development and is to continue to serve its function as a source of understanding and action, it must, while maintaining a significant degree of core stability, also be capable of changing in response both to developments — some even self-initiated — within its own structure and in the world. For this and other reasons, I have suggested that self is, in part, a coalition of elements of consciousness serving an executive function; and that both unity and continuity of self are provided by the particular sense of mineness which is unique to the standpoint of reflective consciousness. However, I also suggested that this analysis was significantly incomplete and so claimed that something objectively psychological beyond the subjective feeling of mineness was needed if an adequate account of self was to be provided. In addition, it was suggested that any purely psychological account of unity and continuity of self was inherently incomplete and had to be supplemented by and tied to an account of bodily continuity.

What prompted the need for these additional criteria, especially the first, was the realization that reflective consciousness typically is not, and perhaps may never be, fully aware of itself. But if this is so, the sense of mineness, as central as it is in the emergence and creation of self (and reflective self-awareness) cannot be the sole criterion of unity and continuity of self. With reflective consciousness not transparent to itself, unawareness is apparently a necessary feature of such consciousness and so any criterion of unity and continuity which is subjectively based must be supplemented by an additional non-subjectively based criterion (or criteria).

But the unawareness which is an aspect of reflective consciousness also creates more specific problems, for unawareness can lead to fragmentation. This occurs when various aspects or elements of consciousness, *i.e.*, those not available to awareness, reflective and non-reflective, control other aspects of consciousness, primarily, the coalition which is self. When the elements of consciousness which are controlling understanding and behavior do not adequately understand themselves and their position in the world, self, in addition to being fragmented, becomes alienated from the world. Thus reflective consciousness, needing to act appropriately in the world, yet capable of misunderstanding both itself and the world, must, if it is to avoid the fragmentation and alienation which flow from the latter, come to grips with the various destructive forms of unawareness which plague it.

Because it is a coalition, the center or self can come apart in various ways and in various circumstances. The question of stability emerges not only with respect to the inherent factor of change given the kind of phenomenon self is, but also with respect to the different degrees of awareness which attach to individual selves, including even the most stable and psychologically centered selves. With this in mind, we need to see what it is which tends to destabilize selves and how such destabilization can be overcome. In a word, we're looking for what, in general, produces fragmentation and alienation and how such phenomena can be turned into integration.

In conjunction with the organism's physiological constitution, self must produce survival behavior. In order to accomplish this, a significant degree of fundamental stability must attach to the coalition which is self. As suggested previously, much, perhaps most, of this core stability emerges from self's relation to the fundamental "economic" dimensions of existence, i.e., the need to obtain food, shelter and clothing. Understanding of what is needed at this level, and how to obtain it, must remain relatively stable and constant if the creature is to survive. However, things of this sort, as well as other things not so fundamental to survival, such as power, prestige and the like, can come to have a meaning and significance other than and beyond that which relates to the primordial level of survival. When this occurs, the stability which attaches to self in its quest for survival can begin to come apart.

What is the new dimension of meaning and significance which develops and how does it lead to destabilization of self? I think the problem involves a misunderstanding of the center or self itself, a misperception of the range and "location" of self. What seems to occur is that self becomes not only the center of the particular creature's existence, but the very center of the whole of existence. For self, its own being becomes not only the center of all that is, but also the most favored and cherished object of attention. Indeed, both in unsubtle and quite subtle ways most, perhaps even all, attention is ultimately focused back on self.

Taking this as a difficulty may perhaps sound strange, for isn't the survival behavior which is the origin of the stability of reflective consciousness itself a focus on the self which is surviving? This, of course, is true, the emerging reflective creature seeks to survive, and, to do so, employs, quite spontaneously and innocently, its developing capacities, including the developing reflective center. Such use and the behavior which flows from it, however, is still considerably determined by physiological factors and is simply a slightly more complex variation of the survival behavior of all creatures, including pre-reflective creatures. The focus on self in such cases is not explicitly, or even implicitly, self-centered in the sense we are now talking about, for the kinds of developments which make such self-centeredness possible are, at this point, only in their formative stages.

The emerging reflective center or self which enables survival is simultaneously the source of its own instability. For given its emergence, it can now take itself as a separate, distinct existent and place itself at the center of all that is. Certainly, the reflective creature experiences the world through its perspective or center or self; but literally to take this perspective as the center of all that is and as what is most important in the world is a factual and an evaluational distortion. It is, I think, the cluster of psychological phenomena which attach to the perception, implicit or explicit, that one's perspective on the world is metaphysically central and valuationally supreme which destabilizes the center or self.

In general, what seems to occur is the following. So long as one takes self as the center of existence, one needs to remain unaware of the actual place of self within the wider range of existence. One cannot fully, or perhaps even partially, appreciate the emotional existence of others within their perspective; nor adequately appreciate one's own limitations including one's finitude, mortality and vulnerability; and, finally, one cannot appreciate the wider perspecitve afforded by a non-self-absorbed view of the developmental process of the universe itself. Such unawareness of reality produces defective beliefs, fantastic desires, unrealizable wishes and distorted and inappropriate emotions. It also produces a denial, or an attempt at a denial, of all the fears and uncertainties which attach to the not to be avoided realities of life. Not being properly aware of the realities of existence and so not capable of adequate emotional responses to such realities, self is inherently unstable in a way that goes well beyond the needed plasticity of the reflective center. Unaware of these dimensions of existence and often unwilling to become aware of and face these dimensions, including its own "nature," self comes apart in the face even of the edges of the awareness of these dimensions.

Such coming apart, however, is a relative matter. In fact, the coming apart, or fragmentation and alienation, of self can even be a more or less common cultural phenomenon. In a culture in which the realities of existence are not confronted directly, indeed are carefully hidden or overtly denied, the common mind set will be one in which significant unawareness permeates everyday consciousness. As a result, selves, at best, maintain a precarious stability.

The need to remain hidden or to deny leads to a situation in which what is acknowledged as self is limited to what is acceptable to a dimension of consciousness which, through a combination of sociological, historical and personal factors, cannot accept the realities of existence. Consequently, self does not adequately grasp its situation and so is not equipped to deal successfully with a variety of occurrences. When the aspects of reality, *i.e.*, the reflective creature's circumstance, which are not allowed into awareness, yet relentlessly display themselves, can no longer be entirely ignored or denied, self, as typically constituted, is not equipped to adequately recognize them and so is not able to deal with them effectively. This can destabilize self at the surface since the dimensions of consciousness which relate to the not properly acknowledged elements of reality can, unbeknownst to the creature, dramatically take over the executive function previously exercised by the apparently, but only superficially, stable self.

As suggested, this is a relative matter. All selves, however psychologically stable and centered or integrated, have areas and occasions of destructive instability. But the degree of such destructible instability does, I think, increase as self and its real and imagined needs and wants become more and more the preoccupation of the self which is aware it is a self.

Why and how does this preoccupation develop? What does it express? What I think is relevant here is roughly the following. As the reflective creature becomes explicitly aware that it *is* a creature, a particular creature, that is, a self living a life, the desire to hold onto this self, this life, becomes virtually overwhelming. The thought that the self which one is, the vantage point which one occupies, will no longer exist often becomes too forbidding even to entertain. Consequently, the self or vantage point is given a priviledged position, one radically incommensurate with the larger realities of the existence of the self, but one which corresponds to the yearned for centrality of the self. Indeed, we so gravitate to this centrality of self that we often find an inherent absurdity in the thought that the self will cease, transpire, as do all things which change, become.

The emergence of self as the limited self-director of life is simultaneously the emergence of the possibility of self seeing and experiencing itself as the very center of existence. What makes *human* life possible also provides the possibility for the distortion of such life. Failing to see and accept the place and limits of self in the flow of life, self needs to keep itself unaware of its situation and of its emotional reactions to this situation. As a result, everyday existence becomes limited, flat, distorted, escapist.

When the realities of life and feeling impinge strongly on awareness, a range of alternatives appear. One is that self, unable to deal with the strength and depth of the forces, massively destabilizes or comes apart. Another is that self may yet seek to maintain the *status quo* by continuing to deny and to remain hidden. There does, however, appear to be a limit to this strategy. But there is a third option, one which is more promising. This is to acknowledge the realities of one's situation, to deal with them in detail, and ultimately to realign one's sense of oneself with the realities of being a self in the world. It involves accepting and making peace with the fact that one is a self-aware creature living a life, but a life which is a limited and finite aspect of the process and which, like all else, comes and goes.

These last very general remarks need to be filled out in relation to concrete dimensions of experience. However, before venturing into these areas, I wish to say something further about the instability of self, for such instability is both the ground for increased self awareness and so growth, and for the breakdown of self as a functioning phenomenon.

As I have argued, self is not a substance, but is a coalition of elements serving an executive function for the creature. As such, self is a dimension of consciousness which grows out of and responds to its environmental and physiological situation. Self so conceived is, of course, dynamic, not static, and so lacks the permanence and stability that attaches to what is static. The dynamic nature of self enables it to meet changes in the world with altered and hopefully more adequate behavior; indeed, it enables self, as it becomes more aware of itself and its situation in the world to change in positive ways, *i.e.*, to grow. So the instability—or, perhaps better, the dynamic quality — of self is the condition for constructive adaptation to the life situation.

But self is also subject to change in another fashion and to this possibility the term "destabilize" applies. The phenomenon in question involves the loss of coherence of self, the increase, to significant degrees, of fragmentation and alienation. The less self accepts and acknowledges its plight, the more it has to manufacture elements within itself, such as attitudes, beliefs and desires, to keep this plight unacknowledged. As this occurs, more and more of self and so of consciousness is pushed into unawareness and more and more of self and consciousness become incoherent. The attempt is made to keep the surface of consciousness coherent, but it is a scissors and paste job, and in any case, the surface and what is below the surface become wildly at odds with each other. Consequently, the whole of consciousness becomes incoherent and so unstable. As the surface but false coherence of self undergoes further stress that, too, can break down and self can completely destabilize, leaving only the causally operating factors of consciousness.

Along the way of such destabilization, misperceptions of situations, along with ignorance of those factors within the individual which produce such misperceptions, produce impulsive behavior, behavior that is controlled by forces and elements within consciousness that the individual doesn't recognize and which are not appropriate to the individual's situation. But while such outcomes are common and may even be necessary as stages providing for the possibility of increased awareness and growth, they are, at the level now being discussed, not necessarily permanent. The dynamic nature of self and consciousness provide the reality within which the various operating elements can be slowly and patiently acknowledged both with respect to their force and appropriateness or inappropriateness. As a result, one can begin to see one's attachments to such elements and so also begin to see alternatives both with respect to attitude and belief, and to action. And, again, it is the dynamic nature of self and consciousness which makes possible the latter set of moves.

II

The above remarks lead into the perplexing and difficult problem of freedom. In the present context, the problem takes the form of whether or not the reflective creature has the ability to grasp its situation in its various dimensions with a new or expanded awareness and to initiate action which flows from or expresses such awareness.

But perhaps this statement of the problem is misleading, for there is little doubt that at least sometimes, some individuals do in fact achieve new and expanded awareness of themselves and their situation and do alter their orientation and behavior on the basis of such awareness. If this is so, the question is not whether or not this is possible, but rather what is involved when this does occur. This in turn, raises the question of the nature of the conditions within which such awareness does occur, including the details of the self (or, more broadly, the consciousness) which attains such awareness.

It is to be noted that freedom so understood is a phenomenon limited to reflective creatures. Pre-reflective creatures, not having the capacity to attain reflective or centered awareness, that is, not having a sense of themselves concerning which new awareness may emerge, cannot be said to be free — or unfree — in the sense now under consideration.

The freedom which is possible for reflective creatures consists of the creature's awareness of its situation, with this awareness involving the creature's *own* perception of the situation. This perception (or perceptions) is in its turn typically, though not always or necessarily, tied to action. From this perspective, it is of course obvious that such awareness (and action) and the freedom this expresses *always* occurs within a given or conditioned context, a context necessarily involving both the historical development within the sphere of consciousness in general and the particular consciousness in question. Freedom, then, is not only limited but indeed is made possible by the historical development of consciousness. It is a concept/experience which can arise only at a certain stage of the development of consciousness, the stage at which consciousness is capable of becoming reflectively or explicitly aware of its situation and attempts to direct its life in the face of that situation.[1] Thus, any notion of freedom which suggests the transcending of the flow of consciousness, the breaking out of consciousness and the world is, from the present perspective, impossible and so self-defeating. Whatever freedom is possible occurs within the flow of consciousness, within consciousness in the world. To think otherwise is to see self as a separate, self sufficient entity and to insure that whatever freedom is possible for human beings will not be attained.

Freedom, then, being one of the fruits of reflective consciousness, is both finite and must bloom within such consciousness. But now we face our daunting question: given that freedom is tied to awareness, self's awareness of its situation, what can we say of that awareness itself? With awareness always occurring in a context which is much deeper and so at least partially hidden from present awareness, do the efforts of the reflective creature have anything to do with producing new and expanded awareness? Or does such awareness flow from, and is it determined by, those deeper elements, irrespective of the efforts of the self? Another way of putting the matter, virtually universal in the literature, but modified to fit the present perspective, is to ask: can one become more aware of one's situation?

When the matter is put in the above fashion, the answer seems to be an unequivocal yes. As indicated above, unless we mean something quite idiosyncratic by "aware," it is quite clear that people become more aware of themselves and their situations. This is true, but as also indicated above, doesn't touch our problem at the needed depth. For what we are asking is: what is the nature of the activity which produces the requisite awareness? Is there an activity (or activities) on the part of the agent which enables a transcending, a seeing beneath not consciousness itself (for this is not possible), but the presently existing awareness of the individual? Or is such expanded seeing, granted that it occurs, simply the outcome of a set of causes working their way through and being expressed by consciousness, with agency being in no significant sense a contributor, but itself being an expression of the operating causes?

Perhaps another way of looking at the problem is the following. For any creature, there is the level of awareness of the moment. Let's call this first level awareness. Such awareness occurs within a wider and deeper structure of interconnected attitudes, beliefs and concepts. This structure provides the framework within which first level awareness occurs and, so it seems, while such awareness is occurring, the deeper structure is not itself available to awareness. Our question now becomes: given that elements of the deeper structure can become available to awareness, what is the process by means of which this occurs and can we call it "freedom?"

Although I think these various statements of the problem of freedom are helpful, I also think they contain two questionable assumptions. The first is that the expanded, second level awareness, is first and last reflective; and the second is that the requisite awareness stems from or is equivalent to a momentary, essentially discrete action. The two assumptions go together: if we think of awareness as reflective, we will also tend to think of such awareness as involving a specific and discrete action which takes place at a particular time.

On occasion, of course, awareness understood as a discrete, reflective act does occur; but I do not think such awareness is the only form awareness can take, or that it is necessarily the most productive form of awareness. Indeed, it often appears to be the best that a fragmented and alienated consciousness can achieve. Although, as indicated earlier, given the nature of reflective consciousness and the place of reflective creatures in the world, such awareness properly achieved is needed and productive, it is not, I think, connected to the core and most fundamental nature of freedom.

If we think of awareness as reflective and as occurring at a particular moment, we need also to think of such awareness as involving action. If we do so, we then have to contend with the question concerning the nature and origin of this act, or the effort (itself an act), to perform the act. Such a model involves a relatively sharp and distinct break with the existing awareness of the agent and leads to the puzzle of the source of the break. In response, we get talk about "effort" and "will" which, understandably, is often dismissed as being mysterious, non-explanatory and simply pushing the problem one step further back.

Perhaps a better model to employ here involves the mode of operation of non-reflective, as opposed to reflective, awareness. If we focus our attention on non-reflective awareness, we do not have to think of the emerging awareness as involving a distinct act for which effort or an act of will is needed. Non-reflective awareness increases when what, in the absence of the agent's awareness, was structuring experience becomes available to the agent, first at the level of non-reflective feeling and then at the level of reflective naming and notice. At the level of non-reflective feeling there is not, I think, a particular action of the agent involved and so no radical, sharp break within present awareness which stems from a particular act of awareness. Rather, there is a lessening of various controls or habits such that what is structuring these phenomena can be experienced, *i.e.*, felt, more directly. The loosening I am speaking of here occurs slowly, over time, and typically involves not one particular, isolable element of consciousness, but rather an overlapping, interconnected set of elements and structures.

But now our previously asked question reemerges: how is it that one, previously unable to directly experience elements of consciousness already in some sense present within the range of consciousness, can now do so? For example, doesn't this ability to make direct contact with such elements involve "effort" or "will?" Well, yes and no. Paradoxically, the more one tries to make contact with such elements, the less one is able to do so. This is because a certain sort of trying involves the attempt to get at something which can only be had, not by trying to get it—for that is to distance oneself from it—but simply by letting it shine forth. Although this may sound mysterious, the relevant awareness arises when one relaxes, ceases efforts to get at something, and allows feeling, emotion, belief, desire, mood, etc. to reveal themselves. At the most fundamental levels, effort doesn't work here, for such is an attempt to control, to make oneself get at that which is hidden; it is indeed, typically, an instance of separation in which one aspect of consciousness is, *within its own terms of operation*, searching out another aspect (or aspects) of consciousness. This other aspect of consciousness will reveal itself as the search for it diminishes and it is allowed to display itself. In a sense, what is needed is a cessation of trying; and, of course, one cannot, in the usual effortful and controlling sense of trying, try to do so.

If this is the preferred model of increased awareness, it allows rejection of the action model of awareness and enables us to see awareness as a slowly developing, interconnected, organic phenomenon. One's freedom involves the ability to gain a centered grasp of one's life situation. This, in turn, hinges on the ability to first become non-reflectively aware of one's deeper life perceptions and, subsequently, to purge these of the distortions which typically characterize them—especially those concerning the nature and range of self.

Having said the above, a number of problems need to be addressed. First, I have been insisting that increased awareness, properly conceived, does not involve a sharp break with existing awareness. But this seems not quite right, for if awareness increases, there is indeed a break with present awareness. The new element of awareness constitutes an alteration of , and so a break with, the present state of awareness. Although this seems correct, it does not, I think, detract from the points being stressed. The present concern is with the nature and origin of the break with present awareness. If we think of awareness as stemming exclusively or even primarily from a particular effortful act, two things seem to follow: 1) as indicated above, the break with present awareness will be radical and sharp; and 2) awareness so conceived would be initiated by what would have to be thought of as an *external* act. Even though the act (or act of will) would originate within consciousness, it would, in a very significant sense, nonetheless be external to present awareness. Such an act would not flow out of the internal movement of awareness; rather it would be instigated or imposed by a controlling aspect of consciousness, one which at the level of felt experience would be foreign.

It is this understanding of the break in awareness which I am rejecting. On my view, the break of new awareness arises out of consciousness itself, a consciousness which through the lessening of controls is able to reveal itself. The moment of awareness may indeed involve a sharp new realization; but such awareness does not originate in an act of will; rather it has been prepared for within the matrix of consciousness and arises organically and spontaneously within this matrix. Breakthroughs in awareness, then, are always conditioned. They occur within a context and maintain a continuity with what has preceded them, even though the expanded awareness, being new, does involve a break with present awareness.

These remarks take us into our second problem. If consciousness has to be prepared, loosened of its controls and habits, so awareness can expand, how does one get to such a point? To push the original problem back still farther: does one have the ability to get to the point where consciousness can reveal itself? And doesn't effort play a role here?

It is certainly the case that if self is rigid and controlling, not allowing the range and depth of consciousness to shine through, a good deal of effort and struggle is needed to alter such modes of operation. But the effort that is here expended is the effort of commitment, of persevering in one's attempt to see things differently. No doubt at various stages of this attempt, especially at the beginning, the effort involved will be conceived by the agent along the lines of a particular effortful act. If self is conceived as a separate entity, then, of course, awareness or insight will be seen as originating in an act of this self. Within a fragmented and alienated consciousness, increase in awareness will be seen as stemming from what in actuality is the source of the unawareness, the fragmentation and the alienation.

At this stage, effort or struggle has to do with self's sense of itself, its ability to see how its sense of itself and its understanding of gaining insight and alleviating difficulties is itself a significant source of the difficulties it is struggling with. But as insight concerning the nature of self and its place in the world surfaces, the struggle slowly subsides and so does the effort that is wrapped up within the struggle. Energy is now no longer attached to the struggle and it can express itself, organically and spontaneously, within the situation confronting self.

Can one — anyone — get to this stage? Theoretically, I think, the answer is yes. I have already indicated that the question is not "can one become more aware?" but rather "what is involved in becoming more aware?" If increased awareness is possible (and indeed actual), there is no theoretical barrier to such awareness and, it seems to follow, that if at least someone could become more aware, then, on that theoretical level, anyone could.

On a practical level, however, the situation is not so clear. Certainly, the more rigidly structured one's consciousness, the more defensively unaware one is, the less the likelihood one will be able to achieve the relaxed, open, trustful orientation within which increased awareness develops. From this perspective, the question concerning the agent's ability to do otherwise involves an essentially psychological or emotional focus, not just a logical one. Within certain psychological or emotional orientations, it is likely that an agent can do otherwise, i.e., can become aware, while within other psychological or emotional orientations, it is unlikely that an agent will have the ability to do otherwise.

Because psychological or emotional orientations are complex, interconnected and multi-leveled, it is quite doubtful that any sharp line can be drawn between the two general kinds of orientation. Perhaps, however, something of a helpful sort can be said concerning the difference between the two orientations. One major reason why certain psychological or emotional orientations can yield increased awareness is the awareness contained within them that one's present situation is marked by dissatisfaction or pain, and that, at least theoretically, there are alternatives available. Having such awareness keeps one from being thoroughly locked up within one's present orientation and provides a channel through which the present, predominant orientation can be opened up still further. In the absence of such awareness, one will insist that one's present situation is optimal and so no awareness which clashes with such optimality will be allowed to register in consciousness, that is, nothing short of sheer catastrophe.

One can, of course, now push the problem back still another step and ask if one has the ability to come to such a significant awareness. And, again, the response must be given in terms of present psychological or emotional orientation, with the added, and repeated, point that the awareness in question arises, when it does arise, not through a particular effortful act, but rather through the slow relaxing of controls, habits and defenses.

But now given that non-reflective awareness can expand — that elements of consciousness structuring experience, though hidden from direct awareness, can reach the surface of awareness — what is the nature of the purging of the distortions which mark non-reflective, and thus everyday, awareness? And, in addition, doesn't often maligned reflective consciousness play a significant role in such purging? Yes, I think explicit reflective awareness does play a significant role in such purging, for it is by means of this mode of consciousness that, via more primary felt awareness, self can make explicit to itself how it is actually experiencing itself and itself in the world — that is, what is believed, wanted, feared and the like. By making the relevant items, attitudes and orientations explicit, self is thrown back on itself and sees itself in a new light, indeed, in the best of circumstances, gains a new perspective. As such, self can confront itself with a new directedness at new levels. In this way, reflective consciousness plays a large role in increased awareness and in the attainment of an expanded freedom.

Reflective awareness, however, does *not* yield freedom simply be accepting as true either the various insights which it has attained through the expansion of non-reflective awareness or the ideals for living which have emerged through the realization of alternatives to one's present orientation. Simply knowing intellectually or rationally that some attitude, desire or belief is appropriate is not equivalent to feeling and living the attitude, desire or belief. In other words, the purging of distortions of everyday awareness is not, most fundamentally, an intellectual activity involving reflective consciousness. Rather, it is an activity — in the process sense of activity — involving the alteration of one's fundamental orientation in the world, of how one *actually experiences* oneself in the world. As a result of such ongoing alteration, one experiences oneself as part of the continuous, ongoing world process, not as a separate entity — a self — over and against the process.

From this perspective, freedom or its absence has to do with the way the reflective creature orients itself both to itself and to its life situation. If self is taken as the center of existence, as the hub around which the world turns, consciousness becomes permeated by distortions. Within such an orientation, freedom is not achieved, for adequate understanding of situations and their alternatives are not possible. Consequently, action will be less than optimal and the condition of the creature will deteriorate.

III

The discussion of freedom and how it relates to fragmentation and alienation, and so integration, has been very general, dealing with matters at a structural level and omitting virtually all reference to specific areas of life experience. It is necessary, therefore, to become more specific; to relate the general perspective not to the minutiae of life experience—even though it also has application there—but to more focused yet still general areas of life activity, such as morality and religion. Providing this application will help us see how, in general, the perspective of integration is experientially instantiated in various areas of activity, and how it informs the notions of "being moral" and being religious."

If, as has been suggested, the most basic dimension and cause of fragmentation and alienation is a misperception of self, an experience/idea of self as a separate, ongoing entity, then all instances of non-fragmentation, non-alienation, i.e., integration, will involve an absence — in degree, of course — of just such an experience/idea. Let's see how this claim gets spelled out first within the moral and then within the religious dimension of life.

If self, and self-identity, as an ongoing separate entity is an illusion, then any perspective on life which leads to or recommends accumulation to such a self must ultimately be distorting and unsatisfying. While accumulating to such a self might very well provide short term and surface satisfaction, in the long run and at depth such a mode of life must be unfulfilling. Feeding an illusion might provide some degree of satisfaction, especially when the illusion remains intact; but it cannot satisfy what is hidden by and beneath the illusion.

These considerations, however, must be seen within the awareness that one must tend to one's basic biological and psychological needs. Such tending is, of course, a tending to self; self, that is, seen not as a separate entity, but as an embodied self-reflective whole or organism existing within a larger life process. In many instances, however, it is no easy matter to distinguish between the distorted and the organic self. This is especially so when the attempt is made to grasp these phenomena within the context of interpersonal interaction. Not only on a theoretical level, but also and quite pressingly on a practical level as well, the complex of difficulties reveals itself in one's relationships with other people.[2]

There are some interesting consequences to the present perspective. If self as a separate ongoing entity is ultimately an illusion, it seems to follow that the person, and indeed *every* person, is a part, an aspect, an expression of the larger ongoing world process—and *equally* so. At this level, and perhaps at this level only, there is a sameness of persons. For as our focus becomes less general and more specific, there is the awareness—the individual awareness—of one's particular existence, with one's idiosyncratic and particular needs, wants and the like. The proper perspective of a reflective creature, then, involves a duality of awareness, though not a duality that implies discrete moments or areas of awareness.

The duality of awareness involves the realization that one is *simultaneously* both an individual *and* a collective being. It is not that one is, on this side, an individual being and, on that side, a collective being. Rather one is an individual being within one's collective being and a collective being within one's individual being. This last remark is not a strained attempt at paradox, but rather the outcome of two different moments in the *development* of reflective consciousness.

As suggested previously, it is out of one's participation in the public world that one gains or develops a sense of individuality. Historically, what is public precedes and makes possible what is private. But, then, out of the sense of individuality and privacy, a new sense of the public or collective *can* develop, a sense whose condition is precisely the awareness that one is a particular, individual creature, but one whose individuality is grounded, and necessarily grounded, in one's collective existence. On this view, individuality cannot—in reality—be separate from one's collective nature, and one sees and experiences one's individuality as including and involving one's collective nature.

However, it is of course possible to fail to grasp the embeddedness of one's individuality within one's collective existence, and so to see self as separate and self-sustaining. When this occurs, and it is almost certainly the predominant orientation of consciousness in our time, a deep wedge is driven between sense of self and the full range of not-self. As a result of this wedge or split, a variety of popular and philosophical versions of egoism have developed. In its descriptive form, egoism claims that human beings are motivated to act only in terms of their perceived self-interest; and in its normative form, egoism suggests that one's only duty is to promote one's own self interest. Inevitably, such doctrines explicate self-interest in terms of a separate, self-sustaining self, acknowledging others and their interests only insofar as these impinge on and thereby have an impact upon one's own interests. Such doctrines do, of course, recognize an element of sociality in the lives of people, but because of their view of self and self-fulfillment, it is an external, not an internal, sociality.

In a very interesting fashion, egoistic doctrines are countered by a variety of non-egoistic, collectively oriented doctrines. These quite common doctrines are also expressed on both a popular and a philosophical level and insist that self is not, and/or ought not be seen as ultimate and final. This perspective, however, is more of an intellectual doctrine or ideology than a felt reality. All sorts of lip service is paid to such doctrines; and, in addition, a great deal of intellectual effort is expended trying to refute the contrary doctrines. But on the level of orientation, desire and behavior—especially when such is not constrained by various negative sanctions—it is the egoistic perspective which rules the day.

At some level, then, there has occurred the insight or insights which lead to the rejection of egoistic orientations; but these insights have not been internalized, they have not become part of the lived orientation, the actually felt perspective of acting individuals. Consequently, the behavior which would express the realization, the *felt* realization that one is, as are all others, part of the ongoing life process typically is not forthcoming. This, however, is not to claim that behavior which recognizes the interests and the well-being of others does not occur. Of course, there is such behavior; but unfortunately much of it seems to stem from some variation or other of the fear of punishment or disapproval or low self-esteem, or the supposition that it is one's duty so to behave. In none of these cases does the behavior flow from and express the realization that the other, like oneself, is an aspect, a part of, the life process. In the instance of "being moral" to avoid punishment and the like, the focus, obviously enough, is on oneself; and in the case of doing one's duty, one typically, though not always, is responding to an externally produced sense of obligation, not an internally originated orientation toward others.

What seems to follow from the above remarks is that for behavior to be *moral*, it must flow from a certain kind of awareness, the experiential awareness that one is not a separate entity but is, like all others, part of the ongoing life process. In its turn this suggests that, most fundamentally, morality is not a matter of action or doing, but rather a matter of character or being. Of course, this does not imply that action is insignificant or unimportant. It only implies that action or doing is not the most fundamental aspect of the moral life and the reason for this is not very obscure. Two bits of behavior can on their surfaces look exactly alike, yet be motivated in radically different ways. One goes out of one's way to help someone in some degree of distress. The motive, the underlying feelings, concern the well-being of the other, the realization that the other is in pain. Here what I would call "moral motivations" fuel and produce the action and give it its moral appropriateness or correctness or, if preferred, its rightness. Now consider another case. The situation of the distressed and the action of the helper are identical to the first case. But in this situation, the motives of the helper involve not the well-being of the other, but the desire to win the confidence of the other so that at some point in the future the helper will be able to take advantage of, and dominate the other. If we say that morality is fundamentally a matter of action or doing, we will have to say that both actions are equally correct, and this seems quite absurd.

For this reason, we are led into a morality of character or being, a morality which locates the appropriateness, correctness or rightness of actions not in their surface features (or in the consequences they produce) but in the inner states from which they proceed.

But there is an additional consequence to these remarks. If motives or inner states determine the rightness of actions rather than either the intrinsic properties of actions or their consequences, then, as we've been suggesting, character or being is more fundamental than action or doing. But if this is so, it seems to follow that the morality — as opposed to immorality — of persons is determined not by their actions but by their character or inner state. If particular actions can flow from a variety of motives — some sublime and some vile — then it cannot be action which determines the morality of the agent. The latter, rather, must be determined by the motives, the inner state which produces action.

These remarks immediately prompt two questions: 1) what is the inner state (or states) which are the mark of the moral person and which produce moral action; and 2) what is the source (or sources) of this inner state (or states)? At the most general level, the inner state (or complex of inner states) which is the mark of the moral person and produces moral action is the *experiential* realization that each person, including oneself, is equally a product, a manifestation, of the ongoing life process. Although significantly different from oneself, each person is also in a significant sense the same as oneself. In relating to others, I am simultaneously relating to myself, but not to myself experienced as a separate entity; rather to myself as, identical with others, a self in the midst of the flow of the life process.

This realization involves what we can call internal, as opposed to external, sociality. It is the recognition of the *organic* or *inherent* community of persons. Persons are fundamentally and necessarily communal; they do not, as separate individuals, come together in any sense to form a community. The experiential understanding that individuality emerges from, and does not precede, the life flow enables one to see others as internally related to oneself, rather than as externally related separate entities who, out of "artificial" necessity, have to be dealt with.

What, then, is the source of the inner state (or states) which produce moral behavior? It is the experiential realization that I am not a separate self over and against others and the life process. To the extent there is the sense that there is an I, a separate self, there will typically be the perspective of me versus others; and in the midst of such a perspective, situations can seldom be approached in a fair, objective fashion. If self is separate and central, this self's perspective is taken as special and overriding. The particularized needs and wants of this self, whatever their merits from a wider perspective, are taken as fundamental and compelling. So long as all, or most, persons maintain this perspective, the likelihood of moral and genuinely caring behavior is meager. What one gets instead is a modified Hobbesian "war of all against all," papered over with various other regarding ideologies and the demands and obligations of "morality."

The above remarks might lead one to think that it is being suggested that all one has to do is cultivate the proper inner state (or states) and automatically moral action will follow. This is not being suggested, for interactions with others are ambiguous, complex and often obscure. Simply feeling a certain way, having a certain orientation to self and others is not, by itself, going to produce moral action — and still less is it necessarily going to produce productive and helpful action.

For the latter to occur, a great deal of thought, insight and the weighing of alternatives must take place. In the absence of such activities, action can be forthcoming which though perhaps well intentioned is neither moral, nor helpful, nor constructive. This comment may suggest an inconsistency with my previous claim that it is one's motive, one's inner state, which determines the morality of action. Here I seem to be suggesting that a well-intentioned act, while perhaps not being immoral, may certainly not be moral. But what is being questioned here is a popular—and sometimes philosophical—sense of "well intentioned" in which such intentions are tied essentially to feelings and kept separate from thought or reason. It is held that feeling by itself is productive of moral action; and it is this suggestion that is being challenged, for to think of morality as flowing from feeling so conceived is to fragment, and compartmentalize the person and so to miss the centrality of integration, the organically whole person, in the production of moral action. The popular and usual notion of "good intentions" exemplifies the fragmentation of self and so almost certainly expresses an ideology concerning morality rather than the genuineness of an integrated orientation toward self and others.

If an integrated orientation toward self and others produces well-intentioned action in a more adequate sense of "well-intentioned," is such action also moral? I think so; but it need not also be productive or helpful. The action situation may be quite complex and obscure and so what appears to be "right" action may yet yield results which are not productive; or the situation may be inherently tragic, allowing only for harmful and destructive consequences. In such situations, the behavior is moral, yet the consequences negative.

Conversely, however, in the absence of the relevant inner states and orientations, moral behavior will not be forthcoming. No doubt actions will be produced which, at their surface, will be identical with what I am calling moral action and which may very well exemplify one's duty. However, I am suggesting that such actions, such compliance with duty, while displaying the form of moral behavior, precisely lack the inner dimension, the core or content of moral action, which can only be supplied by one's orientation to self and others.

There is a distinct sense in which the orientation to self and others which is productive of moral action can be called "love." The experiential realization that one is identical to other persons in the sense that others, like oneself, are particular expressions of the life process, produces a sense of mutuality and intimacy with their existence that enables a very general, yet deep, connection to them. To be sure, the degree of intimacy with others does not match the degree of intimacy with oneself, for the sense of mineness and the realization that I am living a life are experientially uniquely my own. However, the commonality of source of existence and life situation, including the stages along life's way, yields an orientation toward others that is not even remotely possible as long as one experiences oneself as a separate, disconnected self. My suggestion is that it is this experiential sense of mutuality and intimacy, *i.e.*, love, which is the ultimate and perhaps only source of genuinely moral action.[3]

As suggested above, it is important to see that these remarks (and experiential insights) concerning the source of moral action solve no particular problems. Orientation toward self and others establishes the framework within which particular actions are forthcoming. On a day-to-day basis, the orientation of mutuality and intimacy will typically produce behavior which is considerate and caring. Indeed, such behavior will become virtually habitual, not in the sense of unthinkingly and unconsciously regular and rigid, but in the sense of spontaneously flowing from orientation of character. The orientation or stance becomes absorbed within one's consciousness and action can occur with non-reflective awareness, that is, with little or no reflection. But not all moral situations can be handled in such a spontaneous, non-reflective fashion. Often, much reflection, thought and the weighing of alternatives is required. As suggested above, in such situations orientation cannot, by itself, produce solutions; there is no recipe for grinding out solutions to moral problems.

There is an additional consequence to this perspective. It is that fundamentally, morality cannot consist of a set of rules or principles, the following of which yields moral action and a moral person. To be sure, rules or principles can be generated from the orientation of love, but simply acting on the rules does not, by itself, constitute moral action, and whatever justification can be given for the rules is to be found within the perspective from which they arise, not from some standpoint outside any and all perspectives.

Simply acting on rules or principles cannot be equivalent either to acting morally or being moral, for one can accept and act on rules for any of a variety of motives, *e.g.*, one has been told the rules are "correct," one is afraid of being punished if one violates the rules, or one has "reasoned" that such and such a rule is correct, etc. What the rules dictate may indeed be what the loving person would do, but in the absence of the orientation, the motives, of the loving person, the action is probably self-serving and, almost certainly, empty.

There is, of course, no doubt that generalizations or rules or principles can be generated from the orientation of love. Indeed, there may even be situations in which the generated rule (*e.g.*, do not steal) is treated as the justifying element in the complex of behavior. But while this may be an occurrence in practice, I am suggesting that the rule itself has no justificatory power. What, if anything, justifies the behavior—and the rule—is the perspective or orientation out of which it flows. One needs to look back to the source, and the perception of reality contained therein, to see how action might be justified.

This suggestion, of course, leads to further problems, for if we seek to justify behavior and rules by means of the perspective out of which they flow, we will also want to ask about the justification of the perspective itself. Doing so, we will probably seek something outside of the perspective—indeed, outside of all perspectives—because if we do not find such, we will continually be seeking to justify the larger perspective, *ad infinitum.* But throughout these chapters my suggestion has been that when we are talking about the operation of consciousness, there is no possible standpoint outside some standpoint or other of consciousness. We can, of course, seek to justify the perspective of love; but in doing so we will simply be working on, *i.e.*, altering, modifying and expanding this perspective of consciousness. Thus, any justification of any "product" of consciousness must be found within some perspective or other of consciousness.

How, then, might we attempt to justify the orientation of love? We might begin by looking carefully at the human situation. Doing so will help us see how it is necessarily social and how consciousness through its ability to self-reflect comes to have a complex sense of itself, others and the relationship between self and others. This orientation to self and others can then be seen to have a quite large and fundamental impact on qualify of life, both individual and collective. We might then wish to compare two different ways of life: one involving the experiential realization that self is an aspect of the larger life process, not a separate, ongoing entity; the other experiencing self as indeed a separate, ongoing entity.

This mode of justification, then, originates in claims concerning the relationship of self to the life process, in claims concerning the consequences of alignment versus non-alignment of self to this process. But such a mode of justification involves a distinct limitation, for the various claims involved are themselves claims of consciousness. Consciousness is, indeed, in the extraordinary position of having to evaluate variations of consciousness, *i.e.*, evaluate itself.

But this general realization has a more specific and disquieting form. For the orientation of love is a descriptive/normative *ideal* and indeed one which may not and most often is not attained. Consequently, the problem of justification takes on a further, and perhaps even crippling, form. For it appears to be consciousness in its disconnected form which has to determine what consciousness ought to be. With the determination of consciousness internal to itself, and with consciousness having lost its way, the result is almost certainly the creation, by consciousness, of justifications of its ways which are thought of as involving what is external to itself, but are in reality additional and distorted wrinkles of consciousness. Such is a further alienation of consciousness from itself.

There is a sense in which the problem of justification is quite real, indeed pressingly real, for obviously consciousness can generate all manner of destructive nonsense. The problem, however, cannot be alleviated by seeking to transcend consciousness. The human predicament is such that clarification, clarity and connection emerge as consciousness and its situation are plumbed, not by some pristine, non-structured ray of light, but by the very structures of consciousness itself.

IV

The perspective on morality has been set forth within a set of wider considerations concerning the relationship of the individual—and individual awareness—to the larger life process. Although self can be experienced and thought of as a separate entity, this is a distortion; self, rather, is a manifestation or expression of the larger world or life process. It is a temporary, changing coalition or center of various sorts and depths of awareness. As such, there is a unity of self with other selves, though a unity which necessarily involves individuality and individual difference. This understanding of unity, however, does not primarily provide a reason for or an obligation to consider and care for others. No doubt these can be generated from such understanding and also can, in at least some cases, engender action. But reasons and obligations, derived as they so often are essentially from thought or understanding, though laudable, are typically feeble and fragile. They do not, that is, have their source in an integrated orientation of the person. As such, reasons and obligations are not only feeble and fragile, they are also often ideological, expressing what one aspect of the person thinks ought to be rather than the whole person's actual orientation.

The suggestion is rather that as one comes to *experience, feel,* the unity of selves, to see through one's constructed sense of isolated separateness, one experiences others in a new light and behavior develops spontaneously which is less pre-occupied with self and more focused on others in their similar life situation. The moral perspective, then, is informed by a deeper and more fundamental insight into and *relationship* to the world or life process. What yields consciousness, self and others is the world or life process and it is to "this" that one needs to align oneself.

These last remarks propel us into what we can call the "religious dimension of life," that dimension of life which involves one's sense of and relationship to what is felt to be, experienced as, most fundamental or ultimate in life. The use of the word "ultimate" here is at least somewhat misleading, suggesting as it does that there is something, or something or other, which is in fact ultimate. Of course, many religions or religious orientations have indeed seen ultimacy as exemplified in some kind of (at least apparent) entity. While the present work recognizes the notion/reality of ultimacy, it does so *only* as pertaining to the world process itself. From this vantage point, the process is not seen nor experienced as an entity of any sort; nor is it thought of or experienced as creaturely or personal.

Throughout the history of thought, considerable energy has been expended attempting to ascertain the nature of ultimacy. Like all expressions of consciousness, these explorations have been changing and developmental. And as would be expected of a creature who comes to experience — indeed appears to create — the reality of individuated, personal agency, ultimacy also comes to be thought of as individuated, personal agency, though of course eventually on a scale that infinitely surpasses creaturely agency.

This perspective is one instance of the very common, though far from universal, perception of ultimacy as a separate, creative, personal "being" who has made and continually sustains the universe. Within this perception of ultimacy, the existence and presence of this being, God, is absolutely central. It is He who allegedly gives life its purpose and meaning. If God does not exist or is absent, life is said to be without meaning and perhaps not worth living.

It is clear that within this particular perception of ultimacy, a central — perhaps *the* central—distinction is between theists and atheists. Theists accept the existence of God; atheists do not. Consequently, theists are said to have something which atheists do not. The former are connected to, aligned with, what gives life meaning and makes it whole, while atheists are not, leaving them disconnected, alienated and fragmented.

There are at least two things to say here. First, the theist's professed connection to ultimacy cannot simply be one of belief, for as we have seen belief can in any number of ways be ideological and self-deceptive, significantly disconnected from the deeper and actual sources of belief, feeling, attitude and behavior. Thus, we have the spectacle of many people professing their connection to ultimacy or God through belief, asserting their "awareness" that all that is — including, of course, other people — equally expresses God's creation, yet acting in substantial disregard of such awareness.

Second, and more fundamentally, there is the question of the accuracy and plausibility of the theist's rendition of ultimacy. Certainly, there are no hard and fast proofs available in this area; but it is at least suspect when an essentially feeble, and even in some significant ways helpless, creature reproduces itself in a grander variation as ultimate reality; indeed, when it is precisely the emerging development of consciousness, its awareness of individual, separate existence and agency which becomes infinitely and externally enlarged and projected onto the world's screen.

As so often happens, however, I do not wish to get side-tracked on this particular issue, for I think there is a deeper dimension to this problem, one which both theistic and non-theistic orientations recognize, but which is often obscured when all or most attention is focused on whether or not what the theist perceives as ultimacy exists outside of that perception. The deeper dimension is that the critical component in the kind of life one lives, whether it is meaningful and fulfilled, or, alternatively, disconnected and ultimately empty, depends on whether or not one aligns with ultimacy. This, of course, does not eliminate the question of the nature of ultimacy, for if connection to ultimacy is fundamental, we indeed need to have a sense of what ultimacy is. But it does point the way to what appears to be a deeply significant element in the human situation, one whose importance has gained near universal recognition, either explicit or implicit.

If we treat the interpretation of ultimacy as involving a separate, personal being as one particular interpretation among others and focus instead on the larger question of alignment versus non-alignment, we can re-cast the "religious" question in a more fruitful fashion. The question would not be: do you or do you not believe in God? or, are you or are you not aligned with God? but rather: do you or do you not experience life as meaningful, as worth living? On this emphasis, the significant distinction is not between those who do and those who do not believe in God, but between those who do and those who do not find meaning in life, experience life as worth living. The focus on ultimacy as God, and the usual understanding of the theism/ atheism distinction misplaces a more fundamental and central insight concerning the generation of, as well as the inability to generate, meaning in life. In effect, it distracts us from exploring and dealing with our most general and fundamental orientation toward life.

But now our question becomes: what allows some, but prevents others, from finding meaning in life? The answer, I think, is to be found in one's sense of self. If one experiences oneself as separate, as an entity unto one self, that is, as a being which is socially and metaphysically self-sustaining, one becomes alienated from the life process, from ultimacy. As such, one loses one's grounding in what is both the source and the foundation of one's existence. Having done so, there is no possibility of creating *authentic* meaning, for what supplies the conditions for such meaning has been lost. The absence of the needed ground, however, does not halt the quest for meaning. The latter continues, but can now focus only on the particular self. And thus we get a full range of attempts to prop up, sustain and feed the private, disconnected self. Unfortunately, however, the disconnected self cannot manage to fulfill itself on its own. Quite simply, it does not have the resources to do so. To attempt to do so is not only a psychological mistake; more gravely, it is a metaphysical mistake.

Consequently, selves drift in various degrees of aimlessness and/or self-deception. Unthinkingly, the various myths of one's culture are internalized, so that one does not directly experience the aimless drift. In many cases, one seeks to amass things, power and prestige so that one feels substantial and has purpose. But as satisfying and as heady as such accumulation can be in the short run — and sometimes even in the longer run — it is ultimately vacuous and unfulfilling, for it seeks to substantiate one's existence by what is taken into self, not by what constitutes and informs individual existence.

Without a proper grounding in the life process, there is often a deep, vague and substantially hidden sense of malease or disquiet. This sense of malease is often accompanied by a restlessness and frantic busyness, the deeper object of which appears to be the maintenance of the obscurity and vagueness of the malease.[4] All is done to keep one's actual situation from coming to the surface to be seen clearly. To bring it to the surface would involve confronting one's life situation and this, typically, seems too much for a creature who is reflectively aware of its individual existence, but whose understanding of its larger plight is severely limited—probably necessarily so—and whose existence is finite and mortal.

The contemporary preoccupation with the existence or non-existence of God tends to obscure and distort the more fundamental and significant problem. However, the deeper problem — separation from the life process out of which self emerges—has been recognized in a variety of contexts and traditions. In the midst of such separation, one is severed from the ground of one's being and so also the standpoint within which one can create a meaningful, fulfilled life. As a result of such severance, the private self is assigned the status of ultimacy and basic reality. This has dire consequences since it distorts the nature and place of self and so creates an imbalance between self and not-self, i.e., others and the world. In a word, it miscalculates the place of and the importance of self and sets the distorted and fantastic interests of the misconceived self over and above the life process and all its other manifestations.

What is more than intriguing about all of this is that it is consciousness itself in its developmental movement which creates the possibility of such severance and disconnection. Yet, it is also consciousness which is able to recognize the situation and attempt to create a new form of alignment — one which is built out of the actuality and necessity of separate, individual, action-guiding awareness. It appears, then, that consciousness needs to pull itself up by its own bootstraps. And this can, of course, lead one to see a tragic, an unalterably tragic dimension to human life. But it also leads one to see that within the parameters of the life situation, it is consciousness which must create the future. This complex, no doubt, is simultaneously the despair and the joy of the human situation.

NOTES

Chapter 1. Philosophy of Mind and the Problem of Personal Integration

1. A possible exception is that recently a number of philosophers have focused their attention on the emotions.
2. Although this statement of the matter is unexplained and dogmatic, my reasons for such a claim will become clear as we proceed.
3. "Folk Psychology is Here to Stay," *The Philosophical Review*, XCIV, No. 2. (April, 1985), p. 197.
4. "Eliminative Materialism and Propositional Attitudes," *Journal of Philosophy*, LXXVIII, No. 2 (February, 1981), pp. 79–84.
5. (MIT Press: Cambridge, MA), 1984, p. 97.
6. *Ibid.*, p. 46.
7. These matters will be taken up in greater detail in succeeding chapters.
8. These remarks may suggest that I think integration and fulfillment are either/ or phenomena rather than matters of degree. I do not think this is so, but it is easier at this point not to provide all the needed distinctions and modifications.
9. This is a simplified version of a much more complex phenomena. While indifference is not the deeper, actual mental state of the individual and so is not functioning at that level, the belief or insistence that indifference is the individual's actual mental state enables it to function — albeit, sporadically and inconsistently — at the surface level.
10. Unless, of course, such states become a part of our larger network of mental states either by their affecting or being affected by other of our mental states or by our attitudes toward them, or both.

Chapter 2. Conceptual Understanding and Personal Integration

1. This needs qualification and will be dealt with more fully in later chapters. "Total integration" may indeed be possible at a moment. This would occur when one was spontaneously immersed in some activity or other, say, some bit

of writing, or dancing, or conversing, etc. Total integration in another sense would be seen as a fixed state which involves a static, non-fragmented psyche. It is this notion which I think is defective and should be distinguished from an increase or increases in those moments in which an individual is dynamically and spontaneously involved in various activities. Theoretically, the limit of such increases would be a state of total integration, dynamically understood. Whether such can be achieved in actuality is a difficult question.

2. Some of what will be said here is an elaboration and application, within the present context, of remarks made in Chapter 1.

3. It has, of course, been claimed that there are certain *a priori* structures of thought or language or both, and that these have not simply emerged in the course of living. I probably agree with a version of this claim. However, the extreme generality of what could be *a priori* in this fashion does not detract from the historical nature of the content of consciousness, and therefore the relevance of the latter to any understanding of self, consciousness and integration. In addition, if there are ahistorical, *a priori* structures of thought and/or language, these can only be discovered through an exploration of thought and/or language themselves, *i.e.*, through consciousness. In short, the centrality and indeed priority of the standpoint of consciousness in the generation and evaluation of concept and theory cannot be avoided. This, perhaps, is the ultimate *a priori* element in the structure of reflective consciousness.

4. Although much in the way of details and modification is needed here, these remarks are to a significant extent, consistent with recent claims that pre-reflective creatures, *i.e.*, non-human animals, are conscious and have mental experience. (See D. Griffin, *The Question of Animal Awareness, Rev. Ed.*, (Rockefeller University Press: New York, 1981).) Certainly the stress on evolutionary continuity of mental experience is pre-supposed in my remarks, as is the claim that pre-reflective creatures are conscious. Where perhaps I part company with Griffin is in his claim that, although very large, there are only quantitative, not qualitative, differences between non-human animal consciousness and human consciousness. A large enough quantitative difference, however, might produce a qualitative difference. And this is what I think occurred with the emergence of reflective consciousness. Our ability to reflect on our consciousness and ourselves, and so explicitly experience ourselves as separate entities, creates a unique awareness.

5. For Perry, see "Frege on Demonstratives," *The Philosophical Review*, LXXXVI, No. 4 (Oct. 1977), pp. 474–97, especially pp. 487–8; and for Lewis see "Attitudes 'De Dicto' and 'De Se,' " *The Philosophical Review*, LXXXVIII, No. 4 (Oct. 1979) pp. 513–43, especially pp. 524–6.

Chapter 3.   Consciousness and Personal Integration

1. My talk of exclusive or pure physicality as a mark of non-consciousness and "something" more, etc. as a mark of consciousness should not be taken as a commitment to dualism. The contrast is between the sort of physicality which is a property of, say, rocks and the sort of physicality which is a property of conscious creatures. There is obviously some sort of difference and it is that difference I am trying to get at.
2. *The Character of Mind* (New York: Oxford University Press), 1982, pp. 13 – 14.
3. *Ibid.*, p. 14.
4. These remarks might suggest something I denied in Chapter 2, namely, that we have a certain sort of relationship to ourselves. The emergence of a reflective standpoint enables us to have a sense that we are living a life, indeed enables us to provide a name for this life which we are living. In its turn, this ability creates the possibility — expressible in a number of different ways — that we may experience ourselves as separate from that life. This occurrence, I have suggested, is a form of alienation, perhaps the extreme instance of which is amnesia. The development of the standpoint, however, is grounded in pre-reflective immersion in experience. Reflection expands this immersion into reflective awareness of living a life and when this awareness is, in its turn, absorbed into non-reflective awareness, we have a non-separated, unified mode of existence, which is living the life of the person one is.
5. I am thinking in part of the social contract tradition, beginning with Hobbes and continuing through Rawls.
6. An additional possibility, not in principle different from these alternatives, is as a preliminary to, or general locator for, introspection as revelation.
7. And, extending the point, the same question is raised concerning our knowledge of not-self or the world. This variation of the problem will be taken up in the next chapter.
8. In this case, "unconscious" refers to the amalgam of physiological forces — even those or their aspects which can be said to be non-conscious — those elements which could be conscious but are not, and those elements which were at one time, but are not now, available to consciousness.

Chapter 4.   Consciousness, Knowledge and Error

1. Since pre-reflective creatures also act — or behave — in the world, the notion of value, at least in the sense of raw preference, is also applicable to them. Such preferences, however, flow essentially from instinct, not from a constructed reflective standpoint. Thus, the sense in which such creatures "have values" is very different from the sense in which reflective creatures do.

Chapter 5.   Consciousness, Pain and Error

1. This usage of "felt or experienced . . . " is different from its use to refer to the pre-reflective differentiations of pre-reflective creatures. The present usage points to a phenomenon *within* reflective consciousness, namely, the ability to be reflectively aware of the differentiations of reflective consciousness.
2. It is not entirely clear how what is not now pain could have been pain. On Functionalists' grounds, it seems possible that presently non-existing functional states could have existed and could have been pain. What is less clear is whether presently existing functional states now identified with mental states other than pain could rather have been identified with pain. In his "Mad Pain and Martian Pain," David Lewis seems to reject this latter possibility. The paper appears in N. Block (ed.), *Readings in Philosophy of Psychology: Vol. I.* Cambridge, Mass: Harvard University Press), 1980, pp. 216–222. See especially p. 218.
3. However, as suggested previously, the feeling of pain need not be acknowledged in the sense that the pained individual identifies it as pain. This is consistent with our contention that there is a class of pains such that one can be in pain and not know it. For pains of this sort to function, they need not be identified as pains, only painfully felt. However, in the absence of conscious identification, *i.e.*, direct feeling, the modes of operation of such pains may not be typical or obvious.

Chapter 6.   Desire

1. On this point, see R. Wollheim, *The Thread of Life* (Cambridge: Harvard University Press), 1984, pp. 174–176 and *passim.*

Chapter 7.   Belief

1. A possible, though unimportant, exception to this claim would be tautologies, a sentence of the form A is A. A more significant exception would arise from sentences which could be said to be both synthetic and necessary. This is an immense topic which has recently received subtle and extensive attention. See W. V. Quine, "Two Dogmas of Empiricism," in *From A Logical Point of View* (Harper & Row: New York), 1963, pp. 20–46, and S. Kripke, *Naming and Necessity* (Harvard University Press: Cambridge, Mass.), 1980. There is a sense in which some of my remarks can be taken to suggest the existence of "necessary facts" concerning human existence. Perhaps the most obvious of these is my claim that we are always ultimately embedded in experience, that we are always immersed in some experience or other. The certainty here, however, attaches not so much — indeed, perhaps not at all — to the sentence or

statement involved, the reflective awareness of the phenomenon, but to the experience itself. What cannot be the case is that I am not immersed in experience, some experience or other, even if it is not the experience I would describe myself as being immersed in. The belief that I am immersed in some experience or other seems, on one level, to be a purely formal, contentless claim, perhaps akin to a necessary statement, although I am well aware that most contemporary philosophers would not typically treat it as such and that many thinkers not only would deny it a status as necessary, but might even deny its truth. Of course, once a content is provided for such a belief, it is no longer necessarily true, for the characterization of the experience may, in any number of ways, be inadequate.

2. Except perhaps in the case of certain kinds of organic sensations. See Chapter 5 for discussion of this matter.

3. Those, for example, who claim that all perceptions involve beliefs.

4. There is a slight complication with respect to those beliefs directly extractable from perceptual situations, for in such cases there is a phenomenology present. However, it is that of the sensible appearance, not of the extractable belief.

5. Recall, one is *always* immersed in consciousness (experience); there is no non-immersed mode of consciousness (experience). The question is: which mode or wrinkle of consciousness (experience) is one immersed in and with what degree of awareness?

6. These remarks do not negate my previous point that *all* the experiences of reflective creatures are mediated by elements derived from reflection. The form of mediation under discussion is, at least in many cases, an unnecessary addition.

Chapter 8. Fragmentation, Alienation and Self

1. It might be suggested that unawareness is simply unawareness and so cannot be talked about in terms of degrees. At one level, this is probably correct, but what I have in mind are the contrasts available for those elements of one's psyche which are deeply buried and repressed, and those which are readily available to awareness via surface clues expressed in talk, expression, desire and belief. For example, the anger which one may not acknowledge, but is visible through comment and facial expression involves much less unawareness than would the deeper source of such anger originating, say, in certain childhood experiences.

2. However, a substance view of self need not entail an identity without difference view of self, for one could say that the substance itself changed while still being the same substance.

3. Of course a similar inclusion would be needed in the analysis of unity of self at any particular time.

4. If self is thought of, dualistically, as a substance, then mentality and consciousness are also tied, necessarily, to the substance which is self. Thus, the mind/body problem becomes a sub-problem of the broader self/body problem. As a result, the whole problem of self gets distorted, for rather than self being seen as the unity of embodied consciousness, it is seen as other than body.

Chapter 9. Self and Integration

1. The question of the status and origin of this capacity is fascinating. Is it a necessary occurrence of the movement of consciousness, one which will simply occur at a certain stage of such movement; or is it contingent, depending for its occurrence on, and so possibly not occurring without, particular self-initiated acts of awareness on the part of individuals? Or can those two possibilities somehow be combined so the capacity is seen as a necessary occurrence, but one which can only emerge by means of the self-initiated awareness of individuals? But if it makes sense to talk of such necessity, what provides the warrant? And what are we to say of freedom at this level?

2. It might be added that in its most general form, the problem manifests itself with respect to anything which is taken as other than self, *i.e.*, anything to which the sense of "mineness" does not attach.

3. It must be emphasized that the intimacy discussed here is very general and non-differentiating. Genuine, caring involvement with others, of course, demands a particularization of such intimacy, and this can only emerge out of ongoing interaction with others. The present claim is that the particularization of intimacy is grounded in the more general intimacy that flows out of the experiential realization that others, like oneself, are particular expressions of the life process. In the absence of this realization, the particularization of intimacy is almost certainly not going to occur. Typically, what will occur in its stead are various forms and degrees of dependence.

4. This, of course, is only one way of dealing with the malease. There are a variety of alternatives, including, for example, sinking into passivity and seeking distraction through various essentially passive activities, such as drug taking and spectatorism.

INDEX